To Dianne —
with thanks for your transitioning
skills & a heart to share them with
so many.
Wesley White
christmas 2013

Wrestling
Year A

Connecting Sunday Readings with Lived Experience

Wesley White

in medias res

In Medias Res, LLC
Publisher
Onalaska, WI

Wrestling Year A
Connecting Sunday Readings with Lived Experience

© 2013 by Wesley White

In Medias Res, LLC
1009 Quincy Street
Onalaska, WI 54650.

ISBN 978-0-9911005-0-7

White, Wesley, 1943–
   Wrestling Year A: Connecting Sunday Readings with Lived Experience / Wesley White
   1. RELIGION / Biblical Meditations / Spirituality
   2. Christian Rituals & Practice / Worship & Liturgy
   3. Revised Common Lectionary

Foreword

I have known Wesley White longer than I have known most people in my life, and I consider him a dear friend and partner in intellectual crime of the best sort (i.e., challenging the idiocy of what passes for status quo too much of the time). Admittedly, Wesley has always been more irenic than I. Where I seemed more often than not to come out swinging (again, utterly metaphorically), Wesley has been the voice of reason.

That is, until you read his commentary more carefully, and listen to what he is really saying. It is my opinion that Wesley White stands closer to the prophetic/Jesus tradition (prophetic tradition = Jesus tradition) than most of what is found in the institutions that have claimed to stand in that prophetic tradition but are too self-absorbed and culture-bound and, yes, cowardly to stand against the injustice and stupidity and hate in the world, all of which have an upper hand only as long as good people do nothing. So, read Wesley's commentaries and make up your own mind and then, for G*d's sake, DO SOMETHING to make the world a place of greater peace, assurance, gratitude, wisdom, justice, love. Read Wesley's commentaries and agree, or disagree, or dispute, or rail against, or cheer wildly, or make some subtle corrections, or burn the whole doggone thing or make a hundred copies of the book to give to others but for G*d's sake DO SOMETHING. The Good News of Jesus is a radical call to action, in the direction of love/justice. Period. Get on board or hide in the bushes and watch.

So let me comment on just a few things in Wesley's introductory pages. I have read all the commentary, day by day, week by week, and now in draft format, and they stand on their own. What seems to me to be particularly unique and wonderful in Wesley's work is his approach. I agree 100% with 99% of his approach, and the 1% I take issue with is that he does not go far enough. So let me push, and then what you read from him may go down easier.

Wesley's introduction begins with a recognition that "neither I nor anyone could break the Bible or even injure it." That is completely and utterly true, because the Bible is already broken. Broken, broken, broken. Take and eat, for the Bible is G*d's body, broken for you. Take and eat, and remember, as oft as you do it, that it is broken in love. In this library of rotted, torn, fragmented, assembled from multiple arguing textual families (some substantially corrupt), translated and re-translated equally by the best scholars and the worst idiots with an axe to grind, interpreted through a thousand ideological lenses, the passages known as "the Revised Common Lectionary, Year A" are just crumbs, and surely even all of us dogs are allowed the crumbs. Wesley's commentary, which he names as "my vanities... revealed for what they are", is nothing more or less than the labors of a faithful householder gathering what tidbits remain after all these centuries and creating a nourishing platter fit to be a feast.

Wesley's invitation to "listen in... unfocus your gaze... listen deeply... take one more step toward premeditated mercy through basic kindness and acceptance of your importantly small gift and those of others" is without a doubt the heart of Wesley White. Listen to him. If you read nothing else, take this in, mull it, memorize it, make it your daily practice. You could do no better: "listen in... unfocus your gaze... listen deeply... take one more step toward premeditated mercy through basic kindness and acceptance of your importantly small gift and those of others." Indeed. Isn't that also the heart of Jesus' teaching?

Read carefully Wesley's intro section entitled "Process." Read carefully the section entitled "Notes." Ignore the B.S. about his failing English 101; Wesley's grammar is just fine, and the scurrying away he mentions ("the basic rules of grammar scurry away from my intention") is PRECISELY what you, the reader, need to be attending to since it is precisely in the scurrying away that the godhead resides (and I presume I can use the word "godhead" without asterisk since it is in lower case...).

Regarding Wesley's warning about heresy (and maybe now you will read his introduction): This warning is outrageous on the face of it since all language is analogical and metaphorical (the map is never the territory) and so also always heretical. Hooray! Jesus was a heretic; just ask Caiaphas. Rest easy; you are in the very best company.

Thomas D'Alessio
September 2013

Preface

This series of reflections on the Revised Common Lectionary began with a recognition that neither I nor anyone could break the Bible or even injure it by use of imagination -or- unbidden pictures arising in the course of careful reading -or- a host of scholarly resources -or- basic lived experience -or- anything else in all creation. Vain imaginings are nothing new for G*D. My vanities will be revealed for what they are and I will trust in a great premeditated mercy sometimes called prevenient grace (read *Premeditated Mercy: A spirituality of Reconciliation* by Joseph Nassal).

Put another way—Ah, sweet mystery of life, at last I've given up grasping you (if "you" is anywhere near a category that might make sense in this context).

With this confession, here are all too many words about the formation and process behind the following fragments of thought and connection regarding the scripture passages known as the Revised Common Lectionary, Year A.

You, dear reader, are welcome to listen in. May you unfocus your gaze, listen more deeply than any surface denotation would allow, and take one more step toward premeditated mercy through basic kindness and acceptance of your importantly small gift and those of others.

Process

Each comment grew out of an almost lectio divina process I have used for practical matters such as sermon development and for simple listening. While probably not fair to that ancient process that shows up in every reflective tradition (Haggadah/Midrash – Tilawat/ Muraqaba – Samyama – Sravana – Vision Quest – ...), here is my variant.

First, believe that life experience is a positive value. Inasmuch as language attempts to describe experience but can never carry the whole load, every scripture and creed contains a cry for liberation from the limits of a first draft and accreted meaning laden onto it by various powers that be. Scripture and an offhand remark simply mean more than they mean.

Second, slowly read aloud the passage designated for a season until a word, phrase, or image begins to attract attention.

Third and Fourth and Beyond only take a little more than the available time to explore and wrestle with a beckoning of spirit to learn more than was previously available (see John 16:12). All manner of tools are available for deeper listening. In addition to lives important to you are whispers from the ignored lives within and without—variant readings, alternative traditions, and other promptings will all play their part and make a Way to see what else is possible and healing.

When we are willing to open our treasure chest of old and new gifts and apply them in artful ways to the "queen of sciences", we are at a creative edge that integrates our past and future through the medium of this moment.

What emerges may simply be a clearing away of accumulated shoulds and shouldn'ts. This is valuable. An inkling of a new direction for self and/or others may begin arising to be added to later. This, too, is valuable.

These comments are not much more than markers on one journey. May they also carry a blessing of encouragement to go down your "road less traveled".

Notes

Points of clarification that may be helpful:

—Title
Images from stone pillows, dreams, and immanent realities of relationships wrestle within. *Godwrestling—Round 2* by Arthur Waskow encouraged me to work beyond a temptation to reduce an ineffable to certainty.

—Orthography
Regarding a use of "G*D" throughout this book—I follow an idea from Rustrum Roy in his 1979 Hibbert Lectures, *Experimenting with Truth*. Roy uses an unfamiliar cloud-of-dots symbol similar to

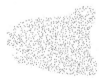

to represent "God". I use an asterisk (*) for the same intent—to blur or thin the boundaries within which G*D has been trapped by language. An asterisk stands for "more can be found elsewhere so look in another place for what is not here".

Later I added "Neighb*r" to help me remember how easily I limit neighbor to those I am comfortable with. May these shocks to the eye slow down your reading to consider what we know about what we say.

There is more to G*D than God, more to Neighb*r than neighbor. A greater degree of humility in our language is in order.

—Format

Even though four scriptures are designated for each Sunday of a church year, they are presented in book order rather than calendar order. While tempted to use the Jewish order for the Hebrew readings, I will stick with a traditional Protestant Christian ordering. This allows reading an over-arching story as a devotional book while also providing a relatively easy way to find the four readings. If there is a question about what the pericopes for a given date are, go to www.lectionary.library.vanderbilt.edu for the official chapter and verse and to www.textweek.com for all manner of resources.

—Sunday Designations

Over time the church has come to name various Sundays for convenience of reference. Naming, of course, has power. It is difficult to study and preach new learnings and have still powerful hymns from previous understandings sung without comment on their content. The same conflictual dynamic is present with Sunday designations. They keep undermining a deeper connection with a dynamic that began them.

An attempt at re-designation of Sunday labels grows out of a pet peeve of labeling particulars as "Holy"—Holy Land; Holy Week. What land isn't "Holy"? What week isn't "Holy"? This labeling is counter-productive for claiming Belovedness for others as well as for ourselves. Any official name comes with a danger of being co-opted for a current power structure.

For example, consider the Season of Epiphany in which the Sundays keep referring back to Epiphany (First Sunday after the Epiphany, Second Sunday after the Epiphany, ...). These Sundays need to move us further along than a simple accumulation of Sundays. Each Sunday might be named for a key component of Epiphany, such as "Guiding Gift". It could then carry an exponent instead of being additive—a Third Sunday after the Epiphany would become Guiding Gift ^{3}.

Such a shift might help remind us that a witness of G*D's steadfast and expanding love is to increase our gifts and use of them, day-by-day and week-by-week. It would also lead to other redesignations such as the last Sunday of a Church Year changing The Reign of Christ or Christ the King to "Evaluation Sunday" where we can look at our growth in graceful living over the course of the last year and know there is more to look forward to.

With exponents there is always a question of what to do with a first Sunday designation. I have chosen the awkward [1] designation. It is not really an exponent, but reminds us to begin moving in that direction. For the Sundays we now designate as "after Pentecost", I have simply used their Proper designation as they would otherwise be confusing in subsequent cycles, but a designation such as "Community Practice" would still be in order.

An Appendix contains a chart of the variations used in this book. I look forward to hearing how you have improved on these alternative names of the Sundays of a Church Year.

—Abbreviations

Abbreviations of the various Bibles used and referred to in this work are found in the Appendix after a chart of Sunday Designations.

—Fragmentation

Two streams of intent, beyond laziness, led to a decision not to develop a fleshed-out commentary. The first is two-fold: I've said what I can say without straying further into justifying my perspective and hardening a position which will delay being able to move on to better insight—and a sense that evocative language will aid others in their own wrestling with their reality rather than either adopting or rejecting mine. Obviously this will lose some along the way who are more attuned to tradition and/or literalism. A second is to honor my appreciation for exploring without a map and to simply lay smaller and smaller bits alongside one another for primitive reproduction purposes rather than to construct them into a Tinker Toy™ frame of a general theory.

The sections that look like poetry are but phrasal fragments strung together in a Cut Up process based on work by William Burroughs.

—Theological Physics

I come out of an Arminian Wesleyan tradition still found in the graceful parts of United Methodism. I presume any reader from another tradition can translate as we all carry a larger picture within our fragment of life. If you are not familiar with holograms and fractals, at least try a Wikipedia introduction to them as they will be helpful models for dealing with these wrestlings.

—Heresy

Some have suggested that these reflections border on and even slip into heresy. I can only say that such is a danger in any metaphoric or literary approach to scripture or life and is a risk well worth taking.

Ancient traditions of midrash and parable are always walking that line. If one is wrestling with a Living G*D, there is no known way to avoid operating out of an out-of-date perspective. Being stuck in the past is a far worse danger than stepping forward with fear and trembling toward a larger vision.

One of my ways of taking such accusations lightly is to set a price for this book at the numerological price of 6.66 (eBook) and 16.66 (paperback) rather than to use some other formula of popular pricing or pricing technique such as starting low to attract volume and then raising it later. In a capitalist society perhaps the greatest heresy is taking money lightly.

—Plagiarism

It happens. I am much more of the old, old school that spends less time worrying about the boundaries of intellectual property than seeing how far the ripples of a thought can travel.

Long quotes have been noted, but many words and phrases are simply appropriated without pause for specific thanks for where I first heard them and general thanks for their journey before that. Thanks Universe.

—Kairos CoMotion

Kairos CoMotion began to bring contemporary, liberal/progressive theologians to the bestilled waters of Wisconsin United Methodism. Along the way its Executive Director, Rev. Amy DeLong, has been tried by her denomination and peers for celebrating a Holy Union and being a lesbian in a partnered relationship. This has led to a several year exploration of clergy relationships as well as developing additional ministries of advocacy known as Love On Trial and Love Prevails. Their current work can be found at www.KairosCoMotion.org and www.LovePrevailsUMC.com.

The first Kairos CoMotion event in 2002 also brought an idea of having a blog that might stimulate an online conversation around a progressive view of the lectionary texts. It turned out that I was the constant voice and, after eleven years of blogged reflections, I have condensed those comments and fragments that some call poetry in three compilations for the three-year lection cycle. Along the way some weeks were missed and new comments have been written for this occasion.

—Grammar

Having failed English 101 twice before receiving a pity-D is not overcome by being given authority to preach. Nearly every sentence I begin begins to get away as internal connections raise their siren-song—eventually a sentence comes to a crashing halt without a clear direction to a next one. Though bright in many areas, the basic rules of grammar scurry away from my attention and intention the moment I set pen to paper or fingers to keys. I welcome your editing.

—Keeping Current

To find a more extensive posting of unedited comments organized by book, chapter, and verse you are invited to browse archived comments at www.wesleyspace.net/lectionary/biblebooks.html and/or to begin following new comments at www.kcmlection.blogspot.com.

Author Influences

This work is a distillation of eleven years of blogging. It is pulled together for distribution to celebrate completing my biblical warranty of 3 score and 10 years. Retired from nearly 40 years as a United Methodist clergyperson, I now have no more official warrant than before I began.

My first tutors were lay people: parents, siblings, Sunday School teachers, and friends. Six writers stand out as early influences: Nikos Kazantazis, Greek Orthodox; Jacques Ellul, Reformed; William Stringfellow, Episcopalian; William Butler Yeats, Irish Protestant/Spiritualist; and E. E. Cummings, Unitarian/Transcendentalist. Two musicians are also notable: Pete Seeger, "God is everything", and Alan Hovhaness, Armenian Apostolic. None of these are priestly.

Over the years these have been added to: Matthew Fox, Roman Catholic/Anglican Episcopal; Arthur Waskow, Jew; Neil Douglas-Klotz, Sufi Muslim; Starhawk, Pagan/Witch; Ursula Le Guin, Atheist/Taoist; Steven R. Donaldson, Unknown; and so many more. Each "religious" tradition has a blessing to share.

Clues about the author beyond such direct influences include a developed fondness for space such as the shore of a great lake or a desert, Asian art, camping, a Quaker meeting—appreciation for unsystematic theology through children's and coming-of-age stories, poetry, mystics, folk music (formal and informal)—a language preference for "response" instead of "answer" and "a" instead of "the".

Regardless of how these fragments of reflection have come to be transmitted through a dark-glass of self, may they urge you one step further along to your next plateau.

—Additional Thanks

Notable folks along the way, with wonderfully different gifts: Betty Lu Anderson from my High School Methodist Youth Fellowship; Walt Wagener from the Wesley Foundation of UW–Whitewater; Kenneth Engelman, preacher; Lucius Walker, an early director of Northcott Neighborhood House; Amy DeLong and the Kairos CoMotion board; and Thomas D'Alessio, kindred spirit and challenger.

Finally

Well, as finally as any of this gets, I wish you well in affirming your own experience as you encounter these comments on Year A. You are welcome to use the content in a local setting without express permission. Attribution is appreciated, but not expected.

Because these reflections were initially written over time, there will be some obvious inconsistencies and even contradictions. In addition to time, nothing is smooth when working at an intersection of "belief" and "doubt". There has been an attempt to do one last edit on the initial blogs, but mostly they remain the same as when first written to honor an impetus of the moment. I must admit that the discrepancies are probably my favorite part and are what we have to play with going forward.

As we say in Kairos CoMotion: "Living within an expansive and expanding Love is a most exciting and life-giving place to be". My hope is that you will take these reflections with many a grain of salt, enjoy their flights of fancy as best you can, and find your own spark encouraged into larger flame.

My dearly beloved, Brenda Smith White, who goes beyond any categorization or singling out, has been heard to say that I only have one sermon: "G*D loves you, so what are you going to do now?" May you catch a bit more of that love and pass on the blessing that is you.

Peace and Joy abound
take plenty
and some to pass around

Wesley White . . . October 2013 . . . wwhite@wesleyspace.net

For the greatest benefit,
remember to read the Biblical text
before proceeding to the comments.

Genesis 1:1–2:4a
Hopeless Hope Vigil — Live Together

To vigil for Easter can only happen after the surprise of a first Easter. Now anticipation of a new event asks us to be ready to revision past Easters and the various doctrines about life that have come forth over time. If we are not ready to be surprised by a new vision, we are not vigiling.

It will be important to consider an ongoing mystery and confusion of Trinity talk. In terms of Easter we have a variety of explanations about Jesus rising or G*D raising. These two models have never lived well with one another and whichever is used leads to differing conclusions about the nature of what traditionally has come to be known as "Father, Son, and Holy Ghost".

The creation story and the only model of G*D presented—that of humanness—can lead to additional models of Trinity. In his *Genesis* for the Interpretation Commentary series, Walter Brueggemann suggests another trinity regarding our sexuality: "Creation, Humanity, Community".

- Sexuality is good. It is part of creation. It is part of fruitfulness and multiplication.

- Human sexuality is not helpful for describing G*D. We are continually slipping up by projecting our experience onto any mystery of G*D. Though sexuality seems to be intended by G*D, it is not constituent of G*D.

- Experienced sexuality comes in a multitude of ways. It is worth noting that verse 27 speaks of our singular and plural sexual identity. We are gendered and communal. Neither Genesis' "his-ness" nor "them-ness" completes a picture of G*D. We still have more theologizing to do from an intersex perspective.

We may have to revisit Easter and Trinity in light of the fecundity of creation and wonder more about G*D and sexuality, but for now claim sexuality as a good gift, regardless of its orientation. There are boundaries of good and bad behaviors in every sexual orientation, but that is another story for another time.

Genesis 2:15–17; 3:1–7
Conviction [1]

A "tree of knowledge" certainly sounds helpful, particularly if it aids one in distinguishing good from evil—even if such distinguishing is as fine as a difference between a white and black thread at the rising and setting of the sun.

Such a "tree" presupposes that good and evil are to be distinguished. If creation by G*D is good and evil only latent until an eye was opened, did evil exist already? If so, how important is a whisper of its existence? Does it take some present ability to distinguish good from evil to desire to better distinguish them?

There is some sense in which stepping between good and evil leads us into confusion.

It is from this very tree that Jesus seems to have also eaten. He is able to distinguish helpful applications of the scriptures (accumulated wisdom of our experiences with G*D) from unhelpful applications. It is not that scripture is automatically helpful. Knowing when to apply which portion is important.

There is some sense in which stepping between good and evil leads us to clarity after an initial confusion. Read again Martin Buber's *I and Thou*, in particular his image of a whirlpool.

Thank you "Adam" for joining "Eve" in engaging wisdom. We are in this journey together—discernment is as much communal as it is mine alone.

I wash my hands in innocence
   again and again
I am washed away by circumstance
   again and again

until I cannot tell
   again and again
truth from falsehood
   again and again

my very same hand hugs my brother
   again and again
that slaps my sister
   again and again

and am joined to the cosmos
   again and again
and divorced from myself
   again and again

so I define and define
   again and again
and am in turn defined
   again and again

redeemed
   again and again
gracious
   again and again

Genesis 6:9–22; 7:24; 8:14–19
Proper 4 (9)

The pericope for today is pretty mechanical. It speaks of building an escape pod that is somehow to be so formative that the blessing/curse genetics of human beings will be reduced to that of only being a blessing for G*D (not by G*D).

It is as if G*D has been talking to "himself" again and plans this re-creation with an initial big negative (flood) and an expanded positive (increasing the food chain to all creatures rather than just plants). I expect this story was to teach us to always acquiesce to G*D because there would always be a threat of a flood (well, a fire next time) poised to sweep us away.

This is a different story than living in a garden protected from the ravages of chaos. How can you expect a future threat, unexperienced, to hold for very long? Here there is concrete evidence of a creator's curse.

Take a look around at today's world, church, and state. If we are to assist making a shift to fruitfully live together, it might be well for us to move away from generalized fears for the future to demonstrate how a curse to come grows from our decisions of today. That is, in both church and state, how do we concretize the presence of fascism in order to clarify the closeness of curse? In both church and state, how do we bring a word of blessing that will open eyes to a rebirth of community (Christian and otherwise).

The selected passages skip through a larger story dealing with the limits of creation. When we read the whole section about Noah, it shouldn't be too surprising to find everyone back where they started—in need of steadfast, rainbow love.

The shifting sands of our life lead us, again and again, to search for a rainbow where we might find an ark-of-gold that will make everything right. We just don't want to have our rainbow come after great turmoil. But until we are more constantly ready for change, these are lessons to be gone over again.

May the certainty of closed heads not erase an exploration by open hearts.

Genesis 7:1–5, 11–18; 8:6–18; 9:8–13
Hopeless Hope Vigil

What a re-telling. All strangeness is taken out of this passage by its unrelenting upbeat nature. Everything seems to automatically work out, unlike in our own lives. Unrealistic expectations of our relationship with G*D rise easily out of this redaction and bowdlerizing.

We don't hear the questions, the doubts, the institution of drunkenness and slavery in a new creation. In not hearing these we lose an ability to deal with G*D and Neighb*r, as well as Self.

A covenant that has to deal with these unflattering realities will be the stronger. Surprises when internal and external events don't go well can be better dealt with through a whole-story arc.

An Easter devoid of betrayal and loneliness/emptiness is not able to deal with the necessary realities of our lives.

Better to read these three chapters in their entirety and to wrestle with how Noah represents "righteousness". This will aid us in dealing with our own "righteousness" and lack thereof.

Noah co-conspirator
in global destruction
can see the benefit
of everything blotted out
leaving him standing
on a mountain top
surveying all as his

Noah comes forth
savoring being a savior
all creation owing him
a debt of gratitude
wrapping a rainbow
about his shoulders
and gets drunk

Genesis 12:1–4a
Conviction [2]

Can one be born again? It happens all the time.

Abram, Sarai, Lot, and more are born again through migration. This is not an issue of legal or illegal. It is a call from G*D, a necessity. Abram ran a risk greater than deportation. He felt in danger of his life and felt this strongly enough to risk his relationship with Sarai.

Elijah was born again while hiding in a cave.

Moses found a birth canal through a burning bush.

A Psalmist found new birth with a song of trust and confidence.

Peter is reborn through questions of his love.

Saul is reborn Paul on his way to Damascus.

To think these folks had only the one rebirth is too limiting. I've had several, myself. What about you? Can you count your many birth canals?

Even folks we have a most difficult time with have had a new birth to get as far along as they have and we pray for more births for them. If we parallel this to forgiveness, as we pray for their rebirth we pray for our own.

---

1 + 1 > 2

my current life
plus my rebirthed life
is more than the two
combined
I now also have
an anticipation
of yet another 1
even if I reach
70 x 7
there is more
for there is no end
of toil
of bookmaking
of steadfast love
of rebirthing forgiveness

Genesis 12:1–9
Proper 5 (10)

Jesus called and was called. Abram and Sarai and Lot and others were called and call.

Call is closely allied to blessing—blessing is where a call is intended to lead.

Call and blessing are so strong that they can overshoot the mark. We catch a glimpse of the extra energy that comes from call and blessing when Abram and the lot make it to the land of Canaan, have it acknowledged that this is the place that was the goal, and then find themselves unable to stop their journey, their call, their blessing and moved on from there to east of Bethel and then south to the Negev.

One could always argue that these subsequently named places are all part of some larger "promised land" and Abram was but staking out various parts of it. If we read but one more verse we find Abram all the way into Egypt. There is a sense of bait and switch here with Abram seemingly promised good things to come and ending up in a famine that pushes him on beyond Canaan. Promise delayed is going to be a theme for a while (still).

You may want to track this in your own life of calls and blessings overshot or delayed. While we usually focus in on just the pericope at hand, in this instance it is helpful to go the extra mile and read a bit beyond the appointed stopping place.

A later reflection on the "overshoot" phenomenon suggests that call and blessing can easily be sidetracked through a mechanism of pride. It appears that call and blessing do not live easily with humility. A struggle, rather than cooperation, between these gifts can delay each of their benefits, for both self and others.

Genesis 18:1–15, (21:1–7)
Proper 6 (11)

Of the stories of responses to G*D—I'll take Sarah's every time. Sarah knew impossibility when she heard it. Just being real was what many years had taught.

We have all too many folks who are serious in their promising to be a particular way before actually being in a situation where a test was applied for real. Their earnestness clutters the communication channels and is a frustration to both G*D and themselves.

We have all too few who are able to simply be, able to laugh in such a way that a way ahead is cleared. Their lightness shines a light upon G*D's behavior. Their laughter finally brings G*D to put up or shut up about serial promises with no action.

What impossible vision has been held out for you? I surely hope you have a good laugh about who you will become.

When that vision comes to pass, I hope you will remember the dismissive laughter of your earlier days and that you will rejoice in unbounded laughter that will grow through the years.

One of the ways to anticipate a really deep laughter yet to come is to cast your mind back to some of the unexpected moves that have led you to where you currently are.

I laugh whenever I think of being a preacher. A tongue-tied youth fearful of how I would be betrayed by what I said—indeed the tongue is both the weakest and the strongest of muscles. Moving my planned study at seminary (academic interest, not ministerial) up 5 years because of the Viet Nam war. Getting a phone message from Bishop Alton while graduating and having my name run through a local congregation and district and conference boards and being ordained a deacon within two weeks—ill-prepared, at best, to be a pastor.

Who would have thought of that result? Surely not I. I've been laughing at the silliness of trying to administer our way to "holiness" ever since.

What's ahead? I can only presume it is more laughter. Won't it be a hoot when I'm called out of a pastoral role! Won't it be a hoot if I die in a pulpit! Won't it be a hoot if ...!

We might as well laugh well now if there is any glimmer of hope that we will laugh well later. In fact, even if there isn't any hope—we might as well laugh. Laughing with and without hope has gotten me through the last several General Conferences and many a local parish circumstance.

Genesis 21:8–21
Proper 7 (12)

Does G*D know everything, including the future, or is G*D still inventing, creating, growing into new life? An old, old question.

Does G*D already know Ishmael will be rescued by G*D and so sending Hagar and Ishmael cavalierly onward is but an opportunity to have G*D be seen in a better light, later?

Does G*D agree with laughing Sarah who is no longer laughing about Ishmael's playing? ("Laughing" can be a euphemism that would make them lovers and "playing" can stand for sexual activity that would be a cause for banishment.) Then is it only after hearing Ishmael's cries (but not Hagar's?) that G*D wakes to the enormity of the consequence for the permission-giving already done?

So who is the good and the bad here? Sarah—protecting her own and giving up another? Abraham—giving a skin of water, so little against a large desert? Hagar—lifting a voice in weeping even if departing without a confrontation? Unnamed—(Ishmael) a nimrod anticipating a later Esau's reversal? Isaac—so young, so symbolic?

Of these six archetypes, which most closely approximates your past? your present? your desire? Note that each is a mixed bag and so this question is not about ideals but the mixture of motives and actions that is you.

How do you play this one from G*D's perspective? Do Abel and a Flood finally dawn on G*D and a rainbow sparkle? Was it in G*D's cards all along? Is Ishmael's inheritance claim upon G*D primary or secondary, a given or an afterthought?

How does this play out within an institutional church? Is it the role of priests to play Sarah and cast out those with whom they disagree or accuse of one heresy or another? Consider how prophets are cared for in the same way as Ishmael—seen as second-class rather than first-born and cast out, but, while crying, cared for.

---

finding our fearless place
pushes us beyond the surface
where crosses around necks
are protective amulets
saving one from so living
that a cross comes to our back

Genesis 22:1–14
Proper 8 (13)

Peace and Welcoming are only proved in their doing. It is one thing to pronounce peace and another to live it. It is one thing to announce a welcome and another to demonstrate it. Both Peace and Welcome are demanding masters. They are such large visions with so much detail within. It is best to be a bit humble while visiting these holy ones in their everyday places.

Welcoming is bedrock evangelism. A first rule of thumb of expressing our discipleship is to love one another and, presuming we are expanding our "one another", its logical extension is that of hospitality.

So we need to welcome the unexpected goat or exile. It saves us from inbred craziness (slaughter of our own) and denial of our common family (if they have been away).

In so doing we will find G*D's absent face wasn't so absent after all and we are part of the generations who experience steadfast love in the midst of every wavering.

Thanks be that we are not bound by our sins of self-assurance and closed doors. Our escape from such is a participation in welcoming.

---

sit in a new-to-you house
experience its idiosyncrasies
wonder where its secrets lie
where children were hurt
what kept blessings from flowing
who was exiled here
or escaped exile
if walls talked
what shame and glory
would come forth
were its doors ever opened wide
or barricaded even more tightly
how will we interact

enough of sitting
though not enough
a start is a cup of cold water
taken through the house
sprinkled here
there and everywhere
that more cups
will be ready
before family stumbles
ere strangers cry out
beckon them in
before they know
their need

Genesis 22:1–18
Hopeless Hope Vigil

Heroic intentions are a dime a dozen. Making a promise not to be attached to a current source of meaning is one thing and quite another to enflesh.

When tested we find out all we would lose. In that hangs an important balance—the weights of the past and the lightness of the future.

Unless in the depth of despair, we will salvage all we can. As broken as life may be, it seems somehow preferable to carry it on as a jockey's handicap.

Transformed minds lose their ability to leap tall buildings and speed blessing onward when laden with the detritus of past significance.

Imagine the relief when an abundance of provision can be seen. It changes the calculus of what is possible. A zero-sum game of required sacrifice is erodible with a choice of sacrifice which sets up an eventual choice of no sacrifice—a blessed legacy.

It was not easy for G*D and Abraham to settle on a sign of blessing—a child, no child, many children. All three signs have their importance.

As we vigil for a "second-calling" we sometimes call resurrection, may your relationship with creation bless many.

Genesis 24:34–38, 42–49, 58–67
Proper 9 (14)

Information from the National Council of Teachers of Mathematics: "On average, a 7-foot (2-m) tall camel weighs 1500 pounds (680 kg) and can drink up to 35 gallons (130 L) of water at one time and about 50 gallons (190 L) of water in a day."

Rebekah's offer to water 10 camels could have been a substantial endeavor.

While the young can be wearied, they can also keep at endeavors—just because. What might be your "young" quotient these days?

For the moment, I'm feeling like there are a hundred camels lined up to be watered. Sisyphus is alive and well.

Meanwhile, Isaac is waiting to find out with whom he will be joined in marriage. Day turns to day-after-day. He also spends time by the water.

Isaac returns from Beer-lahai-roi. This is the place where Hagar opened her eyes beyond her weariness of running away and being sent away. Here Hagar sees G*D seeing her (face to face with no death ensuing) and is able to return to servitude and to move on into G*D's promises. It is a good place for Isaac to visit (later he settles there, 25:11).

Where is your Beer-lahai-roi when you are wearied from waiting? or weary of other conflicts?

What would happen if in the midst of the current Palestine/Israel conflict they might remember a common link through Abraham and also remember that, after Abraham's death, Ishmael and Isaac are connected by the renewing waters of seeing G*D at Beer-lahai-roi?

What would happen if in the midst of any conflict we might lift our eyes from our weariness and see G*D's seeing of us?

Genesis 25:19–34
Proper 10 (15)

We are not determined by the way the world is presently organized. A pronouncement seems to come true that the two wrestling in a womb will become two nations in conflict and the younger will become stronger and the older will become servant.

We can appreciate how next generations need to move away from the combined blessing/curse of an exaggerated emphasis upon first-borns. We also can see an inversion of power simply leading to the power of a different heel, not a healing of power struggles.

Imagine a world not fixated on rights or entitlements. What kind of a story will go beyond the good news of inversion to even better news of conversion? How do we claim our worth to be more than a bowl of soup? How do we acknowledge our envy and jealousy that they not lead us to manipulate another?

Are we committed to seeing ourselves and Jacob as heroes? Are we expecting that our enemies and Esau will always be trodden underfoot?

May we find a way to break the "last shall be first" routine that finds the latest last shall become the latest first, etc., without falling into an equal danger of first always being first. What story do you know that is opening us to a new stage of human development or a new understanding of G*D's mercy?

---

brother wrestler	go out	even here
heel grabber	anguished loneliness	instead of a thorn
stew chef	to accomplish	a sound of singing
lineage stealer	more than you purposed	in the myrtle
flock grabber	to return	an everlasting sign
G*D wrestler	a brother's embrace	none are cut off

Genesis 28:10–19a
Proper 11 (16)

Why would one climb Jacob's ladder if "the LORD" stood beside Jacob and the ladder?

There is a lot of archetypal stuff that has gone into this scene from outside it. Somehow it has become an image of a gateway to heaven, rather than a presence of G*D in a paradise of a present.

---

what's G*D doing
at the bottom of a ladder
while angels climb
up and down down and up

angels are a diversion
while G*D sneaks up
as imagination soars
with the ladder

angels bring not messages
from above
but store promises
with the rain

together they fertilize
our present
to bring forth much future
growing up

promises spoken
are carried on high
to baptize tomorrow
resurrect a day after

Genesis 29:15–28
Proper 12 (17)

With a passage like this we could go riding off in all directions. There is no prioritizing of one theme over another. While appreciating a trickster getting tricked, I am more interested in a review of what it means to be "wifed". How do you read these NRSV verses?

(21) Then Jacob said to Laban, "Give me my wife ...."

(28) ... then Laban gave him his daughter Rachel as a wife.

To be wifed is more than to have been "gone into". Leah had been gone into without being acknowledged as a wife. Child bearer, yes; wife for Jacob, no.

To reduce a relationship to the genitals, as The United Methodist Church has done to define away a gay or lesbian relationship, is to reduce love for Rachel to sex with Leah or one of the maidservants. This is certainly not a story that translates well into our time and place. Nonetheless, it is helpful to aid us in not limiting our discriminatory inclinations to simply one style of culturally regulated sexuality.

"Wife", in a relationship of any orientation, is a word loaded with tons of overtones. It is not a subordinate role or a directorship. Consider the many ways you have been wifed or you have wifed another—this is not a sex term—it is a relationship beyond gender or role.

Rachel was Jacob's wife more than 14 years before he went into her. For more years than either anticipated, there were no children. Neither a ceremony, nor sexual partnering, nor children make a wife. Rejoice and make a parable out of this story—How would Jesus retell this story to make it come alive again? And you?

---

before prayer
a sigh
before knowing
a call
before covenant
a thanks
before serving
a love
before presence
a parable

Genesis 32:22–31
Proper 13 (18)

Jacob wrestles with an angel; disciples wrestle with a crowd. In both instances they learn something very important.

"Wrestling Jacob" is significant in the Wesleyan Tradition (Charles Wesley's poem is now found as "Come, O Thou Traveler Unknown"—386/387 in the 1989 *United Methodist Hymnal*). G*D is identified in the original publication with the special typography of LOVE and UNIVERSAL LOVE, similar to LORD in the King James version or G*D in this publication.

Jacob wrestled with his father, brother, father-in-law, and self. Neither winning or losing tricks, having little or giving away much, could be counted on for either power or meaning. A blessing is worth much more than any of these or a sore hip.

The disciples wrestle with a crowd and learn their perceived limits are not so—Jesus' ordered method allows folks to sit together and look at one blessing and see within it an abundance not previously glimpsed.

In the midst of everyone looking every which way (searching for their own best advantage), two loaves (loves) and five fish seem mighty puny. Even if Jacob were to send ahead in time that which went to Esau (200 she-goats and 20 he-goats, 200 ewes and 20 rams, 30 milch camels with their colts, 40 cows and 10 bulls, 20 she-asses and 10 he-asses), it wouldn't add up to much more than puny for such a one-time crowd, much less a next one. When we look together and opportunity is identified as a blessing—things change.

Given that Jacob and Jesus' disciples have been willing to indenture themselves to achieve some heart-felt desire, will you as willingly wrestle with an unknown nature of G*D for 7 seconds, or 7 minutes, or 7 hours, or 7 days, or 7 weeks, or 7 years or 70 years?

May you receive a wrestled blessing and offer an audacious blessing in return.

Genesis 37:1–4, 12–28
Proper 14 (19)

A promise: I will send you to those who hate you,
who cannot speak peaceably to you. –WW

So Joseph responds to his call as a prophet, "Here am I", and goes to his "brothers." So Elijah hears as a prophet hears, in great silence, and returns to those seeking his life. So the disciples enter the chaos of the deep, of wind and wave. So the faithful strive not for heavenly stairs or power to change the past, only a word and heart for this day's need.

This promise is repeated continually. Some hear and are renewed. Some almost hear and fear. Some do not yet hear, but are called, nonetheless.

---

sent ahead
we know our own
times of famine
made worse by tired feet
starved of peaceable speech
as well as of daily bread
our insides and outsides
stumble on

sent ahead
without a clue
we take
what we know
and join it
with what others know
silently singing
steadfast love to action

sent ahead
into unfamiliar chaos
we battle wind and wave
until we can step aside
from our fears
until our words
turn to healing
for the nations

16

Genesis 45:1–15
Proper 15 (20)

The second in command, economic advisor par excellence, still identifies as, "I am Joseph." His concern is not just about surviving a coming famine, but, "Is my father still alive?"

Finally, with those who betrayed him he makes an audacious claim, "I am your brother."

Joseph—Jacob's son, brother to eleven—this Joseph, sees his life as, "Sent to keep alive many survivors."

There are many ways to try to keep many alive. These can contain the infamous, "We had to destroy the village to save the village." Under Joseph's leadership, many lost their land and freedom for a better chance at survival. Were they better off? Certainly his family became better off, until Joseph's efficient planning was forgotten.

How might you keep "many alive" this day? How might you keep yourself alive this day? One way is to refuse to label and be labeled. Drop the titles; claim your name.

---

gifts and calling
irrevocable
deniable

our life
is our gift
our calling

whether rued
or rejoiced
life calls

gifts once dead
remain ours
to reveal

Genesis 50:15–21
Proper 19 (24)

Two excerpts from Walter Brueggemann's *Genesis:*

> [Joseph's] encounter with the brothers is concluded with "comfort" (v. 21). The issue of guilt has been completely overcome. The agenda has moved beyond any concern for *retribution* to the larger issue of *vocation*. Twice now [Joseph] has said to them, "fear not" (vv. 19,21). Their alienation, fear, and grief are overcome. As is evident in Isaiah 40:1–2, "comfort" is an exile-ending word....

> This way of presenting Israel's faith is at the same time deeply believing and radically secular. It does not doubt the plan of God in the least. But at the same time, it accepts responsibility for the plan. Joseph does not "leave it all in God's hands." But he also does not believe that "God has no hands but ours." He accepts his vocation.

So where is your vocation? Where do you accept responsibility for being a participant with G*D in a process of working forward from a gift of creation?

When we get to the point of claiming our vocation, issues of guilt and shame can finally be laid down. Clarity of vocation frees us from fears of retribution over any detail—comfort and hospitality become real (both our being welcomed and our welcoming).

Progressive Christians find themselves wrestling with a bothness of being "deeply believing and radically secular." We are not willing to have one be subservient to the other or to separate them as though there were a choice to be made between them. This is a quality that can help move a church into its next stage of life, so rejoice in living this bothness.

May this bothness enhance our following of Isaiah's dictum to "speak ye comfortably" to one another, as well as to Jerusalem, and reveal another sign of having accepted our vocation as exile-enders.

Exodus 1:8–2:10
Proper 16 (21)

There are many gifts. In the Moses story there are folks who have the gifts of disobedience, secrecy, complicity, adventure, subversion from within, etc.

In the Jesus story there are gifts of Baptist John, Elijah, Jeremiah, and other prophets that help to define who Jesus is and isn't.

Likewise there are gifts in each of our lives as we interact with those closest to us. This includes those we yet name as enemy as well as friends who challenge and/or support and feed us to become more than we currently are.

There is no one else's story to tell but our own. So the disciples were told not to tell the gift of Jesus; that was for him to reveal. So, too, no one else will tell the secret of who you are—it is yours to reveal and this is a good time to reveal it.

Are you someone whose gift of compassion will not allow you to go along with the dicta of society? Are you a gift willing to give birth to something new even in the face of overwhelming evidence that such is not desired? Are you willing to be practical enough to let go of your child and gift it another space where it might yet grow, knowing your own space is too risky for it? Are you gifted to reach out to the forbidden and make it your own? Are you willing to participate in the irony of life that flourishes within your own non-ironic life?

---

how shrewd we are
as we look around
to the dangers
and opportunities
to enhance our power

our very shrewdness
turns all too readily
to ruthlessness
we only perceive
as extra shrewd

being so shrewd
we fail to find
the irony in ruthlessness
that destroys
its beginning shrewdness

somehow it is never our fault
that what we have set in motion
will come back to haunt us
through the very structures
of our elite electedness

we move from "us"
who are fearful
to restrictions
that fall apart
at the next "I"

Exodus 3:1–15
Proper 17 (22)

Pharaoh's daughter was surprised in the midst of her daily life to find a baby floating toward her. Moses was surprised in the midst of his daily routine to find an unconsumed burning bush before him.

Any division between sacred and secular, holy and profane, or any other duality we might mention fades in the face of a mystery beyond all the sacred and secular, holy and profane distinctions we so easily draw or glibly pronounce.

Lived experience leads "holiness" in strange directions. Pharaoh's daughter adopts a male Israelite her father has condemned to death before the little guy was born. Moses returns to face down the ruler who had condemned him and a whole people. He returns to bring those people out of slavery, to be "somebodies".

In the midst of the daily we, ourselves, have been called to do what is right even in the face of power to the contrary. We, too, have wondered whether we could do what needs doing. We, too, have sometimes needed a sense of authority larger than ourselves (although, note that Pharaoh's daughter didn't have the same recorded reservation that Moses did).

Sensing that most of us are more in the situation of Moses, unprivileged or even less than that, we do look for a talisman to carry with us into the difficulties ahead. What we know about such is that if it is too specific it won't hold up in changing circumstances and if it is too general it will float away before gaining traction. And so we hear the specifics of Abraham, Isaac, and Jacob and the much broader I-AM-WHO-I-AM (in all its various tenses). Moses holds together these two gifts, the specific and the general.

May you hold your contradictory gifts together that you might further the models Pharaoh's daughter and Moses offer you of doing the right thing to honor life—the life of a condemned child and the lives of enslaved relatives. Those same gifts are needed in today's world. Of particular need is a move toward an integral worldview, where our current world-centric pluralism and relativism (seemingly too accepting and unwilling to stand against wrong) are transcended and included into a critically evaluated, more systematic, whole.

[collected from written background material of
www.bodymindspiritworks.com and www.IntegralLife.com]

Exodus 12:1–4, (5–10), 11–14
Courage Thursday– Proper 18 (23)

Have you marked a first month for the rest of your life? Not only do we remember the first month for the Israelite community, I am now writing as Ramadan comes around again. These are lunar holidays, not solar. Their perpetualness is enhanced by the peripatetic nature of a maddening moon going its own way, marching contrary to the regularity of evenings and mornings. The moveable nature of these months makes intentionality all the more important. We have to plan more for them. They interrupt all our other plans.

What are you to do when a whole nation and its power is against you? Clarify a needed change and affirm your basis of authority. Say, "No." Say, "Let people go." Say, "Past, Present, and Future Life is calling."

Let us continue to be about a business of loosening (never again slavery) and binding (rituals to remember freedom).

To best be about this business of setting people free, attention to the realities of beginnings is important. A danger of ritualizing beginnings is that an on-the-ground pain is covered in a patina of glory. The whole Exodus story goes back to a Pharaoh who forgot. We need rituals that help us remember the whole story and not just a dramatic moment.

In election times there are frequent attempts to define a starting place from whence we can arrive at a solution being offered. Pay attention to political theatre to see if you agree with their assessment of the issues. Who best gets a "Remembrance Award" that honors all people and shares common-wealth equitably? Remember that Pharaoh wanted to continue being on the top of his wealth gap over others, even if that meant their enslavement to the economy of his day. Remember you can chose to "Think Different" than a Pharaoh.

Would you have participated in this first Passover? Just because Moses says so? His track record wasn't the greatest. If pests and boils won't work, why would blood on the door and shoes at the ready?

This challenges us to attend to a moon that breaks all our solar-based routines and to hope beyond current evidence.

From a vantage point after an Exodus we wonder how
our crying out for G*D to come to us was reversed
to plead G*D to pass over us, miss us.
You just never can tell with G*D.

Exodus 14:10–31; 15:20–21; and 15:1b–13, 17–18
Hopeless Hope Vigil

"Weren't there enough graves in Egypt?"

This question reminds us of the difficulties which have moved from the horizon to smack us square in the face. When we finally have to face up to the on-going messiness of life and feel hemmed in, we shift our memories according to our latest fantasy of utopia and how all things are to work out to our benefit. (Otherwise what is the value of our current utilitarian G*D?)

Not liking to be thought culpable in our own circumstance, our difficulties can easily shift over into our making life difficult for some vulnerable sub-group among us. We love to hate someone not like us.

Whether bemoaning our own situation or trying to make it seem better by seeing to it that someone else moans louder than ourselves, there is a healing word to be heard—"Don't be afraid. Stand your ground".

When we shift from unanswerable questions to affirmations beyond previous limits, we find we are on the way to opening a new way. On this way some folks make this shift faster than others. They begin assessing the options and eventually find a foreground/background shift as in an optical illusion and can never again only see a blockage without its resolution. There were many options evaluated before only the sea ahead could fully be addressed.

Seas are chaotic for creatures of the dust of the ground. Seas dissolve us. We go down to the sea again to visit the mystery of other and death.

In a gentle lapping of wave on shore or a typhoon beyond categories, we remember how it felt to have been so bound by a too-large question and the relief when it became clear that avoiding disaster is not an option, only how we will respond to it—not fearing death and dissolution, but claiming our best hope to stand upon.

Resurrection is hope renewed, but only after the fact can we incorporate it into a next time we face our grave again. Fears will have to be faced again and hope is key to seeing a path in the midst of a deep blue sea threatening drowning and obliteration. We may yet drown, but, like the Mary Ellen Carter, rising again is not out of the question.

Even so, we cannot avoid the eventuality that death does come. May it be said that we stood our ground and danced with our best hope.

Exodus 14:19–31; 15:1b-11, 20-21
Proper 19 (24)

Moses baptized those Egyptian charioteers "real good." That perspective is questionable from many directions.

With that silliness aside, remember that Moses not only dealt with water that rock might be revealed, but later he dealt with rock that water might be revealed. We are always finding balancing points.

What needs to be passed on from this "saving"? The Gospel lection associated with this passage (Matthew 18:21–35) says forgiveness (a kind of saving/healing) is to beget more forgiveness. How might ways be opened for those who are finding themselves no less trapped than the Israelites of old? Is there an economic component to this "saving" for those whose job has moved? Is there a political component for political theories (such as the liberal or progressive which has taken such a PR beating in the last generation or third-party platforms) to be revived? Is there a racial or gender or sexual orientation discrimination that hangs on long after legislation was to have done away with it or in the face of current and new legislation further marginalizing a people? Is there an educational component in the face of cultural boredom?

By and large, none of the Abrahamic religions has done well in expanding salvation past its own self-interest. How are you doing on a personal level?

---

transgressions removed ahead
a welcome road sign

hope for myself rises
to return to
an original blessing of good

disgust that it might be
for every Jane and Jack
or my favorite enemy
rises even quicker

and quick as a wink
my special welcome sign
becomes a road closed detour
onto winding rutted paths
leading 70x7 times back to this marker

23

Exodus 16:2–15
Proper 20 (25)

Where two or three are agreed, ask! See what happens when a whole company asks!

Apparently the half-life of blessings is just a tad longer than that of plagues.

All too soon we forget. It will only take folks 6 days to forget what to do on a 7th. After a plague is passed we seem to immediately return to our previous normal and reverse any learning that had gone on.

Yet, big lie memes seem to catch so quickly and last forever. What is a thoughtful person to do?

"Mercy" can easily be translated as "manna". (Aren't we still wondering what mercy is?) Are two or three of us crying out for mercy or have we left it in G*D's hands, forgetting our responsibilities as images of or partners with G*D?

We cry out for mercy. When asked about a consequence of receiving same it is so easy to start bargaining, talking about works that one will do in response. You give me mercy and I'll do whatever you say. Give me mercy and I'll hedge myself round with the law so I will never have to ask for mercy again.

A more difficult route is to receive mercy and humbly ask for more. This presumes that there is not a static juridical balance point for blind justice. Receiving mercy is to live boldly again, not to hide away in respectability. Receiving mercy is to pass mercy on, not handy one-liner proverbs or aphorisms. Receiving mercy is to see one's secret heart, to know creation is good, and to experience the spirit of the law. Yes, to be law-observant or dutiful is a minor virtue. To live mercy is the better part of virtue.

On this last point check out the whole Charles Wesley hymn, "What Shall I Render to My God" based on Psalm 116[1].

[1] www.ccel.org/w/wesley/hymn/jwg06/jwg0614.html

Exodus 17:1–7
Conviction 3 — Proper 21 (26)

There are so many riddles in life. Is baptism divine or communal? Can a staff that brings bloody water also be a staff that provides drinking water? Do the generations support me or am I the culmination of them? Does G*D give water to Moses at Meribah to support moving toward "a promised land" and hold Moses back at River Jordan on the eve of entering that land?

How we read the story seems to depend on where we are situated. Are we focused on the divine (religiously/priestly) or the human (community/prophetic)? We will come at things differently and be more attuned to one part of the story or another. A grand trick of life is to keep experiencing until we can appreciate both, though at any given time one or the other is more called for.

When is the hardship of evacuation important and when is the comfort of temporary housing crucial? There is a time and a place for both and either can get in the way if we focus on it at the wrong time.

Are we oriented toward anticipation and prevention or on response and band-aids? Both are needed but in differing proportions as time goes by.

Am I really on my own before G*D or are we in this together so none will be saved until all are saved? Our understanding of this basic relationship between creature and creator, between G*D and Humanity, will go far in determining how we interact between ourselves. Wherein, really, lies the distinction of social sin we all are part of and individual sin we are all part of? Trying to cut this Gordian knot with a sword of individualism is no more satisfying than smashing it with a club of generational determinism.

So many riddles, so few eternal verities. Perhaps the best we can do at the moment is to hear a larger positive intention of G*D to keep dealing in hope when we hear such a lament as, "I have no pleasure in the death of anyone."

The staff used to dry up water becomes the staff to bring water gushing forth. Around it goes. Can you see yourself as a staff of life drying and gushing as needed? So often we image things moving in only one way when back-and-forth is closer to the mark. The stuff of life is too great to be limited to one way of operating (as though everything were a nail because I have a hammer). So be a staff of life, able to be present and helpful in each differing circumstance.

Exodus 19:2–8a
Proper 6 (11)

In the middle of a wilderness it is comforting to receive word that, of all the possible people, G*D has chosen you.

Whether in the wilderness of racism (overt or subtle) or sexism or homophobia or poverty or abuse or whatever, it is important to hear a word of specialness.

A temptation is to turn specialness into a proprietary holiness which separates rather than helps us all toward interdependence.

What happens if we turn this into a generic story? Whether one is from a Native People in the Americas or a woman in Afghanistan or gay in a straight legal system or poor in a land of special interests or a child clobbered from any number of directions or whatever—you are special—you are a priest and a prophet between G*D and others who have been wounded by one or more of the 7 Deadly Sins times 70 Other Sins.

What does it mean to be a "holy" nation brought to G*D on eagles' wings? Do we not help G*D hear other cries, as ours were heard? Do we not help those who are crying by honoring both their tears and their value as we fly them to G*D or fly G*D to them? Do we not structure our common life in such a way that our experience of captivity is redressed and offered as hope for others?

Generosity in the wilderness! Generosity in your wilderness! Count on it. With the whole earth to choose from, G*D chooses you in the midst of your wilderness and also chooses those whom you have placed into wilderness settings through your inattention to their pain. Together we are chosen. How generous!

Exodus 20:1–4, 7–9, 12–20
Proper 22 (27)

To have 10 words from G*D seems pretty straight-forward. When their interactions and common direction are considered, a double handful is plenty enough to keep us busy.

ReligiousTolerance.org indicates at least three different numbering systems for the 10 community guides:

- Ancient Judaism, Reform Protestants, & Eastern Orthodox
- Current Judaism
- Roman Catholics, some Lutherans

and makes this comment: "Lack of agreement among various divisions with Christianity and Judaism would make it very difficult to reach a consensus about how the Ten should be printed for display in public locations." [You may want to spend a little time at the rest of ReligiousTolerance.org if you are not already acquainted with it.]

What was probably once very clear to folks has been broken into several different traditions and all the king's horses and all the king's men can't seem to put it back together again.

How are you playing back and forth between Law and Freedom and the varying number schemes?

---

a medium is a message
it lops off the ends
one size fits all
average is good enough

a medium whispers
stories behind stories
believable and not
what you see is not all

a medium well
is recommended
to burn out illness
and blood guilt

a medium nurtures
biologic experiments
testing theories
confirming evidence

a medium colors
pale lives
with pigments
life experienced

a medium law
keeps us from
in medias res
and attendant glory

a medium life
bounded by rules
binding with same
unconscious errors

Exodus 24:12–18
Mountain Top to Valley

We have so bought into the imagery of things being carved in stone, good for eternity, not transfigurable, no matter what else might change, including changes with the carver, that we don't know how to keep that picture in tension with the experience of a devouring fire that could even dissolve stone tablets.

It turns out that much of the injury of the church (both to itself and others) has to do with this business of stone and fire. One set of folks is sure it is one while others are sure it is the opposite. To be caught between the devil and the deep-blue sea or a rock and a hard-place is kid's play in comparison to finding oneself between stone and fire. Being in the presence of the symbols of the law and the prophets (Moses and Elijah) requires a transformation, a transfiguration, that life between these polarities might remain steadfast in the presence of faithlessness—that of calf-dancing or inept healing or whatever you are having to deal with. Blessings upon us as we deal with the building of new land from lava, burning stone.

So, for what purpose are the tablets of stone given to Moses? It is to build community. How might one tell a community has been built? Might it be the personal sense of belovedness experienced by each member of the community and a shared sense of compassion for one another? Between these two commandments—an experience of being loved/loving and mutual encounters with compassion—will lie the whole of the law and the prophets. Without them stricter and stricter laws will come. Eventually the goal is to live out of assurance and compassion.

As might be expected, it takes time for a community to become clear about its internal workings and external relationships. For Moses it was a 40-day slow-grinding-of-the-gods to come down a mountain and go to work engaging issues of assurance and compassion.

Other tales say it took a second try because the task looked so large while viewing life through the lens of a golden calf. But, first try, second try, or fortieth try, we look beyond a need for stricter laws to the over-riding issues of personal assurance and communal compassion. Look again, there is no law against these. Let's nurture them.

Exodus 32:1–14
Proper 23 (28)

G*D had a second thought that caused a change in G*D. Hooray! Is this not a sign unto us as significant as rainbows and pillars of fire and manna and circles within circles and mangers?

Evil threatened turned out not to be evil done. A disaster was averted through a second-thought.

In the midst of an ever-present current economic "disaster" we might wonder how many second-thoughts were allowed to come to fruition and how many died aborning?

In the midst of whatever personal "disaster" (again, perception is significant here) we are experiencing, we would benefit from a reflection on our second-thought process. The same goes for a congregation or other institution.

One of the blessings of the progressive movement is its ability to see beyond what is purported to be common-sense or orthodoxy. We are freed through a second-thought process to visit any number of situations again for a first time. In such a manner are idols best rooted out and extraneous baggage (then and now, gold) released.

In this case Moses and G*D sharpened each other. May you continue to sharpen your second-thoughts by honing them against your current "opponent" (again, ...).

---

a most beloved phrase
And the LORD repented

and Moses and you
and I and we and all

the most specific
the one and only

LORD ever constant LORD
LORD the same LORD

repented then and now
repented again and again

And the LORD repented
a most beloved phrase

Exodus 33:12–23
Proper 24 (29)

Goodness can be blinding. This comes from both the sparks of new life that burst forth as a result of goodness and a turning away from goodness by those who fear it will lead them where they would fear to tread.

Whatever its origin, goodness comes to be too much to look upon directly or in advance. We prefer to deal with goodness after the fact.

When we begin to attribute goodness as an expected quality, it isn't long before we are disappointed. Likewise, when we intend goodness to flow from a present action, we are soon discouraged by the number of unintended consequences that also come forth.

Oh, that we would temper our anticipation of someone good arising to lead us out of our current situation all too clearly connected with our past decisions. That goodness will not be forthcoming. Likewise to come at decisions more humbly, we will do the best we know to do at the time without universalizing it. Decisions always take place in the gray areas of life or they wouldn't be decisions.

What we are left with is the backside of goodness. We can recognize it by what comes to pass. This leads us to simply rejoice at the presence of goodness in the midst of so much that isn't. As folks made in G*D's image, having Glory within us, we are called to do all the good we can, with all the folks and all the time we have. This, however, needs to be carried out with the humility of backsides. May it be our everyday life to sow seeds of kindness and tend them as they sprout. Much later there will be stories told not only of John "Appleseed" Chapman but (your name here) as fruits of simple goodness—mature and nourishing.

---

to set out to trap another
is the surest way to be caught
steering god the way of our ammunition
    in thus getting caught
    in our own attempt to trap another
    we are set up for Jesus' jujitsu theology
        when our trap's premise
        is exposed we fly head over heels
        bowing before our previous blind spot
            now comes the revelation
            malice's short-run effectiveness
            will ever reveal its long-run fallacy

Leviticus 19:1–2, 9–18
Guiding Gift [7]

Those of you in Wisconsin know the governor is playing games with the jobs of public workers. Threats are made to jobs themselves, wages, benefits. Threats are made to bring in the National Guard.

It is difficult to read this passage and then face ideologues whose sense of economic realities is as small as their compassion.

Though it can apply to any party, the current Republican dilemma includes a promise to deliver $100 billion in spending cuts—and its members face the prospect of Tea Party primary challenges if they fail to deliver big cuts. Yet the public opposes cuts in programs it likes—and it likes almost everything. What's a politician to do?

Once you think about it, it is obvious: sacrifice the future. Focus the cuts on programs whose benefits aren't immediate; basically, eat the country's seed corn. There will be a huge price to pay, eventually—but for now, you can keep the base happy.

Paul Krugman in a February 14, 2011, *New York Times* article, "Eating the Future", ends his column, "And so they had to produce something like Friday's proposal, a plan that would save remarkably little money but would do a remarkably large amount of harm."

Do you hear in this that there is nothing left for the gleaners, for the poor, the alien? Do you hear the defrauding, slandering, and profiting from the blood, pain, loss of your neighbor?

We have here a huge grudge borne against Neighb*r. We have here a denial of community. We have here a false idol of Market.

And so the people do as G*D does, rise in opposition to theft of common-wealth. Demonstrations Today and Tomorrow!

Sing along with the noontime Solidarity Sing Along in the Wisconsin state capitol by getting your copy of their Song Book at: http://dl.dropboxusercontent.com/u/1940227/52%20songs.pdf

Sing Along Sample

It isn't nice to block the doorway
It isn't nice to go to jail
There are nicer ways to do it
But the nice ways often fail
It isn't nice, it isn't nice
You told us once, you told us twice
But if that is Freedom's price
We don't mind

Leviticus 19:1–2, 15–18
Proper 25 (30)

Two phrases from Everett Fox's *Schocken Bible* translation:

> Verse 2
> Holy are you to be,
> for holy am I, YHWH your God!
> Go for it. Be not afraid of holy being. It is you.

> Verse 18
> be-loving to your neighbor (as one) like yourself,
> I am YHWH!

Fox notes: "The meaning of this phrase, and the concept, have been widely debated throughout the ages." So where is a debate about this in our age? Who here thinks they get it? Start talking about "be-loving" and see how far you get.

Where do you see this intersecting with other portions of Leviticus? Pay particular attention to the lives of gays and lesbians (in today's understanding of same). What will change in our culture when those heterosexually oriented be-love those who are oriented otherwise? Just more be-lovedness.

Where do you see this intersecting with neighbor Iraq (or the enemy of the day)? And what are you doing about what you see? Can you see the apoplexy of a SECRETary of deFENCE like Donald Rumsfeld when he finally gets it, "Be-loving to Iraq who is like America." What, like America with weapons of mass destruction, etc.!? Yes.

Numbers 6:22–27
Naming Day

Context is always tricky business. Are we continuing the past, attending to a present situation, or anticipating a next step?

This famous blessing is located just after instructions for rededication as a Nazirite after they have had a brush with someone's death. It comes just before setting up and anointing a tent specifically for encountering G*D's presence. In its singularity it is a corporate blessing.

This blessing is a group (Aaron and sons) to group (Israelites) blessing. A resultant question for us is, "As a representative of G*D, what group are you and a group you are with called to bless?"

Will a plural "you" keep the blessing internal or include other classes, nations, and even enemies?

---

receive assurance
walk in blessing
before – behind –
right – left –
above – below –
into every dimension

this energy
lights paths
yours and many
to illuminate
graceful options
ever present

wonder
holds us together
countenancing
new engagements
to spread
expansive peace

Numbers 11:24–30
Energy to Witness

A power-sharing process leads to prophesying and inclusiveness enough to welcome Eldad and Medad and folks of all languages.

It is of great importance to note that a power that was set loose in a desert and a locked room both came through a power-sharing mechanism. To focus on a process of power-sharing is prelude to making Open Hearts, Open Minds, Open Doors more than a slogan, but an exciting reality.

If there were one thing I would covet for congregations it is a greater sense of needing everyone to be involved in decision-making. To have a vision of building a better decision for the present and future is a source of creative energy that is helpfully bounded by innovative pictures and responsible reservations. These parentheses bring fruitful growth that is both deep and wide.

Numbers 21:4b–9
Relic Day

Imagine that—people become impatient on the way. It happens at every transition we make. Individuals and communities alike get edgy as they approach a boundary between leaving behind and moving on. We know we won't be able to go back again and yet we want to take enough of our old way along to comfort us.

We don't do transition well. Resistance to potential loss of what little power we may have comes in a variety of ways. Legislation sometimes contains a "poison pill" to lessen its chance of passage. Through this gruesome story we see the poison of resistance to new realities as we drag old habits, rituals, and entitlements along to vaccinate us from having to change.

In this scene, though, poison doesn't keep us stuck with what is but encourages us to break out of old ways. To stay with yesteryear is to poison one's self—Moses just reveals a poison already present.

Impatience can be said to be an outward and visible sign of past responses not knowing what to do in a new setting where they cannot be relied upon to be effective. Impatience needs to be seen for what it is—a panic-attack dependence upon a past way—before we can breathe deeply enough to welcome a new path.

Curiosity is a helpful tool to help us not be consumed with impatience. A non-attached wonder does wonders for attending to figuring out what is next. It is helpful to consider what you, or a group you are part of, have as a ratio between impatience and wonder. It will give a clue about your relationship with larger movements within and about.

Try imaging impatience being crucified. Might it set wonder free?

Deuteronomy 8:7–18
Thanksgiving

So often we have a long prayer before a Thanksgiving Feast. Note here that thanks is given after we have eaten our fill.

This is an excellent piece of advice. Our tendency when full is to expect more. We have been privileged and grown accustomed to such. The Deuteronomist is very clear that danger lurks exactly at the point where we might give thanks, but, instead, we expect G*D to fill our growing expectation of ease and comfort.

To intentionally give thanks beyond ourselves puts a buffer between our pride and our deserving of more. Thanks, here, is not mouthed piety. Rather, it is steely-eyed reality thankful for how far we have come, but recognizing that none will be whole until all are.

"Take care lest you forget and your heart grows haughty and you forget Freedom's source is not your own power or worthiness." Freedom comes through desert hardship and is most fragile in the midst of fertile ease.

It may help to turn to the Black National Anthem, "Lift Every Voice and Sing", as a Thanksgiving Hymn. It is to be preferred over "Come, Ye Thankful People, Come" that looks to a claim on some future heaven, forgetting to work toward paradise in the present.

———————————————

Sing a song full of the faith that the dark past has taught us;
Sing a song full of the hope that the present has brought us.

Stony the road we trod, bitter the chastening rod,
Felt in the days when hope unborn had died.

We have come over a way that with tears has been watered;
We have come treading our path through the blood of the
    slaughtered.

Lest our feet stray from the places, our God, where we met thee;
Lest our hearts drunk with the wine of the world, we forget thee.

Selected:
Words by James Weldon Johnson
Music by J. Rosamond Johnson

Deuteronomy 11:18–21, 26–28
Guiding Gift [9] – Proper 4 (9)

Blessings and Curses abound. Our tendency is to focus on one or the other. This is a great theological divide between people—as great a division as the languages at Babel.

Is your initial orientation to life a glass half-full or half-empty and how do you account for the experiences of life that point in the other direction? Between recognizing our proclivities and overcoming our resistance to change lies the experience of Pentecost or any other epiphany.

Habituation is one of the realities we need to take into account as we attempt to stay up-to-date with a next stage of growth in our understanding of ourselves and our experiences. After we walk past the same picture for a week, it becomes a space holder. We know what is generally there but it has lost a connection with our latest experiences and is either misapplied to them or lost track of.

We take our last learning and codify it. Then we tack it up or carry it as a hammer to adjust every new situation to the way we have decided it should be.

To bind a past experience to our life is to blind ourselves to a current choice able to lead us beyond a mere continuation of the past to a jump to a preferred future.

Yes, write down your experiences. Interpret them along the way. But be ready to thank them for bringing you thus far along the way and to bid them as fond a farewell as you have to teddy bears of yore. There is a new choice to be made and a new basis for making that choice.

---

mementos in hand
cry out for eternity
never satisfied
for a moment

choices arriving
set a new moment
yearning
for a chance

Deuteronomy 30:15–20
Guiding Gift [6]

Jesus' statements "You have heard it said, but ..." remind us that one of G*D's nicknames is Freedom. After being kidnapped by government forces in the 2011 "Arab Spring", Wael Ghonim said, "This is not the time to settle scores. Although I have people I want to settle scores with myself. This is not the time to split the pie and enforce ideologies."

Here is a choice as stark as those between a scripturally heightened rhetoric of "Life and Good" or "Death and Evil" or "Fire and Water". Here we have "Violence and Retribution" or "Freedom and Cooperation".

We have heard and lived in cultures of "Power Over" and again we see the gift of "Freedom Growing" from beneath. After remembering an old Egyptian poem,

> *The Nile can bend and turn,*
> *but what is impossible is*
> *that it would ever dry up.*

Professor Mamoun Fandy remarked, "The same is true of the river of freedom that is loose here now. Maybe you can bend it for a while, or turn it, but it is not going to dry up."

The choice to be free, to hear "you have heard it said, but ..." is basic to life and therefore to G*D and therefore to us as a goal. Not to choose beyond enforced consistency is a hobgoblin of little lives (no matter how large they project themselves).

Simply put, we have not been commanded to side with or be wicked, nor have we been given permission to tear down others to aggrandize one's self. We are in this together. I rejoice when you can stand tall for the Freedom of G*D [rendered into Olde English as "Kingdom of G*D"] right where you are. It encourages me to stand tall where I am. I'll do what I can to return the favor.

A G*D of Freedom again sets before us a choice—settle scores or build new blessings.

Deuteronomy 34:1–12
Proper 25 (30)

What vision is larger than yourself? Is glimpsable though not achievable in your life or life-time?

Is that not worth pursuing with all one's presence and passion and prayer?

One way of coming at this is to listen for what promises ring most true. Another way is to listen to your heart's desire.

Both ways are dependent upon listening as well as Moses did whether he was observing injustice, noting a strange event in nature, remaining persistent in the face of seeming failure after failure to have people freed, believing rocks and water contain each other, receiving mountain-top inspiration, etc. So, listen for a vision and follow and share.

What do you see that you will not be a part of, other than as an extension of what you are doing today?

This vision will help keep your sight unimpaired and your vigor unabated. To drop your eyes to where you are presently standing and to only find ways to keep standing there is to cause one to weep for oneself rather than weep for others.

Lift up your eyes to the world you want to see and live as though it were already present.

Then, when death comes, it is just a next thing to do.

Joshua 3:7–17
Proper 26 (31)

Let's see, YHWH says, "You are still on a journey of freedom. Instead of raising your staff like Moses, send the Ark ahead into the water and the barrier will become dry land."

Then, as in the Garden a long time ago, come additional interpretive words, "The sign that G*D is with us is not a repeat of nature miracles, but acts of genocide."

Ouch. Like conversations in the Garden, Joshua says more than he heard. How often do we say more than we have heard (making it up as we go along)?

True enough, back in Chapter 1, YHWH speaks of possessing or inheriting the land. All manner of justifications have been used for a "holy curse" or "holy war" that Joshua uses. My own favorite excuse is that they couldn't help using this technique because it was a matter of survival—the end justified the means. For those of us who follow the story of Jesus (Joshua II) the issue is not survival, but faithfulness unto resurrection. Put the ark of your body into the fear and trust it.

My own sense is that those who use a "holy curse" will die or be exiled by the same. This perspective seems never to be seen by those who use this technique (whether on the right or the left). It is very effective in the short-run and so devastating to everyone in the long-run.

We still live in a time of "holy curse" within United Methodism. If you have a question about this, look at the attempts of the religious right to conquer the traditional Methodist wedding of personal piety with social mercy by causing a divorce between them and giving all the proceeds to the personal. In this scenario General Conference is the promised land and majority rules is the ark. Leaders past and present of The Institute on Religion and Democracy, Good News, Confessing Movement, etc., rejoice in playing a current role of Joshua with their additional interpretive and justifying words.

I suppose that just saying this much puts me in the same camp where a first and last response is, "Off with their head." I pray for better from me and you and others.

Joshua 24:1–3a, 14–25
Proper 27 (32)

I do wish this lection had continued to verse 28. Then we would have heard about a stone that heard everything that G*D had said to the people.

Every General Conference there are huge volumes of verbatim from the floor. Toting them around is like carrying a stone. In them we hear everything that people say to justify themselves. Included in those volumes are sermons that are preached. (Supposedly these contain what G*D is saying to the General Conference delegates. My experience is that there is a huge disconnect between the sermons and the actions of the delegates. The sermons run up against predetermined bias and fade away before an amen is heard.)

It is as though Joshua really understood us.

"Choose this day!"

"OK, we choose G*D."

"You're not up to that promise."

"Yes we are."

"We'll see."

I'd like to have stones piled up in a place of worship so the stones can clearly hear the prayers and scripture and preaching and music of worship. Then, at the end of time together, dismiss the people (along with a listening stone given to them) each to their own "heritage" or "ministry". The instructions would be to carry the stone with them during the week and to regularly take it out and listen to what it heard during worship. May we remember and be glad.

Judges 4:1–7
Proper 28 (33)

Jabon and Sisera are used by G*D to punish Israel. Deborah is used by G*D to punish the punishers, Jabon/Sisera, for their 20 years of punishing. And around we go.

In regard to punishment, how is G*D using you? Are you to help punish someone G*D is mad at? Are you to punish someone who has been one of G*D's past punishers? Is punishment a helpful category?

If we posit an eternal reciprocal engine that runs on punishment, stroke-by-stroke, what would cause us to look for an alternative energy source since anger seems to be eternally renewable?

On the flip side, we wait for G*D to set life up for us. We spend our time and energy attempting to get ourselves in the right position to take advantage of G*D's setup. This attempted readiness seems, more often than not, to have some ritualistic element to it according to the wisdom of the day about how to get on G*D's good side.

Barak had it easy. Just go and wait and G*D will manage to have events conspire in your favor. We continue to look for this sort of intervention—that G*D finally has set things up for us to win. No lottery odds for us—we want to know G*D is on our side and has actually arranged for us to win in the short-run—none of this pie in the sky, by and by, stuff.

We find it very easy to be over-reliant upon G*D, exempting ourselves from any responsibility for the events of life. Zephaniah's phrase, "rest complacently on their dregs", fits well here. We can also fall into despair that allows us to simply keep on keeping-on in the easiest manner possible—G*D not seeming to do anything, either healing or violent.

Being willing to do our part to partner with G*D—to encourage, and push G*D along and even go so far as to set things up for G*D—would shift this eternal punishment model. Come, let us counsel together that we might short-circuit our respective knee-jerk responses to life.

1 Samuel 2:1–10
Elizabeth and Mary Meet

Exultation is a category unto itself. Whether on the way up or the way down, whether currently rich or poor, powerful or forlorn, exultation is available.

Where we catch a glimpse of more than ordinarily expected we are on the verge of exultation, leaping to a new level of awareness and participating in the mystery of a deeper common good and a better future already incarnating in the present.

Exultation is equivalent to a shift in an elemental valence—energy is expanded and released far beyond expected every-day levels.

When invited to exult the only pertinent question is, "How high?"

Might you exult in exalting your next visitor?

Well, of course.

Alright, then, will you?

Uh ....

1 Samuel 16:1–13
Conviction 4

Samuel may help us into a question of "blindness". Early on he was deafened by his own name and not able to hear beyond it. Here Samuel is stymied by his fear which feigned grief. Later Samuel is blinded by Eliab's physical attributes. After anointing David, the last and least of Jesse's sons, he sets out for Ramah, anticipating a later scene of Rachel's weeping grief for her children.

Blindness is not just personal, but corporate. As we talk of social holiness, so we need to speak of social blindness. To translate this to modern concepts—I think we could say that someone or a whole culture may not be blind, but they might be "blinded". If something is in a person's blind spot, they won't see it. If a light is too bright, they won't see it. If there are too many distractions, they won't see it. It is the same with hearing deafness; if a sound blocks people's voices or if we are in a room with a lot of echo, we are "deafened".

Samuel got caught in a cultural appeal for a king, fearing a king out of power, and not able to recognize a next king. In each case his blindness and deafness did not lead to playing a mean pinball. Things fall apart and we fall with them. Things are crookedly put together and we are misshapen in crooked's image.

In the end Samuel returns home to Ramah—a high place for idols—that systemically, culturally, blocks a new word and later will be a place of slaughter (always a prime indicator that blindness and deafness are present in high places). Samuel returns home after this scene and the next we hear of him—he died.

Though fondly remembered, Uncle Samuel, is one who wrestled long with not hearing and not seeing.

1 Kings 3:5–12
Proper 12 (17)

Solomon's disposition in the beginning was for wisdom. Where did that go wrong? By the end of his reign things were falling apart. It is difficult to maintain wisdom in the midst of power.

Is a part of the issue before the church and world a continuing constriction of where G*D can be found? Here at one of many local shrines, wisdom can be sought. In the one and only temple, power can be found. How are we constraining G*D these days through space and scripture and specialness?

Solomon begins where Adam and Eve do, looking for the difference between good and evil. They find evil in the blame game (it's your fault). Solomon will find evil in power (it's my right). Where do you find evil? Searching out a difference between good and evil may be a beginning spot for wisdom, but in the long run wisdom needs more than this. It also needs to find a way for a prophetic judgment that difficulties are also my fault and blessings are also your right.

1 Kings 19:9–18
Proper 14 (19)

Can you tell any tonal difference in Elijah's two explanations of why he is off dreaming in a cave when he might be engaged in the danger that is life?

When you read this passage aloud do you read verse 10 the same as verse 14?

The first question about what Elijah is doing at a cave comes after 40 days without food. The second question comes a 1st day after the symbolic 40 and after feasting on sheer silence.

Elijah's first response reflects his not finding G*D in all the usual in-your-face places. Elijah's second response follows the hiddenness of quiet or silence.

With the same words do you sense a shift from edgy, defensive, blaming to calmly centered, clear, ready to take part?

How's your stress level today? Is it time to be intentional about casting about for a gentle whisper that will reorient your attention and fortify you to re-engage?

Quiet is a place we do well to regularly cultivate. It must be noted, though, that silence is not a natural place for many and it can take earthquake, wind, and fire to move some toward it. If nothing else noise will eventually deafen us and so consider finding a vast and reorienting quiet before it is required.

Job 14:1–14
Absent Saturday

Will we live again? Will release come? These questions are as deep and unanswerable as the "why" questions of life. We never know.

We wait in the unknowing. All we have to hang on to is an expectation that steadfast love is accessible, even while we don't know. So we cast about asking, "Are you a taste of steadfast love?" ... "Is this a new recognition of steadfast love?"

We wait in the unknowing. We fret and fear. We hardly hope.

Yet, we wait in the unknowing. We go one more day. We go one more step. We take one more action for what we understand to be wholeness for ourselves and others.

We wait, unknowing.

Psalm 1
Proper 25 (30)

Remember your joys. Live your joys. Anticipate your joys.

Then take a next quantum leap:

remember joy; live joy; anticipate joy.

No matter in what order you proceed through this trinity of joy, you will find yourself embarking on other aspects of love.

An excellent start to the Psalms; an excellent start, period. Now that it has begun, keep it rolling.

---

a tree by water
lives forward
season by season

chaff in the wind
is left behind
seasonless

if a choice were needed
polls show trees
well ahead

hulls have protected
tender seeds
and been jettisoned

their servant's role
finished
they're blown away

having come to serve
we thank the chaff
and are happy

Psalm 2
Mountain Top to Valley

Holy Hill! Holy Mountain! Holy, Holy, Holy! Holy Land!

We do invest our spaces with meaning. We find the unremarkable has become remarkable; the mundane, sacralized. This process goes on and on.

When we look around we find a mountain is not a single entity but a seven-story event. We find our hill is not a molehill but an occasion to play King of the Mountain and compete with each other for preeminence.

Transfigurations can move contrariwise and we can find our laughter not being laughter *with* someone but *against* them in derision. Our experience of forgiveness can turn quickly to avenging past wrongs without ever getting to healing or restoration. Mercy received is not passed on. This may be why, in casual conversation, if you toss in the word "transfiguration" it is so easily heard as "disfiguration".

Mountain top experiences are real, but short-lived—a healer before; a healer after—a rascal before; a rascal after.

A transfiguring moment actually sets a different course. When we look back on the best of our transfiguring moments we can see they were more in an interpretation than the actual event.

May we be good interpreters of the experiences which come our way.

May we be good interpreters of the experiences of others.

Psalm 8
Naming Day — New Year's Day — Live Together

The first seven Psalms are prayers for help. Symbolically that would be all the prayers for help that would ever need to be prayed. Then comes Psalm 8, a hymn.

It seems appropriate to have this be a hymn, for, after praying prayers for help, we do finally have to give that over and simply sing for yet being alive. We begin to catch a glimpse of how our prayers for help might be settled without divine intervention.

First, we recognize a gift of creation—vast and venerable. There is a soft, far-off hymn of creation and new creation going on independent of ourselves. How, then, can we keep from singing?

Second, we claim an important spot in relationship to gods and angels. We have authority to make a difference in the situations we find ourselves.

Third, we know such importance does not mean domination. Our dominion, care, is not exploitative of creation nor over one another.

When these three become clear, we sing our little hearts out.

------

a food chain mystery
is no less a mystery
than a unitized trinity

we eat another's lunch
and in turn are eaten
but wait there's more

circles can end
children's songs
drown marching orders

Psalm 13
Proper 8 (13)

In the face of steadfast love there is but the moment.

To begin addressing the imponderable question of "How long?" it is helpful to return to a baby game of "How big?" — "So-o-o-o big" that becomes "How long?" — "So-o-o-o long".

Through the depths and heights, joys and sorrows, time and yet time again, forgotten and remembered, we have this portion of "So-o-o-o long". It is just long enough to raise a glass in toast and to raise a voice in song.

Come from mud and moving to dust we join in another chorus from St. Woodie:

> So long, it's been good to know yuh;
> So long, it's been good to know yuh;
> So long, it's been good to know yuh.
> This dusty old dust is a-gettin' my home,
> And I got to be driftin' along.

When time becomes part of steadfast love and allows alternatives, Abraham is set free from having to sacrifice. Isaac is set free from having to be sacrificed. Lovers are set free from any co-dependency. Righteous folk and thirsters after righteousness are set free from creedal restrictions on their actions. Angels are set free from having to tote sheep to high places.

Whether "So-o-o-o Long" turns out to be long or short, we have an on-going choice:

> This dusty old dust is a-gettin' my home,
> I choose kindness while driftin' along.

Psalm 15
Guiding Gift 4

Who lives without blame? This becomes particularly poignant if we ask to whom and to what we are paying attention during our everyday life when little things count as much as big things.

To be honorable, through and through, means living from and to the heart—from our heart to the heart of another (whether that be G*D or Neighb*r). So how are we doing?

Blessed are those who ...

walk blamelessly (who are poor in spirit)

speak truth from their heart (who mourn)

do no evil to friends (who are meek)

do not reproach neighbors (who hunger and thirst for righteousness)

stand by their oath (who are merciful)

do not lend money at interest (who are pure in heart)

do not take a bribe against the innocent (who are peacemakers)

shall not be moved (who are persecuted)

In so doing we honor the hope of our creation—caretakers and co-creators.

Psalm 16
Hopeless Hope Vigil — Assured [2]

"The boundary lines have fallen for me in pleasant places."–*NRSV*
Hear this word from John Wesley's *Directions for Renewing our Covenant with God*, Third Edition, 1784.

> Christ hath many services to be done, some are more easy and honourable, others more difficult and disgraceful: some are suitable to our inclinations and interests, others are contrary to both: in some we may please Christ and please ourselves, as when he requires us to feed, and cloath ourselves, to provide things honest for our own maintenance, yea, and there are some Spiritual duties that are more pleasing than others; as to rejoice in the Lord, to be blessing and praising of God, to be feeding ourselves with the delights and comforts of Religion; these are the sweet works of a Christian. But then there are other works, wherein we cannot please Christ, but by denying ourselves, as giving and lending, bearing and forbearing, reproving men for their sins, withdrawing from their company, witnessing against their wickedness, confessing Christ and his Name, when it will cost us shame and reproach; sailing against the wind, swimming against the tide, steering contrary to the time; parting with our ease, our liberties, and accommodations for the Name of our Lord Jesus.

Do you find these boundaries to be pleasant for you?

---

desperately seeking G*D
we search old haunts
apply old creeds
looking in all the old places

blundering with old swords
charging new cannon
with old canon
charging backward

honorable folly
is folly still
honor the past
by not repeating it

Psalm 17:1–7, 15
Proper 13 (18)

All who acknowledge G*D's right hand will find refuge there. Those who don't, won't. This is very convenient when we are convinced that our cause is just, our good looks quite sufficient, our perspective on any given issue at hand—accurate down to the last detail.

Because of our special relationship, G*D is as good as a trained hunting dog—ready to sic our point and fetch whenever we identify our prey, our enemy.

This is so comforting to us and so dangerous to others.

After catching on to this dichotomy we might listen to Eugene Peterson phrasing the last verse, "And me? I plan on looking you full in the face, when I get up, I'll see your full stature and live heaven on earth."

Whether or not there is a plan for our lives or a purpose to be aligned to, there is a meaning to be participated in—living heaven on earth. Regardless of external/internal mechanisms, we are called to "live tomorrow, today."

It is this that leads us, again and again, to a deserted spot where we don't have to give directions to G*D (as per this psalm) or receive some eternal answer to every question. When we simply are able to let circumstances be what they are and to stretch into a new way of being with others and with our self, we are (paraphrasing Holly Near) angry and gentle people, singing for our lives, doing what we can to live heaven on earth.

Psalm 19
Hopeless Hope Vigil — Proper 22 (27)

What does Madame Day teach every morning? and Professor Night each evening?

Is this a trick question simply because speech is not used?

Probably not. It is an opening to hear other important parts of your life that are also beyond being put into words. For instance, the whole category of sins of omission. How do you see what you haven't done? How do you hear about what you failed to say?

May you pay attention to the macro as "Madame Day holds classes every morning." –MSG

May you pay attention to the micro as "Professor Night lectures each evening." –MSG

May you additionally pay attention to the every-day as "Sister and Brother bring their perspective each mid-day and mid-night."

These are voices not heard, yet they go out through all the earth!

In the Psalm, "they" are the creation sequence—the evolution of creation—the elements basic to life.

In Scripture, "they" are also the poor, the widows, the children, the alien.

None of "them" has a voice and yet they cry out as mine-canaries deep below every political, economic, and educational system.

Have you heard "them"?

Do you add to the cry for G*D to attend to the vine, the creation, the poor?

Whether it seems your voice is heard or not, even whether you want it to be heard or not, it is important to know where you identify, what you listen to, what you pass on to G*D.

Listen well; speak clearly; act humbly.

Psalm 22
Annihilation Friday

I would prefer one longer Psalm that would bind Psalms 22 and 23 together.

This new movement would go beyond a sense of entitlement betrayed and beyond a simplistic, "G*D is everything."

A larger movement is from our sense of broken entitlement to a renewed understanding of living more largely than we have. It was our initial limitation of scope that led to the cry of abandonment.

Since this is a reflection on "Good Friday", the end of Psalm 22 leaves us without ourselves. Everything is G*D. This is as much as death, to become a proclaiming puppet.

If this is all there is, we have moved from being individually forsaken to being forsaken as a series of generations.

We still yearn for a participation in life and life's conflictual realities. Overflowing cups and resurrection invite us to live in light of goodness and mercy, no matter what the consequences.

Even as we have some down time here with this Psalm, it is not the end of the story.

Psalm 23
Conviction [4] — Assured [4] — Proper 23 (28)

When something gets so familiar that we skim over it because we know it, there is a need to turn it around. Have you tried reading this Psalm backwards?

Throughout the length of my days, I am forever in the presence of Creation.
Every step I take reveals goodness and kindness and mercy.
A Flood of Blessing is so overwhelming I am emboldened to feast with everyone, including enemies.
Comforting Strength guides and guards my encounters with evil, no matter how pervasively heavy it might seem.
Grace points to safe paths that lead to life renewed.
Sabbath Rest and Milk and Honey beyond wanting, are gifts.

My whole life long I shall dwell in the house of G*D;
    all the days of my life lead to goodness and mercy.
My cup overflows; my head is anointed with oil;
    my enemies become feasting partners.
I am comforted by Rod and Staff, signs I am not alone;
I fear no evil even though I walk through the darkest valley.
For G*D's sake I am led in paths of righteousness.
G*D restores my soul with waters of rest and verdant pastures.
I shall not want for G*D is my shepherd.

Do note the plural on "paths of righteousness" and consider how many different ways lead there.

Psalm 24:7–10
Old Welcomes New

Here comes a 40-day-old baby and we image a fanfare of doors opening.

An unresolved task of the church is to move from the particularity of Jesus to every child, including those who have grown.

Wherever formal or informal discrimination shuts doors on people for simply being, the church is complicit in that discrimination if it is not actively breaking discriminatory laws or attitudes. No matter the number of resolutions passed or encyclicals published, a closed door closes a ministry of Jesus.

This is a fun and exciting passage even though it seriously mistakes a baby or a messiah for a battle-hardened king. This error has been compounded down through the ages as the church, as an institution, becomes ever more institutionalized with bigger doors to slam on some and to open for a privileged few while most just watch from afar.

As an alternative to mighty doors, you might want to consider returning to a paganish Candlemas nicely positioned astrologically and lift a flickering candle for the fragility of a babe-in-arms—all of them.

Psalm 25:1–9
Proper 21 (26)

"Integrity and generosity are marks of Yahweh..." –NJB

These are issues we need to focus on, again and again.

What does it mean to have integrity? My *Webster's Third New International Dictionary* lists as its first definition: "An unimpaired or unmarred condition: entire correspondence with an original condition." We are creation-centered. We listen for the refrain, "It is good." We measure ourselves against what we understand G*D's intention for creation was (not how far we have fallen short). We encourage everyone to work together. We are like the prophets, always returning to creation as our plumb-line.

And generosity? Try this same dictionary's definition: "Liberality in spirit or act." There is an expansiveness here that goes beyond definitions of the status quo. This may have something to do with the line "be fruitful and multiply." If it does, that means more than literal procreation. There is also a suggestion of working from a mind and heart-set of abundance rather than scarcity. We have enough experience of G*D's merciful hospitality toward ourselves that we can let our cups overflow with this same generosity toward others.

Keep practicing. Keep encouraging others to so practice.

Psalm 26:1–8
Proper 17 (22)

"I never lose sight of your love...."
–MSG

"I love the beauty of your house and
the place where your glory dwells."
–NJB

We enjoy courting moments. We draw and are drawn.

What are other parts of a constellation of love/beauty/glory?

This would be an interesting way of evaluating decisions so that if we are fooling ourselves about love (and that is so easy to do) that we might catch ourselves on the beauty or the glory aspects of a decision.

If we can't trust the overuse of the word "love" as a basis for action, might we ask if our decision will bring more beauty, more glory? Will the world be a happier place? Will the ratio of peace and justice jump higher? Will we choose to bless at every moment because at every moment we know ourselves blest?

Psalm 27:1,4–9
Guiding Gift [3]

In the midst of a roller-coaster that is life—

Up—confidence in G*D

Down—evildoers assail

Up—I'll still be confident

Down—days of trouble

Up—praise

Down—abandoned

Up—taken in

Down—violence

Up—courage

—are you a glass half-full (bottom-half awaiting more or top-half anticipating a fall) or are you a glass half-empty (bottom-half, all that's left from being of service, or top-half, covering emptiness)?

If called, will you go hesitantly or enthusiastically? In the midst of disagreement are you a hands-on bridge-builder or hands-off they-deserve-each-other trumpeter?

Is our one desire to live in G*D's house or skin? This would take forgetting a number of other things we know about G*D. We are likely to still have a sense of uncertainty while inside G*D's place. G*D seems to have arguments with G*D and to repent G*D's own actions and experience. Why wouldn't we, who are filled with G*D DNA, find ourselves likewise divided wherever we find ourselves?

As we live in the midst of divisions where it is all too easy to claim our good as very good and the bad of our adversary as very bad, remembering we live in a tension with ourselves as well as with others will help us along the way.

Is it true that my good isn't good enough yet because it hasn't adequately taken your good into account?

Psalm 29
Beloved

"May we be blessed with peace"—everyone's favorite easy answer to the question, "What do you most desire this year?"

Working backward through the Psalm, we find ourselves a-shoutin', "Glory!" Why would we do that?

Might it be as a result of what G*D has thundered over the waters of chaos since time immemorial—"Beloved!"

G*D dreamt, "Beloved", and light came to show it. G*D whispered, "Beloved", and division came to reveal a blessing of particularity. G*D said, "Beloved", and seed came to carry it on. G*D spoke, "Beloved", and cycles polished it bright. G*D intoned, "Beloved", and multiplication arose to show a growing universe. G*D thundered, "Beloved", and burst into infinite images of beloved caring.

G*D saw creation was good and is good and will be good.
St. Julian saw, "All manner of things shall be well".
What do you see?

Want peace? See Belovedness everywhere (beauty ahead, behind,....). Thunder Belovedness everywhere.

BBaep/toivsemd (password/code starting with Baptism)
BBealpotviesdm (password/code starting with Beloved)

Whether you begin with Baptism or Belovedness, the two are intimately intertwined.

Psalm 31:1–4, 15–16
Absent Saturday

Eventually we run out of options. We raise our hands and surrender. Seeing no way out of a net made of our own expectations, there is a time to appeal for help.

Even then an old joke comes into play: While hanging onto a cliff by a fingernail and importuning G*D to intervene, a voice from above says, "Let go," to which we respond, "Is there anyone else up there?"

We can't trust ourselves to get us out of our pickle. We are unwilling to trust any other wisdom, particularly if it stretches our disbelief farther than acceptable to us.

Whine all you want about your distress or loss; our experience is that dead means dead. Only a great mystery will do here, not a quick answer.

On a Saturday like today we are experiencing a hell in our lives and not experiencing Jesus bringing his new perspective. Sometimes there is no explaining forlornness. We no longer live in hope and can but hope that hope still lives in us.

Psalm 31:1–5. 15–16
Assured [5]

A purpose of a refuge is to gather courage to reenter a fray, not to simply be cared for forever.

We who have received a gift of compassion and extension of that beyond our own certainly do need courage to keep expressing such a gift in every circumstance. I have yet to see a system or structure of this world that values compassion. Oh, the appearance of compassion is a selling point ("compassionate conservatism"), but more than fooling the people one more time, compassion, itself, does not come highly valued.

Intentional refuge is an interesting image that raises a question about sabbath being a prophylactic or a treatment. Do you use sabbath time as preparation time or recuperation time? Probably some of both, but there may be one that you use more than the other.

Whichever way you have been gifted, may you find your experience of refuge to refresh your courage.

If you are finding your courage and boldness waning as you engage principalities and powers, it would be good to engage your faith community or a spiritual director in an investigation of the state of refuge or sabbath in your life.

Psalm 31:1–5, 19–24
Guiding Gift [9] — Proper 4 (9)

be steadfastly courageous
act as though assured of refuge

assumed haughtiness
desires entitlement
claimed through
a contentious tongue

assured of refuge
be steadfast in courage

blind to self-traps
too far below
what is deserved
we trip over ourselves

freed from expectation
comes expansive new refuges

Psalm 31:9–16
Premature Fear Sunday

I hear the whispering of many—"terror all around!"

If those are the last words we hear from this Psalm, it is a sad song. No wonder we hedge our bets and get as strong as we can possibly get. Paying attention to that whisper may help us to be as wise as a serpent. Paying overmuch attention to that whisper, so it appears to be a din, will lead one to being a snake and preemptively terrorize.

To lead us back toward the innocence of a dove we have to hear about trust and steadfast love, even in the face of terror.

What is today's pervasive whisper of terror? It has been heard in Syria, Iran, North Korea, percentage of incarcerated in the USA, racism and all the other isms dividing one from another, and global rape of labor, not to mention all the etceteras. May we listen more deeply to an eternal trust that involves us in living out steadfast love, no matter what else we hear.

"Be gracious to me, O Lord, for I am in distress .... save me in your steadfast love."

Can't you just hear G*D reply, "April Fool! I already am gracious to you and all. You are already saved."

April Fool's Day comes to puncture our seriousness. It arrives to grant us a renewed perspective. It is so easy to get caught up in the Sturm und Drang of life and not see our next step so we give it over to some deity or other. Thanks be for April 1and a Sunday after Easter when a court jester can play to our ruling self and point a better way. Would that such were several times a year.

Psalm 32
Conviction [1]

Blessed are those forgiven a choice to follow temptation.

Blessed are those able to now clarify a temptation facing them.

Blessed are those whose temptations have been chosen against.

Blessed are those steadfast in choosing against temptation.

Psalm 33:1–12
Proper 5 (10)

How new a song can be sung? Wherein lie the limits of G*D's creation and G*D's favor?

This is one of the questions with which we wrestle. There is value in tradition and continuity. There is value in breaking new ground (earth) and new hope (heaven). Between these two we usually find ourselves trapped into valuing tradition and continuity more than we value new ground and new hope.

The risks in turning this value system upside-down are often too great for us—so we emphasize G*D's designs and plans and will as eternal and constant. G*D's people are G*D's people and those who aren't, aren't. The Psalm ends with G*D's steadfast love being called our own. This is a pretty old song—I got mine, too bad about you.

A new song would be to call G*D to love all there is with all the love G*D has. A new song would risk the joy of our own hearts being loved, by living as if that joy is not complete until it also springs forth in others.

A mystery of this new song is that there is more than enough Babel (counsel of nations) in each of us to separate us from one another and there is more than enough of G*D's love to bind us together. May you live in the larger mystery of G*D's love and sing a new song.

Psalm 34:1–10, 22
Honoring Day

Hear again this song of blessing for deliverance from trouble. Saints are able to look beyond a current difficulty to a blessing yet to come. Saints are thus able to experience *dayenu* and *l'chaim* amid any suffering, not beyond it.

When we have tasted a feast before it is set before us, we can claim our whole being (mouth, tongue, lips, eyes, ears, face, bones) knows more than a moment. This makes a difference in the way we engage others. It makes a difference in how we are experienced by others.

The poles of response by others runs from adoring fans waiting for our next pearl of wisdom to deadly enemies for bringing them a choice in their behavior. Both of these run a danger of our being defined from the outside. Saints have a gift to humbly wait with G*D to see what will develop next.

Since troubles are so universal, we have plenty of opportunity to practice encouraging others to engage the saint within them and to be encouraged by others to engage ourselves as saint.

When connecting with our internal saint we sense a cloud of witnesses of those who have participated in their own journey of seeming mad in the face of their culture's norms and fears. We are welcomed to dive deeper into life and have a choice to continue onward or to return to the safety of everyday existence.

May we be proud of the saints we have known and may others eventually be proud of having known as much of the saint we are becoming as they can grasp.

Psalm 36:5–11
Clarification Week Monday

Let's begin with a renaming: Clarification Week, not Holy Week.

Our very distinction of "Holy This" or "Holy That" belies the "holiness" of life in all things. With too much coded holiness we move into unhelpful dualities that end up splitting spiritual and material.

The Psalm begins with plotting in bed—nightmares continued into the day. I suppose this could be seen as a foreboding of Judas' journey between Palm Sunday and Maundy Thursday.

Even so, the larger story is not that of betrayal but a continuance of steadfast love (salvation, if you will). We participate in this love and add our part to its continual revelation. Hold hands; do not be driven from this reality.

This pericope could have continued to the end of the Psalm. This would have brought us back around to doing-in those identified as evildoers. Instead it ends with a simple call for protection: "Bestow faithful care on those participating in greater justice who are caught in traps set by those claiming entitlement to continue their ways."

We cannot follow Jesus' way, differentiated from that of Judas and Religious Leaders attempting to continue a privileged status of money or power, without seeing beyond the usual visible spectrum. This seeing into the infrared or the ultraviolet is to see deeper into creation, into G*D. The Psalmist puts it this way, "By this light do we see light."

Even though this is a week with great sadness, we find a bubbling fountain of life in mercy far outweighing betrayal by encompassing it.

Psalm 40:1–11
Guiding Gift [2]

"I waited and waited and waited for God."
Psalm 40:1a –MSG

Remember how far it is from Jesus' birth to baptism? It is far longer than the twelve days from Christmas to Epiphany. Traditionally it was a 30-year wait. Less than a 40-year wait in the Wilderness, but still a long time. How many died for no good reason during that wait? How many were born? How consistently perfect were our heroic figures?

"At last God looked; finally God listened."
Psalm 40:1b –MSG

The wait was about a direct encounter, a sense of belovedness strong enough to stop waiting. Enough, G*D, of the active listening. Enough, G*D, of the appreciative inquiry. Enough, G*D, of the anticipatory waiting. Enough.

Now, with a firm grasp of mercy beyond repentance, Jesus rises out of chaotic waters (even as Moses put his sandals back on after that mystery of an unconsumed burning bush). And you? No matter how great your repentance it will always be outdone by mercy. So you might as well get on with it—receive great mercy; give great mercy.

No matter how long it has been, living a moment in mercy more than balances all the years of waiting (well, if your view is long enough and you don't want to apply fairness or justice to each opportunity faced). Perhaps we only need to affirm that mercy is a more wholesome approach to life than is an insistence on repentance.

May you find a new song of mercy on your tongue and in your life.

Psalm 40:5–10
Creation's Conception

Stories begin in the middle of things (in medias res). In the middle of wondrous deeds we can look back and see that ritual sacrifices fall far short of being an adequate response.

In the middle of steadfast love we can look ahead by responding with our life, not someone else's.

Here we are, in the middle of a story gone on for generations before us and promised for generations to come.

In the middle of my story, G*D's story, and our story, it is a joy to reveal blessing following blessing.

Blessings have been present all along, even if dimmed by preoccupation with one construct or another. This is another day for them to be announced.

This is a good day to start a new habit of your heart.

1) Actually go outside

2) Turn to the West and give thanks for the blessings of yesterday on which the sun set

3) Turn to the North and wait to hear of blessings being unthawed for today

4) Turn to the East and announce a blessing you intend to have become real

5) Turn to the South to receive energy to follow your intention with action

6) Proceed

[Note: In the southern hemisphere the directions
would be ordered West, South, East, North.]

Psalm 42 & 43
Hopeless Hope Vigil

Where is your G*D?

Let us offer a word of Thanks to our "enemy" who, in one way or another, raises this basic question. However it comes, we are blessed through a focus on an important question that we resist asking ourselves.

Here G*D is closely allied and associated with Hope and experienced through a steadfastness of a "love song" that touches deep places beyond any of our usual markers—beyond hope, beyond faith, beyond love. There is a yearning here that will not be satisfied with any of our usual measures—hope is not enough; faith is not enough; love is not enough.

This is a Jewish koan: "Where is your G*D?" No response is sufficient. Every response leads deeper. Some responses are more enlightening than others, but none are wide enough to hold for all time. This is instructive when we make an opportunity to sink deep within this question. This existential question balances an Edenic question from G*D, "Where are you?"

So we seek each other, we bump into each other, face-to-face and back-to-back, calling to each other, "Beloved, where are you? Come out and play."

Finally, an openness to this question leads us toward becoming G*D, doing greater things. It resets our compass that has gotten confused with secondary priorities. Thankfully, if we have stopped asking the question of ourself, our favorite enemy raises it in ways we cannot avoid. It leads G*D toward us, doing humbler things. It reveals, within every everyday day, another facet of rainbows and empty tombs.

So, where is your G*D and what is keeping you from moving in that direction?

Psalm 43
Proper 26 (31)

Well, soul, why so down in the dumps?

Have you not noticed what is going on around you and within you? How oblivious can you be?

Oh, right. Yep, pretty bad out there and in here. And so it was a day ago and a millennium ago and three before that. In fact it probably will be tomorrow and a next whenever as well.

That sure cheers me up!

Facing that reality wasn't intended to cheer you up, but to remind me that, none-the-less, hope really does abound.

Hope?

Yep. In fact it's living within you right now and will be visible when you're ready to recognize it.

OK. I'll take your word for it. But, I'm still down in the dumps.

OK. I'm still with you.

OK.

Psalm 45
Creation's Conception

This version of an annunciation to Mary of a child to be born has the great benefit of being sensual. Enough of a magical virgin birth. An annunciation without a love song isn't worth hearing.

The sterility of a transaction and made-up creed pales in the face of a basic beauty of sexuality.

If hormones are not blessable, no part of creation is.

Listen to Chris Smither's song, "Origin of Species" to hear about G*D's "unfolding plan" to make DNA for all, "from paramecium right up to man". Chris, filling in for Gabriel, announces for G*D,

> They'll have sex
> And mixed up sections of their code
> They'll have mutations ...
> The whole thing works like clockwork over time.
>
> I'll just sit back in the shade
> While everyone gets laid.
> That's what I call
> Intelligent design.

Whether through the instantaneous or some eon-long version of Isaac Azimov's foundational psychohistory, a G*D worth its/their salt can raise up bones and stones and can do the same with any and everybody. We need to tell a new story that you and I and all carry dominant Messiah genes. May yours be seen and may you announce those you see.

Psalm 45:10–17
Proper 9 (14)

Enjoy a comment from *The New Interpreter's Bible* on verse 17 —"Memory and praise promise permanence to the king (or perhaps the princess)." Ahh, yes.

May you reconnect memory and promise. These polarities reinforce one another. Wherever you find yourself, may you find memory and find promise.

The Psalmist uses a rare loanword from Akkadian in referring to one who will become queen—"consort". May memory and promise consort with one another.

Remember G*D consorting with Adam and with Eve. Remember Adam and Eve consorting with one another. Remember all of humanity consorting with the rest of creation.

Hearken to a promise to till the ground and bear a next generation. Both promises keep us grounded in the reality of flesh. These pull us into watching our decisions for the next seven generations that they might well remember their ancestors.

When we bring together a Paradise of yore and a Heaven of yon we find Earth. Now we can see the burden and the joy of participating in creation as a "stewardship" strictly accountable to that which is put in your care.

As the wedding recounted proceeds, the consort changes relationships and possibilities. This is part of the reality of a consort, not just someone to stand beside, but to share rib-deep. Consort well.

Psalm 46
Hopeless Hope Vigil — Proper 4 (9)

To be a preparer of a better way is indeed a high calling. It is one within the reach of everyone.

Sometimes we strive for some better part, to be a hero/heroine in whatever situation we find ourselves. Sometimes that is not only possible, but achievable. For a given time and place, we are an obvious catalyst to move things along. More often we would do better to cast around for simply a next baby step that someone else will be able to build on and bring to fruition.

It is amazing how often this role of a preparer of a better future revolves around issues of forgiveness. Time and again a gift of radical forgiveness is needed to clear space for a better time. It is this forgiveness that provides a better picture of salvation and ways in which it might become clearer and stronger in our living.

In this last moment of the year we might cast our hearts and minds back over the past year to see the proportion of our experience that found us humbly preparing a better way compared to those moments where we were a final capstone put in place. My hunch is that we will all find ourselves more often in a role of preparer. Now that we have cast back, we might be able to more forthrightly and joyfully fill more of that role in the year ahead. This will lead to a greater fulfillment by this time next year.

---

there is a river
whose streams make glad
habitations of the heart
whose strong flow
sees us through to dawn

streams pre-river
sea post-river
play their part
along a way
of new life

gathering
holding
connected
river-wise
courageous

Psalm 47
Our Turn to Witness

> "*God has gone up* led Christians to associate the psalm
> with the ascension of Jesus to heaven; *with the sounds
> of a trumpet* led Jews to associate the psalm with *Rosh
> Hashanah*, New Year's Day." –*NISB* note.

Ahh, how a perspective one brings along determines what one
sees and hears and experiences.

So, is this the best of the Psalms to associate with Jesus' ascension? Probably not, given the overlay of subjugation that is present. It
simply adds to our propensity to turn an ascension metaphor or experience into unredeemable judgment. Somehow we keep turning
G*D's little artistic touches into additional excuses to subdivide people, losing many along the way.

Ascension is in some way a confirmation of our orphan-hood. We
are no longer simply disciples being filled, but a next generation of
folks attending to and pointing toward G*D's presence. Time to get on
with it without trying to get everything to fit into a nice, neat package.
Time to risk what it might mean to take another step in perfecting
love.

---

everywhere we go
people want to know
who we are
so we tell them
we are trumpeters
we are shouters
we are journeying

they scratch their heads
and still want to know
what in the world
we are trumpeting
shouting and where
we are going

and we jump up and down
and trumpet our shouts
the louder
repeating and
repeating

our shouting
their scratching
our jumping
cacophony

shifting strategies
everywhere we now go
we whisper along the way

what's that—they now say
and we pause to talk

finally joy

Psalm 50:7–15
Proper 5 (10)

A Word calls forth each and every piece of creation. Happy and blessed are those who respond to their call and participate in creation.

A Word turns away the limitations of sacrifice. Happy and blessed are those who refrain from ingrained habits of yore.

We are called to affirm affirmations that bring forth and to deny denials that limit and squelch.

Can you name an example of both? Were you able to make them interact in the same arena so a dynamic tension increases your spiritual strength? Or did you come up with examples that didn't intersect?

Here is one example: affirming universal health care as a right while at the same time providing loopholes that erode a general welfare through giving corporations a "religious conscience" able to withhold certain health benefits or subsidizing corporate profit through ridiculously low minimum wage requirements.

Psalm 51:1–17
Self-Recognition Day

Here are some words you may not be familiar with. In regard to a medicinal use of hyssop, various sources indicate it promotes expectoration through its stimulative, carminative and sudorific qualities. Definitions include: expelling gas from the stomach or intestines so as to relieve flatulence or abdominal pain or distention, causing or inducing sweat, and discharging matter from the throat or lungs by coughing or hawking and spitting.

Combine hyssop with white-washing and we have internal and external cleansing, a making whole or healthy, through and through.

We yearn for a restoration of joy. It is this energy source that turns us into evangelists (in a good way—O how we yearn for a day we won't have to distinguish helpful from manipulative evangelism, but for now there is too much bad "good news-ing" that goes on). What are you most joyful about? This is what you will plant more of in the world. For a helpful reference you may want to check out *Unbinding the Gospel: Real Life Evangelism* by Martha Grace Reese.

Here we are at Ash Wednesday, setting an agenda for the rest of the Lenten season—renewed health and joy. What disciplines for yourself or your congregation would be helpful this year? What will clean your insides and what your outsides?

---

language can be off-putting
as off-putting as off-putting
technical terms get bandied about
pulling the wool over some eyes
too often used approximately

this season may need plain-speaking
monosyllabic words
five syllables meaning one
hmmm, there's a long way to go to
help—way—joy

Psalm 65
Thanksgiving

Ask G*D, "Who is family?" The Psalmist sees G*D responding, "Creation!"

Creation is a needed perspective for our current economic and environmental politics. Living any part of creation is a daunting task by itself without trying to have dominion over everything else.

The Psalmist perceives G*D's goal to be to find a dynamic balance, at least for the moment, when each part sings for joy, together, with the others. Less than joyful singing comes when one perspective or presumptive value trumps the rest.

The Center for Christian Ethics at Baylor University reflects in their series on faith and ethics, *Economy of the Earth*[1], how G*D's family of creation can be separated from one another and G*D by market forces and capitalism, that which has an investment in seeing their corner increase in value regardless of other needs.

Three of their study questions would be helpful to reflect on that your thanks might be creation-wide:

1. Discuss the idea of an *ecolpreneur*. How would such persons overcome the limits of capitalism in caring for the creation?

2. How could communities have greater control over the excessive power of corporations? Are these steps necessary and wise?

3. How would fresh applications of the Sabbath and tithing help us tend the creation?

A question before us is that of having the eyes to see "family" in contexts other than human biology. With a clear picture we can identify those parts of the family that hold us back and those parts that call us to move on whether they be economic theologies or Gaian limits.

[1] www.baylor.edu/christianethics/GlobalWealthStudyGuide3.pdf

Psalm 65:(1–8), 9–13
Proper 10 (15)

Since we have a potential break after verse 8 or a start up at verse 9, we might wonder about who the "You" is at the beginning. If you start with verse 1 you might be tempted to claim it is G*D. If you were to hand this to someone starting at verse nine, they might think it was about them.

Try reading 9–13 as a reference to yourself.

> You visit the earth
> and make it abundant,
> > enriching it greatly
> > > by God's stream, full of water.
> You provide people with grain
> > because that is what you've decided.
> Drenching the earth's furrows,
> > leveling its ridges,
> > you soften it with rain showers;
> > you bless its growth.
> You crown the year
> with your goodness;
> > your paths overflow with rich food.
> Even the desert pastures drip with it,
> > and the hills are dressed in pure joy.
> The meadowlands are covered with flocks,
> > the valleys decked out in grain—
> > > they shout for joy;
> > > they break out in song!
> > > > – CEB

- Have you decided something other than to provide for the earth and people?

- What then might your decision point to?

- How's that going for you?

- Have you recently heard a shout for joy regarding your decisions?

Psalm 66:8–20
Assured [6]

Blessed be G*D—
  my [our] need has not been rejected and
  I [we] remain loved.
  –WW

Whether a personal or communal prayer, it is that word "because" that sticks in the craw. I got the "love" I bargained for for myself or ourselves, but it remains eternally suspect and fragile. It continues to need positive results. For in another moment we may be cursing G*D when we find ourselves not rescued on our terms.

Escape from Egypt and Wilderness, Wildfires in Alberta, recent record floods of the Assiniboine and Mississippi rivers, and winds throughout the American midwest all bring forth individual foxhole prayers and blessings.

How will G*D continue to prove to be a G*D worth blessing? By continuing to show how exceptional we are—we can let a roulette wheel ride on red for 47 continuous turns and we win each time. Odds be damned. Realistic projection be damned.

Is it "hooray" for flush times and "boo" for the thin? Doesn't this make G*D captive or me entitled? Might this be the flip-side of "If you love me, says Jesus, you will keep my commands"? Now, how do we step outside this house of religion built on so many conditions? It is as though Easter has been commodified. Only six weeks out from the astounding, dumbfoundingness, of "empty" and we are trying to stuff ourselves with the empty calories of privilege.

Psalm 67
Proper 15 (20)

- May G*D be gracious to us. Let all peoples praise G*D.

- May G*D continue to bless us. Let all the ends of the earth revere G*D.

- May the earth yield her produce. May all people everywhere hold G*D in awe.

Thoroughly plural in nature, the Psalm moves from a time of sowing to a time of harvest hoped to extend sufficiently to a next harvest. There is a sense of timelessness within time.

At the same time it gives direction from the "us" of the chosen to the "us" of others. Here time runs its usual sequence: first me, then you.

This interplay of creation's fecund increase and human's unequal participation in love or healing brings us to the usual paradox of praise—praise in anticipation and praise in response. Praise is not just praise but also technique to get some other goal met.

It might be helpful to question whether or not your sense of praise these days is that of anticipation to be completed or that of result accomplished and established. A hunch says, wait a bit—it won't be long before it switches and we will need to operate out of the other mode in order to make any sense out of present circumstances.

---

selah music	selah praise	selah living
pauses	breaks patterns	finds sabbath everywhere
interrupts	connects across time	harvests where it does not sow
accentuates	calls to account	praises in disaster
makes light of	completes	heightens paradox
tosses aside	drives onward	looks beyond today
flouts	keeps a beat	sounds like silence
rejects	raises questions	slows a tango
weighs	brings us to all	speeds a polka
balances	and all to mind	and rests

Psalm 68:1–10, 32–35
Assured [7]

It is difficult to connect the body of this psalm with its conclusion: Blessed be G*D!

Up to the conclusion everything is digital. It's either on or off; it's this or that; it's 1 or 0. In this zero sum world, one benefit is balanced by one imprecation. The concluding line about blessing comes from the winning folks on one side of the equation.

Our Wiccan friends often conclude their psalms with a simple, "Blessed Be."

If we are to talk about grace abounding, we need to find new ways to express ourselves that are not limited to a blessing of G*D without there also being a blessing of Self and Neighb*r. As you proceed in this day, notice where your blessings come, how they are directed, and how they might be enlarged.

At The United Methodist General Conference today we ground out the last of the items with financial implications. Oh so many tangled webs we wove as money is so fundamentally tied up with worth and power in a capitalist system. The jockeying for position was its usual marvel to behold. From a distance, it's almost funny. While in the middle of it, it is addictive to the extreme—emotions run high; voices crack; threats are made; the body is broken.

I'm not sure if there were any blessings today, other than the formal kinds. The word that came through most clearly to this listener was a young person calling others of their generation to begin working on a system that is more responsive in time than the accumulation of protections we have piled one on top of the next. Legislation for particular purposes eventually becomes a barrier to the very purposes it set out to address.

Interested in being a friend of G*D?
Befriend G*D's family.
Yes, all the family.
Particularly the desolate.

What is found in thus trying to draw near to G*D is the transformation that shakes rain from the heavens to water the parched earth. In caring for the extended family of creation it is our own dried up hearts that shake loose and we find the presence of G*D through tears of compassion.

Psalm 69:7–10, (11–15), 16–18
Proper 7 (12)

Are we patient or demanding when a result we would have is so slow in coming?

Patient: "at an acceptable time ... answer me." –NRSV

Demanding: "God, it's time for a break!" –MSG

Whichever tone is taken, is G*D's time now or later?

Now: "But I pray to you, O Lord, at a time most favorable to you." –CCB

Later: "So when the time is right, answer me and help me...." –CEV

Ah, the joy of many translations. Which one do I choose? For what reason?

Is your habit to look at choices through one lens or several? And what, would you say, are the pros and cons of your habit? Are there certain choices where you tend toward a single lens and other choices where you gravitate toward multiple lenses?

Knowing how we choose helps us clarify where a growing edge is for us and also gives hints about what sort of assistance we need when stuck.

At any rate, in the midst of choices, may we know G*D's freedom as our own.

Psalm 70
Clarification Week Wednesday — Proper 27 (32)

We are surrounded by a cloud of witnesses to a cloud of behaviors within. Today the warring of sore throat, bloated belly, and constricted head are all things I would leave behind. Along with them I would leave all the helpful family system techniques that are so helpful in conflictual settings (internal and external). I would also sit out any race someone is trying to sign me up for. I'll take any kindness offered, even from a hand that tells me I am dead to them. I don't care if I am supposed to be nice and conciliatory, whatever is hurting me—get rid of it, now!

Hurry help along the way. May it race to me even if I can't race toward it. Here in the middle of preEaster week the wrestling happens between Demonstration Sunday three days ago and Betrayal Thursday just around tomorrow's corner.

It all comes together into a perfect storm, inside and out. All that is left is perseverance and not even that looks doable. Soul's Dark Night arrives again. It has passed in the past but that is little comfort in the present.

Psalm 71:1–14
Clarification Week Tuesday

Listen in on the disciples as they continue trying to make sense of life as it swirls about them.

"We don't know how Jesus does it. He keeps talking about dying and yet there was Sunday's parade. We were a bit apprehensive with all his Jerusalem death talk. This may be a place of refuge for him."

"Whew! Dying here must be more of his incomprehensible parabolic language. So let's get back on track to shift the power balance so we can rescue Jerusalem and instruct the Romans, "Begone!", and demand the priests stop their current propping up of the state."

"I continue to hope all the talk of resurrection will fade away. After all, that would first entail dying. What we need is for a simple revolution to take place so our gifts for leadership will be duly noted."

"G*D has delivered us from Jesus' fantasy of dying because of the way he has lived. Palms! Hosannas! We're good!"

Psalm 72:1–7, 10–14
Guiding Gift

The oppressed, facing violence in their lives, cry out, "Give the king, the premier, the president, the prime minister, the leader of any title, your justice, O G*D!" with an implication that the reception and implementation of such justice can be measured by a reduction and removal of oppression and violence.

As always, the language of our appeals needs to be simultaneously individual and communal. Should the leaders of community have the justice of G*D, they would find a way to distribute both their leadership and their justice.

It is not sufficient that one leader be just if the system around them perpetrates injustice.

A sign of a just leader is an increasingly just community with fewer and fewer needy calling and fewer and fewer weak needing pity. There is a presumption here that the gap of justice between the rich and the poor will be narrowing, not widening, and a sign of this is that those who have much will not have too much and those who have little will not have too little.

The psalm might be translated for the economic barons, middle managers, forepeople, laborers, union organizers, and religious leaders from chief priests and popes and bishops to chairpersons of altar guilds. Each one needs to see her/himself as the one to whom justice is given. Until we each understand our life as a fulcrum point of justice, the plea for justice will continue to ring out.

Justice delayed is justice denied. Justice for some is justice denied. Justice is not simply individual, but communal.

Justice is an important light to lift for us to see and to imagine the epiphany it might yet bring about in our midst.

Yes, demand justice from others, particularly those in recognized positions of leadership, but do not forget to put your own name and vocation into the list—Give me and those who are with me in my vocation your justice, O G*D!

Psalm 72:1–7, 18–19
Needed Change [2]

Give justice to the king, O G*D, give justice to all!

Every political system needs to have justice and righteousness flow through it that it might flourish as when rain nourishes grass without flooding it.

Listen to a section from Matthew Fox's *Wrestling with the Prophets: Essays on Creation Spirituality and Everyday Life*—"Meister Eckhart and Karl Marx: The Mystic as Political Theologian":

> In a society that was as aware of privilege as was Eckhart's, the thesis that all are aristocrats is a far from subtle rebuke of the caste system then prevailing. But it is more than a rebuke—it is an imaginative alternative that Eckhart is suggesting. According to historian Jacques Heers, what characterized the popular uprisings of Eckhart's period and place was that even when the "people" overthrew one aristocracy, another immediately took its place. We see then how truly radical and imaginative was Eckhart's alternative: not to confront aristocracy but to recreate it entirely by baptizing all into it. Eckhart does not put down nobles and aristocrats, and he refuses to substitute a new dualism of the lowly over the privileged. Instead, with a dialectical imagination that only a mystic could muster, he makes the peasants into nobles. Instead, therefore, of putting down anyone, he elevates all ....
>
> Thus Eckhart reiterates his marvelous admiration for the nobility of the human person. Eckhart does not stop short of claiming that human beings give a home to the divine within them. For in us 'God has sowed His image and His likeness, and ... He sows the good seed, the root of all wisdom, all knowledge, all virtue, and all goodness, the seed of Divine nature. The seed of Divine nature is the Son of God, the Word of God.' Eckhart's theology of personhood does not concentrate on sin and redemption but on divinization. In this regard he drinks fully of Eastern Christian spiritual theologies.
>
> The seed of God is in us. If it was cultivated by a good, wise and industrious laborer, it would thrive all the more and would grow up to God, whose seed it is, and the fruit would be like the Divine nature. The seed of a pear tree grows into a pear tree, a hazel seed into a hazel tree, a seed of God into God.

So what would it mean to have this Advent be an advent of your rising beyond the caste system of your culture, your society? Bloom where you are!

Psalm 78:1–4, 12–16
Proper 21 (26)

We tell old, old stories for a variety of reasons. One of them is that of reclaiming the joy of an overwhelming experience that it might inform the darkness of a present confusion.

Who knows how close to the experience came a first interpretation? Well, no one. But, as time has progressed we have found ourselves circling back to the stories until we can just tick them off. We put our fingertips together and intone, "True." In some sense we have become as trapped by our archetypes as we are set free by them.

> in Zoan's land and in the sea
> with cloud and fiery pillar
> through rocks that weep
> we rehearse limits and leap horizons
> –WW

Our old stories are made new with each experience and our new stories morph into old. From every direction wonder abounds for those ready to hear and tell stories old and new, ready to chew on parables and pictures beyond words. May these old chestnuts not trap us in reverie, but set us free to wonder, "Why not" and proceed to find out.

What experiences are equivalent touchstones in your life? As you tick off moments of life shifting, what stands out? If you were to pick 5 to carry on one hand, what they would be?

That's pretty easy. How about just 4 or 3? For extra credit, can you cut it to 2 key experiences that would reflect your journey?

Now the tough one—1?

I expect it will have something to do with what you have done, not believed. Yes, actions are shaped by thoughts. They can even hem in what we are willing to do. But, bottom line, it is the doing that best describes what we mean by the space we take up and the energy we expend over time. Blessings on redeeming this trinity of $es^2=d$ where energy times space squared equals doing, and vice versa.

Psalm 78:1–7
Proper 27 (32)

Incline your ear in this direction to hear an unraveling of the past that we might bequeath more light to future generations.

And when sufficiently riddled, what is to be heard? Hope and don't forget that which builds community. This is not something gathered by easy pronouncement but worked out in the tangles and perplexion of real life.

Imagine dark places being made plain through riddling enigmas! Isn't there another way? Perhaps, but nothing is more astute than Edward Albee's line, "Sometimes it's necessary to go a long distance out of the way in order to come back a short distance correctly", and that is the gift of a riddle, a dope slap, a demythologized reperspectivizing.

So where is this leading—to the middle of the Psalm (vss 37–39):

> Their hearts were fickle;
>   they weren't faithful to covenant.
> But G*D, being compassionate,
>   kept forgiving their sins,
>   kept avoiding destruction;
>   took back anger so many times,
>   wouldn't stir up all wrath!
> G*D kept remembering
>   that they were just flesh,
>   just breath that passes
>   and doesn't come back.
>   –WW

What a puzzle G*D is. What an enigma we are. What mystery that there is no difference. What a long way to travel to arrive at a new beginning.

Psalm 80:1–7, 17–19
Needed Change [4]

To what do we need restoring? Or is it G*D that needs to be restored (come back)?

This relationship is a complicated one. Who's related to whom and in what way?

Rather than choosing a particular way to look at this, it will be helpful to hold the question open. It will be important to wait for the multiple ways of relating to reveal themselves.

If it is simply "restore us" or "come back to us", it is a bit too us-oriented, which limits the effectiveness, usefulness, or application of the psalm. If restoration is more object oriented than relation oriented, we lose its power.

Another way to look at restoration is to rephrase it:

Restore us = Reveal our relationship

Let's proceed to encourage each other along without an upper limit of only being restored to a current set point. Journeys apart can enrich us and pull us onward.

———————————

After writing the above I read a column by Jim Taylor that could be fruitfully paired with this Psalm. My condensing of his column[1] follows:

I've often wondered why death diminishes us.

The most satisfying answer I've found comes from philosopher Ken Wilber. He argues that we humans are not individuals but holons.

"Holons"—I dislike the name; I love the concept. Wilber says that everything is part of something else. Each thing has its own identity, but it is always part of something bigger too.

We delude ourselves when we persist in believing that we stand alone as individuals. That would make us only half of a holon.

When someone close dies, they do not just vanish. They are still part of our holon, our whole.

"No man is an island," mused poet John Donne. A death never happens just to an individual. It ripples through the web of connections that made that person whole, and that makes each of us whole.

It's not just the loss of someone else that hurts. It's the loss of part of me.

[1] www.edges.canadahomepage.net/2011/11/23/1152/

Psalm 80:7–15
Proper 22 (27)

Let your face shine on us and we shall be safe.
Smile your blessing smile: that will be our health.
–WW

While these words are directed toward G*D (for our benefit) they might also be directed toward ourselves (a benefit for others).

What would it be like for you to imagine that your smile is a smile of blessing? What is it that gets in the way of identifying yourself with blessing? How do we get beyond the culture of "cool" to the warmth of blessing?

———————————

Smile well.

Smile often.

Smile.

Psalm 84
Old Welcomes New

And how blessed all those in whom you live,
whose lives become roads you travel.
    –MSG

Happy are those whose strength is in you,
in whose heart are the highways to Zion.
    –NRSV

Blessed those who find their strength in you,
whose hearts are set on pilgrimage.
    –NJB

Happy those whose refuge is in you,
whose hearts are set on the pilgrim ways!
    –REB

Your lively heart is both the substrate of the movement of a living G*D and a journeying response to the presence/strength/refuge of G*D.

Now, how to communicate this?

It is important to note that just after this line a large breath is taken (larger than e.e. cumming's circus tent?), a selah pause or refrain or instrumentation bridge, in anticipation of moving to a next part of the journey.

Let's all take a large breath, large enough to slow us down to walk with G*D (3 mph) and large enough to energize us to enjoy a never-ending pilgrimage. Then let us live in the bothness of poetry that breaks us open to joy and joyfully receives such brokenness. Let us bring together hopping sparrow and swooping swallow, the poor and the rich, the outcast and the privileged, the past and the future, heart and soul.

Let's depart in peace with peace for all.

Psalm 85:8–13
Proper 14 (19)

God's saving justice blazes the trail;
it is the condition of peace and happiness.
—NJB notes on verses 12–13

Done any trail blazing yet today?

Have any trail blazing planned for later in the day?

Will that come through your "right living" or through forcing others to toe some mark?

Blaze well.

Psalm 86:1–10, 16–17
Proper 7 (12)

Here we are—poor and needy, sunk in deep mire without a foothold. We look around for a way out and there is none.

Our behavior is that of bargaining with G*D. What else is there to do? Oh, yes, plead. We plead with G*D.

Both of these behaviors indicate a grief we are still feeling from the metaphoric time of garden leaving. The kids recognize this and murder most foul is afoot. Time after time we find ourselves going awry and trying to get back into good graces on our terms.

This is a tough cycle to break. If we remembered that G*D was outside the garden as well, steadfast in presence, if not in rescuing us from consequences, we might open our eyes to the possibilities of life and thankfulness and not focus quite so much on the disasters and petulance.

In an abundance of steadfast love there comes a crack in our defensiveness, our sense of entitlement. Let's not settle for being free in terms of our enemies, but simply because freedom is what it means to be present to the Freedom of G*D. Whether rescued or not, we are already free to decide how we will live. It is G*D's intention.

---

have an eye to Hagar
extend her complaint
from survival to shaming

desiring rescue
to put it to those who
put me in harm's way

buttering up G*D
gets what I want—
revenge

listen to actual language
and our intentions for same
hypocrisy is sown in this divide

flowery language for base motives
our internal disconnect
salved by honest echoes

Psalm 86:11–17
Proper 11 (16)

It is always astounding how we take the universality of G*D and narrow it down to my present situation. If G*D is going to be wherever I am, even Sheol, then I am set free to take that off my hyper-alert list.

However, a temptation is to keep G*D me-sized (even mini-me-sized). G*D may be with me in Sheol, but G*D wouldn't be with you at any time for G*D is on my side! So go the fundamentalist of any age or faith. Even prophets get into this kind of state. This temptation seems to be as universal as G*D.

So it seems to nearly always be appropriate to examine our hearts for the ways in which we have narrowed the wideness of G*D's mercy.

We pray, "As people whose constricted lives show forth in constraining others, we have finally recognized that we have narrowed your love into our hate. We now look for renewal. Show us anew the light of a larger and dynamic creation that we might again work together for a common good."

---

teach me your ways —
　　Lover
　　　Rescuer
　　　　Kinder
　　　　　Tender
　　　　　　Mercy-er
— in the midst of opposition

let us join strengths
in the presence of bullies
to continue
receiving and passing on
loving rescue
through the kindness
of tender mercy

Psalm 89:1–4, 15–18
Proper 8 (13)

There seems to be a gap between our frailty and misery and our dream of steadfast love, sometime, somewhere, putting an end to our sense of forsakenness.

Through our lifetime we entrust a whole series of idols to keep this dream alive. It's a wonderful picture, being rescued in the nick of time. It has a long heritage.

And yet our experience is that of angels with flaming swords, no rescue by going back. Exile transforms our insight and energy into rigid rules and survivalism. Even an Exodus paradigm ends up separating the 12 tribes from one another and the tribes from the indigenous. Internal betrayals are rife. Crucifixions keep cropping up to lay us low.

It would be helpful to practice an awareness of steadfast love in the midst of all this, as our ground of being, rather than its being separated from our present, only coming later to set everything right that can't be set right without destroying its character.

If the hospitality of steadfast love is not present right now to show mercy in every experience, helpful and unhelpful, then it is very close to simply being a figment of our imagination, a bite of pickle at bedtime, a spot of spoiled cabbage only good for haunting.

---

a throne for all generations
nothing is beyond the generations

we dream of ideal kings
only to be enslaved

not hearkening to Samuel
we want our battle king

so kings ruled and battled and
it came to pass that kings passed

back to where we started—imagining
guaranteed life, solid and lasting as rock

Providence, G*D's beauty, is no illusion
dance in the beauty of trust beyond kings

Psalm 90:1–6, 13–17
Proper 25 (30)

Dwelling in a shadow of one most high is problematic. Our proclivity is to presume that means the one casting the shadow is all that much closer to the source of light and therefore has some inborn right to overshadow our casting a shadow to reveal G*D's presence in relationship to our being. Being in another's shadow undefines who we are.

Being "shadowed" is here taken as a safe place. Unfortunately it is so safe that we become passive. We have need of some direct light, even if it leads us into risky places beyond our seed stage. To come from under the shadow of the soil that has incubated us is to face the possibility of drought. Without this risk, however, the beautiful flower and fruit within us might never be seen or tasted.

----

those who love me
I will deliver
in fact
I will deliver
even those who don't

when they call
these lovers and others
I will answer
I will be present
to all callers

come sweet ones
let me show you
my salvation
ready to satisfy
the longest life

Psalm 90:1–8, (9–11), 12
Proper 28 (33)

When dealing with violence (here spelled, "wrath"), the antidote is not stronger redemptive violence, but mercy. Admittedly this is not effective in the short-term, but the question must be raised about what would be. If we try the redemptive violence in the short-term in order to open the option for mercy to come, our experience is that we get bogged down in redemption protection and never get around to the mercy, for when would it ever be safe to let one's guard down?

When it comes to a thousand years equaling one yesterday the whole concept of short- and long-term flies out the window. We either are on the way to being who we desire to be or we are not.

An interesting question comes: How are we to deal with G*D's contemptuous violence toward sinners and other creations that don't currently or have ceased to measure up? How does one show mercy toward G*D? I keep going back to Bernstein's *Kaddish* to hear the human soothe G*D's fevered brow and to bring rest and sleep to an over-stressed deity:

> *Rest, my Father. Sleep, dream.*
> *Let me invent Your dream, dream it*
> *With You, as gently as I can.*
> *And perhaps in dreaming, I can help You*
> *Recreate Your image, and love him again.*

These issues of violence and mercy go back to a Creator and are in our very bones. How long we have been playing this game! How long before our heart is wise enough to regularly choose compassion?

Psalm 93
Our Turn to Witness

Ascension is enrobement in simple mystery, not resplendent majesty.

Note how many ascensions you have had as you moved from birth to your current state of life.

There is an organic transition from one stage of life to another. We can look back and note what could not be seen at the time.

Having seen our journey, there is a slight easing of anxiety over what is coming next. Whatever it is, we will have yet another dying and rising and ascending a next stage.

Psalm 95
Conviction [3]

Good ol' G*D wants to be proved once for all. Don't test G*D or you'll get it in the neck or somewhere. One test in the desert will keep you out of a land of milk and honey. See, don't test G*D. And we want to yell, "I'll stop testing you when you stop testing me!"

More moderately, we might say, "Relationships are always being tested for how else could there be growth of each part and the whole." We wonder why the mood swings of G*D. Is there not enough lithium in usable form for G*D? How much can we keep new creations from crossing our mind and being followed even should we be threatened with destruction? There is something about our being an image of G*D that keeps us pushing boundaries. Or perhaps it is just the kid in us learning as we go.

Mystery I can abide. Rules without reason are not helpful. Rules that run contrary to experience are hurtful. A rule of not testing G*D is unconscionable; it is not part of our original job description. How else would one know if G*D has grown past a past response? How else do we find what image is our image?

Blessings upon your testings (both those you receive and those you make).

Psalm 95:1–7a
Evaluation Day

The Christian Community Bible finds the following prayer by Teilhard de Chardin to be fitting here.

In the distance, the sun has just illuminated the remote outline of the first Orient. Once again, under the changing cascade of its rays, the live surface of the earth awakens, shudders and begins again its amazing labor. O my God, I will offer you the desired harvest of this first effort. In my cup, I will present to you the sap of all the fruits which will be crushed today.

O Lord, I will bring to your presence the depths of my soul widely open to all the forces which, within a moment, are going to go up to every point in the world and converge toward the Spirit. In former times, the first fruits of the harvest and the best of the flocks were brought to your temple. The offering which you really seek, what you mysteriously need daily to satisfy your hunger, to quench your thirst, is nothing less than the development of the world urged by universal progress.

Receive, Lord, this whole Host which Creation, moved by your attractiveness, offers you in the new dawn. The bread, our effort, is not in itself, I know, more than immense decay. The wine, our grief, is only a dissolving drink. But in the heart of this formless mass, you placed—I am sure of it because I feel it—an irresistible and sanctifying desire which, from the wicked to the faithful, makes us all shout: "Lord, make us one."

What prayer would you raise? Can you sense "universal progress" and be present to a continuum "from the wicked to the faithful"? What imagery holds things together for you—Rock, Dawn, ...?

Psalm 96
Blessed Body, Proper I

Even before a blessed event we affirm the blessedness of not only "the" event, but every event. This sort of willy-nilly blessing is to be looked at quite carefully for it doesn't allow exclusion of any for there is no such thing as equity, an eye for an eye.

When it comes to confession, it is the contriteness of the confession that is important, not the consequence that goes alongside it. A ritual of penance simply calls to mind that a change is happening in our life so we can return to rejoicing always, even in penance.

Equitable judgment, from a "holy" perspective, is not that the sinners will get their comeuppance, but that righteousness and truth will be set free from their prisons—our fear that we will be found deliberately ignoring the options of righteousness and truth on a regular basis and miss being transformed to that way of living.

On this Christmas Eve we recognize that tomorrow is blessed. Prior to a big day we claim its blessedness. Tomorrow is not only tomorrow, but today. Did you find blessedness this day? Are you anticipating a blessing from an ordinary tomorrow? Profligate blessing before the fact is a blessing indeed.

Psalm 96:1–9, (10–13)
Proper 24 (29)

[YHWH] is coming to judge the earth;
[YHWH] will judge the world with saving justice and
the nations with fairness.
–NJB

To envision this as a reality in process is to begin to change our sense of interaction with issues of justice and fairness.

We either acknowledge that such judgment is already underway and so it is a major influence in our actions, or we see such judgment as not applying yet and so we can get away with one more injustice or one more unfairness.

In my viewing of the American war-rumoring scene I can only conclude that we are blind to reality when we use judgment language about going to war against Iraq or anyone else and torturously justifying it any way we can. We have no sense of balance regarding the damage we have already done with economic sanctions and the damage we yet intend to do with regime change. We have positioned ourselves so there is no face-saving way to avoid war or dividing the United Nations. How diabolical we have been and we consider ourselves to be on the plus side of judgment, pulling G*D along with us.

This Psalm is a paean to G*D's saving power, evidenced in the past, and a call to participate in that by singing a new song (living a new way) ready for a justice yet to come for today's living. May we regret the consequences of our plans aforehand and change them accordingly. (Unfortunately for you and me, this applies to us individually as well as nationally. This is not just something we get to yell at others without taking it to heart ourselves.)

Psalm 97
Blessed Body, Proper II

In verse 2 we hear about a foundational parallel between "Righteousness" and "Justice". Many times we pair "Peace" with "Justice". A helpful perspective here is that righteousness and justice correspond with an internal component of our lives. Peace has a greater tendency to be external.

By the time we come to verses 10 and 11 we hear this clarified. Peace/Justice is paralleled to external actions of guarding and rescuing. Righteous/Justice is paralleled to internal responses of light and joy.

If we begin to bring these together we need to ask about what light we might shed on situations where someone or some part of creation needs to be guarded. Immigrants and ocean gulfs come easily to mind today. We also need to investigate a connection between joy and rescuing. If you have been on a mission trip of some sort, you probably have a sense of this and a question about why you don't do it more regularly.

Without having to posit an externalized anthropomorphic "Lord" to be "king", we might better recognize a mystery larger than ourselves in qualities of righteousness and peace, in guarding light (no not the soap opera Guiding Light where little guarding went on), and rescuing joy which are much to be sought and lived. In some sense LORD language puts a focus on being authorized rather than our own inherent integrity and integration (so close in sound and so distinct in derivation).

A guiding and guarding Light and rescuing Joy bend our lives, our journey trajectories, toward steadfast Love. They do so in measurable ways so that we can begin to use them to further explore a vast universe of multivalent justice ready to be employed in any number of ways.

In like manner, Righteousness and Peace bend our lives, our journey trajectories, toward steadfast Justice. They do so in measurable ways so that we can begin to use them to further explore a vast universe of light and joy ready to be set loose in any number of life's arenas.

Psalm 98
Blessed Body, Proper III — Hopeless Hope Vigil

The word "victory" shows up three times in the *NRSV* in the first three verses. In our current ears this sets us up to hear this psalm militarily, not relationally.

Imagine what some word substitutions for "victory" could do for us. First they would put us in a better position to hear the action of G*D at the end of the psalm to be the health of the whole system of creation. Victory doesn't really get us to that spot.

Here then are some words that we might substitute for "victory":

- partnership
- love
- friendship
- joy
- relationship

The whole "victory" approach leads us to the dead-ends of "Truth" with a capital "T", Orthodoxy that emphasizes a style of reporting a G*D experience rather than the experience itself, and Creeds that purport to be the last creed needed because it is the best we can do today.

If joy is to be expressed because of G*D's presence, it needs something larger than a victory that we know will always be ephemeral, partial, and a set up to more conflict.

------

sing a new song
G*D remembered!
hooray
finally

sing a new song
help G*D remember!
woe
now

sing a new song
past the past
beyond tomorrow
sing

Psalm 98:1–5
Relic Day

This sing-a-new-Psalm is paired with the impatience of the Israelites in Numbers 21:4b–9. So we are caught again between a frustration of seeing no measurable movement toward big promises coming to pass and their completion. These two passages would make a good pairing for "Holy Week" Saturday between "Good" Friday and "Pascha" Sunday.

This day is not to just celebrate that a smidgeon of authority's desire for compliance and security of the state was unearthed, but that we can see what the threat of torture and public humiliation has come to—a mere splinter of itself.

To commemorate the cross as cross leads to a veneration of the surface rather than the depths. Lifting high a cross is not lifting high a "triumphant sign", a victory. That honor is for an empty tomb and it is rather difficult to lift.

We have a difficult time holding a physical cross together with a physical resurrection. However it is that brains work, our attention seems to keep sliding away from a new possibility to old limits.

A cross relic might more fruitfully be seen as street theatre performed by a prophet. "See, see, what a feared cross has become—a pale splinter of itself. Put down your current fears that are hemming in your option to participate in steadfast love wherever you look, even to the ends of the earth."

To focus so much attention on the cross numbs us to the sublime music of a new creation drawing nigh. This is not a time of vindication or avenging the past, but a mature forgetting what is past to press on to what yet lies ahead. Forward!

Psalm 99
Mountain Top to Valley — Proper 24 (29)

G*D "loves justice" [*NRSV*] and so creates or "established honesty, justice and uprightness." [*NJB*]

We often think about creation as a physical reality. What would it be like to envision creation not in terms of 7 days of stuff but 7 virtues? Imagine creation from the Bushido tradition to help open up our thinking about virtue.

In the beginning G*D.

G*D created Justice and experienced its goodness—a first day.

G*D created Courage and experienced its goodness—a second day.

G*D created Benevolence and experienced its goodness—third day.

G*D created Politeness and experienced its goodness—a fourth day.

G*D created Veracity and experienced its goodness—a fifth day.

G*D created Honor and experienced its goodness—a sixth day.

G*D created Loyalty and experienced its goodness—a seventh day.

What virtues would you point to that shape your days?

How is this different than trying to hone one's days to end up at a particular set of virtues?

Psalm 100
Proper 6 (11) — Evaluation Day

Hooray, I'm a sheep in G*D's pasture, lying down in good green pastures.

But then I have to consider: Am I a fat sheep (boo hiss) or a lean sheep (ta da)? Well, what day is it and what time in such a day? It seems my constancy as a sheep is not constant in its sheepiness— sometimes acting fat and sometimes lean.

And then I have to consider whether I might be a goat in G*D's pasture, also enjoying a green pasture instead of a sandy one with only patches of dry grass. And what of being a snake in G*D's garden, with or without legs?

Oops, too many thoughts twirling around. I may have started to respond to a different issue and now can't get out of the rut of this one.

Perhaps, with all the other talk of judgment, it may be important to simply remember a variant of the last line:

> For good,
> steadfast love enures forever, and
> faithfulness generates for all.

Note:
"Endure": to undergo (as a hardship) especially without giving in. From Vulgar Latin through Anglo-French—to harden.

"Enure" is a variant of "inure": to accustom to accept something undesirable. From Middle English—to put into practice.

Though close enough to mistype, there is sufficient difference to help one wonder about how we deal with adversity or describe a blessing. Have we hardened or are we continuing to practice?

Psalm 103:(1–7), 8–13
Proper 19 (24)

tenderness and pity –NJB

mercy and grace –MSG

compassionate and gracious –REB

merciful and kind –CEV

Tempers of G*D. Created in G*D's qualities, these are also ours. They are internal/external values that can be applied anywhere along the polarity process between "deeply believing and radically secular."

To move methodically toward these qualities, make up an hourly chart starting now. Each hour, indicate how the previous hour went in regard to you and these qualities. (Using a scale of 1–10, with 1 being lousy and 10 being fantastic should be sufficient.)

Don't forget to do this for sleep time as well as wake time. Our dreams and fantasies need maturing as much as the rest of our life.

Try it again and again, as a regular exercise, to gather data about your progress in becoming G*D-like—a most worthy goal.

Time	Tender	Pity	Mercy	Grace	Compassion	Kind

This doesn't take deep pondering. Put down your first response. Three weeks of charting will show remarkable results.

Psalm 104:24–34, 35b
Energy to Witness

It is always interesting to see what doesn't make the lection. In this Psalm the wisdom of the church was to leave out the sentence (legal sentence or judgment), "Let sinners be consumed from the earth, and let the wicked be no more." –NRSV

This is one of the hallmarks of a progressive movement—being up-front about an agenda of focusing on and rejoicing within the abundance and diversity of G*D's creation.

This is not to say that sin is ignored or lessened in its terribleness or impact, but that the blotting out of sin and wickedness would do us all in and so a healthier way for G*D/humanity/creation to go is that of working with sin and wickedness that it might mature into love and community. This is by far the more difficult route to go (far easier to say, "begone"—lost and gone forever—than to say, "bygone"—it's in the past; now let's live differently).

What will it take for us to continue to support and encourage one another not only to cut this sentence out of the lectionary, but to cut it out of our lives? Worth working on, don't you think?

Psalm 105:1–6, 16–22, 45b
Proper 14 (19)

Consider this Psalm in light of a day of remembrance of Hiroshima, held about this time, and a nuclear plague set loose on the world. The overall tone of this psalm is difficult. How do we divide out one part of the whole of life as we search for a needle of providence in a haystack of difficulty?

Given the tone of America attempting to preempt terror through terror, there is a feel that we could paraphrase the whole psalm through the lens of American capitalism and militarism. For instance, the beginning and ending:

> Alleluia!
>
> Give thanks to America, call on its name,
> proclaim its deeds to the peoples!
> Sing to it, make music for it,
> recount all its wonders!
> Glory in its holy name,
> let hearts that see America rejoice!
>
> Seek America and its strength....
> America gave them the territories of nations,
> it reaped the fruit of other people's labors,
> on condition that they kept its statutes,
> and remained obedient to its laws.

How might a background of providence be glimpsed when a foreground of self-interest is so distracting?

[Note: You might be interested in reflecting on the hymn "God Weeps"—#2048 in *The Faith We Sing* with a tune name of "Hiroshima". Dean McIntyre comments: "This hymn will not be a favorite of congregations, but it will be one of the most powerful that they will sing. Worship leaders must exercise great care and caution with this hymn. It must be sung only with preparation of the people beforehand. You might consider concluding the singing with a time of reflection, silence, and prayer, perhaps including a unison praying of 'The Prayer of Saint Francis,' number 481 in *The United Methodist Hymnal*."—www.gbod.org/live-the-um-way/haiti/resource/the-faith-we-sing-hymn-interpretation-god-weeps-number-2048]

Psalm 105:1–6, 23–26, 45c
Proper 17 (22)

Hallelujah!
Praise the Lord!

?

Playing Monday morning quarterback regarding history is a strange way to receive praise and glory. With this process everything is either carefully arranged or yet to be revealed.

The rubric here is lifting G*D up so whatever rewrite is necessary will be done. As we are reminded in Orwell's *1984* those who control the present control the past and those who control the past control the future. It is that tendency to revisionism that raises questions about cutting up a psalm in this fashion.

Here we are weighted too heavily toward only the divine. Just like the infamous Dolly—what G*D wants, G*D gets. In coming at things from this perspective we lose a ring of authenticity and participation in salvation history.

If you were to cast about for a Psalm to deal with betrayal or call or living well, what would you choose? This one is just too pat and not helpful in reflecting upon the other three lections for the day. We need scripture to rub against scripture in a way that will bring more light, not just stay on message.

PS—I just noted that this is post 601 in this blog. I don't know what to make of this information other than I missed an opportunity yesterday for a celebration. Since we are a virtual bunch there is probably no reason not to have that party today and no reason for you not to party today, where you are, on behalf of the rest of us.

According to www.vandlar.com, this year was an auspicious one in the Vandlarian calendar: "601—King Mordacus III leads an expedition through a portal to the fey realm. King Mordacus returns from his journey mysteriously appearing to be 20 years younger than when he entered."

May you find yourself rejuvenated as you celebrate a mysterious 601 in your own setting.

Psalm 105:1–6, 37–45
Proper 20 (25)

Thank goodness for selective memory. Here we have a memory of the end results of some very difficult times. This psalm would have to be four times longer were the circumstances reported which led to such positive outcomes.

As you look back on previous haunting experiences, is your focus on the difficult moments or a final way through?

A psalm could be constructed to only cry out for a difficulty faced. It would start a new category of a complaint psalm. Even laments have a turn or action involved that begins to redeem a time of difficulty. A question is whether complaint only would be valuable. In like manner, we might ask whether a psalm of rejoicing only has value.

As with most of life, it is moments of transition that are key. Hopefully you can learn from past transitions and can see the beginning of a next transition even as a difficulty of the moment continues.

I doubt that we will get around selective memory and intentional revision, but it is helpful, from time to time, to look at what we are remembering and how that shapes where we head. About this time of year we have opportunity to reshape our interpretation of a national event—September 11, 2001—that we cover-up with the short-hand of 9/11 to avoid finding a better response to a difficult experience.

This might be a good time to do another timeline of how long you think you have been working toward joy. What might a transition be that would get you out of a complaint-oriented approach to working or hungering?

Psalm 105:1–11, 45b
Proper 12 (17)

"Make known G*D's deeds among the people." This is a call to tell parables, not to construct creeds.

Since G*D is notoriously obtuse in being revealed (whatever the motivation, plan, personality, or distractibility that is behind that quality), a part of our partnership with G*D is to let others know how we have experienced G*D.

Here G*D is like a real-estate agent in a time of volatility (perhaps not unlike our own). This agent has found a real fixer-upper that appeals to our participatory spirituality. The terms are almost favorable, just a bit more wholeness or perfection on our part and we'll be able to engage it directly.

While we are not yet able to sign on a dotted-line, the agent continues to be supportive and encouraging. "Canaan has you written all over it." "Don't give up." "Keep building up your reserves." "It will be worth it."

When you are finally settled in, remember with thanksgiving the agent that facilitated what will become a blessing for us and others. Start planning now to add on rooms in which ourselves and all will be welcomed to continue growing in love with G*D and Neighb*r.

Covenants and prophecies are only confirmed by their deeds. Here we have a perspective that says a particular understanding of cause and consequence have conspired together to affirm a prior stating of a covenant. And so an appropriate response is, "Praise the Lord" or "Amen" or "So be it".

One of the questions this psalm raises is that of sufficient evidence that a past understanding is confirmed. Is it time to continue standing in its light or time to turn out that light so some more helpful glimmer might be glimpsed? So, time for a second thought about our underpinnings—on what are you basing your next action—A past covenant? A newly received prophecy? An openness to what has yet to arrive?

Psalm 106:1–6, 19–23
Proper 23 (28)

An unsung super-hero: *The Deflector*.

In the presence of a gap between the powerful and the un-powerful, the privileged and the un-privileged, and the "holy" and the "un-holy", *The Deflector* simply stands.

This seemingly inconsequential act of standing does make a significant difference. It keeps all the un-people from being utterly abolished or annihilated. This is an honorable task for a super-hero. In fact it is a quite doable act by anyone.

- First, *The Deflector* has open eyes to recognize gaps between people.

- Second, *The Deflector* analyzes the relationship.

- Third, *The Deflector* moves into the gap and turns to face the more powerful, privileged, and "holy" to hold their passion and purpose away from the vulnerable.

- Fourth, *The Deflector* at some point transforms into *The Reflector*. By this shift the powerful catch a glimpse of what schmucks they have been and the un-powerful catch a glimpse of how pathetic they have been. In this manner the powerful pause and the un-powerful perk up—field and relationship are leveled.

How are you doing in being recruited as a next *Deflector/Reflector* in your community? If not yet acknowledged, are you at least practicing? When this post is not filled, a lot of people are hurt and social injustice runs rampant; personal injustice rears its head.

Who do you know who is calling you to stand before them thinking you will be deflecting injustice away from them and will be surprised to see their own power revealed to them so they too can stand? If you have only a hint, it is enough to call you to the ranks of Holy Moses and Saint Syzygus and carry on a tradition of doing your best for the un-people.

Psalm 107:1–7, 33–37
Proper 26 (31)

Imagine announcing that today we will only sing verses 1 and 15 of our next hymn. We will also only pay attention to the 2nd and 10th amendments of the U.S. Constitution. Of particular concern will be commandments 4 and 6 (depending on how you count).

In these selective ways we can avoid responsibility for the whole of life or the benefit of another if it competes with my own desire. We can divide up and set one important part of life against another.

In this case the elided verses are pretty repetitious. They are also looking for G*D to take responsibility for our hard times and going back over old hurts.

What this condensation leaves us with is an image of bringing the destitute to a place filled with potential. The response looked for is a return to being stewards of current resources, not revengers of past harm.

We end with Eden revisited. Now comes a decision on our part of how we are going to practice stewardship in our current setting—how are we going to invite the hungry into the bounty we have and join us in a next cycle of sowing and reaping? This is not a "when" question, but a "how" question.

A blog conversation after this comment:

(Reader) said...
I'm preaching on this psalm, and adding verses 7–9 to the mix... since I want to focus on the idea in verses 5–9, especially 9: For God satisfies the thirsty, and the hungry he fills with good things. You have touched on the precise point I want to make: in our gratitude for this steadfast love that feeds us, we, in turn, feed the world.

Thank you for this blog.

(Blogger) said...
Blessings upon your preaching. A deep upflow of steadfast love is basic. Constriction of such leads us to constriction of one another.

An additional image for me is in *The Message* equivalent of verse 35, which begins with "Then..." We need to see which side of the "then" we are on: a wasteland or an oasis. This is also a choice between control-over or participation-with.

Thanks for leaving a comment.

Psalm 112:1–9, (10)
Guiding Gift [5]

happy are those who practice being G*D
regardless of their station
steadfast love
can be expressed
on every-day paths
through grace and mercy

generosity and justice
inform one another
grounding what has happened
within desired happenings to come
assured of this firm foundation
fear of a next best act falters

freeing minds and hearts and guts
opening hands and doors
beyond their current crack
that more light for all
shines unveiled
happy are those who practice

Psalm 113
Elizabeth and Mary Meet

The poor are raised from the dust and the needy from an ash heap.

What might be a sign of this ancient promise, this source of every revolution?

Unexpected births?

Whose hopes are more barren than those of the poor in the face of the power of those who have accumulated for themselves under the aegis of whatever economic system has captured the imagination of the time? Mammon demands its pound of flesh in the form of the poor and needy, the widow and orphan.

Yes, unexpected births!

And so Elizabeth and Mary meet and greet a new dawn even knowing it is darkest before the dawn. Based on the experience of the poor everywhere, what else could they expect from the unexpected than their hopes would somehow be beheaded and strung up? The moment is hopeful, the outcome doubtful.

And more.

We are not looking to simply reverse a current order to throw the lofty into poverty for a cycle to repeat. Note the little phrase "set among" or "sit with" in verse 8. This reconciliation of our self-inflicted divisions is the work of G*D and those partnered with G*D.

And so.

May the unexpected sign of "you" join in the parade of the many unexpected signs we summarize with Elizabeth and Mary and bear much good fruit as we journey toward an expected sitting together.

Psalm 114
Hopeless Hope Vigil — Opened Heart Evening — Proper 19 (24)

In looking back at events of power and loss of life, the Psalmist most remembers what was experienced as G*D's presence changing things.

This helps put the Exodus from Egypt and entry through Jericho in a different perspective than simple victory and to keep us from celebrating the body count of our enemies.

This is an encouraging word. Where are the blocks in moving to freedom these days? Well, a way is being prepared through that block. You are asked to participate—raise your arms; raise your voice; raise your prayers; raise your energy; raise your resources.

Could it be as simple as voting? Could it be as difficult as being a candidate?

Focus this day on the presence of G*D; fear and terror then are seen for the shams they are.

Psalm 116:1–2, 12–19
Courage Thursday — Proper 6 (11)

Consider how this hymn is the same and different than the psalm. In particular, where do you think the line, "and humbly ask for more" came from?

Methodist Hymnal 1879 — C.M. Psalm cxvi — Charles Wesley

1 O THOU who, when I did
 complain,
 Didst all my griefs remove,
 O Saviour, do not now disdain
 My humble praise and love.
2 Since thou a pitying ear didst
 give,
 And hear me when I prayed,
 I'll call upon thee while I live,
 And never doubt thy aid.
3 Pale death, with all his ghastly
 train,
 My soul encompassed round,
 Anguish, and sin, and dread, and
 pain,
 On every side I found.
4 To thee, O Lord of life, I prayed,
 And did for succour flee:
 O save (in my distress I said)
 The soul that trusts in thee!
5 How good thou art! how large
 thy grace!
 How ready to forgive!
 The helpless thou delight'st to
 raise:
 And by thy love I live.
6 Then, O my soul, be never more
 With anxious thoughts distrest!
 God's bounteous love doth thee
 restore
 To ease, and joy, and rest.
7 My eyes no longer drowned in
 tears,
 My feet from falling free,
 Redeemed from death and guilty
 fears,
 O Lord, I'll live to thee.

= C.M. SECOND PART

8 WHAT shall I render to my God
 For all his mercy's store?
 I'll take the gifts he hath
 bestowed,
 And humbly ask for more.
9 The sacred cup of saving grace
 I will with thanks receive,
 And all his promises embrace,
 And to his glory live.
10 My vows I will to his great name
 Before his people pay,
 And all I have, and all I am,
 Upon his altar lay.
11 Thy lawful servant, Lord, I owe
 To thee whate'er is mine,
 Born in thy family below,
 And by redemption thine.
12 Thy hands created me, thy
 hands
 From sin have set me free,
 The mercy that hath loosed my
 bands
 Hath bound me fast to thee.
13 The God of all-redeeming grace
 My God I will proclaim,
 Offer the sacrifice of praise,
 And call upon his name.
14 Praise him, ye saints, the God of
 love,
 Who hath my sins forgiven,
 Till, gathered to the church
 above,
 We sing the songs of heaven.

Psalm 116:1–4, 12–19
Assured [3]

"Because!"

We are a results driven people. Something good happens and G*D did it for G*D can do no wrong. Something bad happens and we did it for we can do no right. Sometimes we claim the good that happens and blame G*D for catastrophic "acts of god".

In focusing on the outcome and working backward we find a multitude of ways to avoid simply being thankful for an opportunity in which to live and move and have our being. If there is not a direct tie to an outcome, our current behavior is dismissed as irrelevant.

The word "because" is still a valuable tool, but only if it works in a forward direction, not reflexively. Because I am doing the best I can, I can stand whatever result comes along.

Being part of a larger system and systems within systems, there is not a single cause and effect. To denigrate what I can do based on immediate results or quarterly financial gain is to put Ourselves and G*D and Neighb*rs and even Enemies in impossible situations where miracle is the only out available.

So, if we give up, we still have our supporters who can carry us onward. If all we can do is stand mute in the face of unfairness, it is a valuable revelation of the meanness of the principalities and powers. If we engage injustice with all our will and skill, the fears of a broken community can still overwhelm our witness as well as process and decision-making. If we are dependent upon the outcome, that which occurs "because" of a specific action of ours, we never get to rejoice in the relief, delight, and triumph of the mystery of adding our part to a transformation of this wobbly old world into a new paradise on earth.

May you avoid the trap of "Because!" things didn't turn out the way I wanted, what I did was valueless.

Instead, may you have a Garrison Keillor's Powdermilk Biscuit forward-leaning perspective, thankful for "the strength to get up and do what needs to be done"—regardless of the result.

Graphically you can see this in one of the artifacts of a church trial—*loveontrial.org/pages/2-store.html*.

Psalm 118:1–2, 14–24
Assured

The phrase "head of the corner" in verse 22 can point in the direction of a keystone at the top of an arch or a cornerstone holding two sides of a building together.

A stone rejected as a cornerstone for lack of squareness yet has an opportunity to be just the right shape for a keystone. This sways me in the direction of keystone.

Once moving in that direction it can be seen how a keystone can rescue an out-of-line cornerstone. It will take the weight, the stress, the pressure of misalignment. This is a more helpful image than that of rule-giver that comes with cornerstones. A keystone is also more humble. Cornerstones often have a date carved on it and a special memory box hidden away inside, while keystones quietly keep things from falling apart.

Easter—a last stone in place to confirm an arc of meaning?

Easter—a first stone in place to set the direction of future growth?

And the ratio of these in your life?

---

right hands and left brains
left hands and right brains
have different sensibilities

when it comes to glory's gate
being opened for me and thee
right or left makes no matter

if it takes both hands
and both brains
just open the door

imagine Alphonse and Gaston
as godly comic gatekeepers
holding open a door for all

Psalm 118:1–2, 19–29
False Dawn Sunday

Steadfast Love—Forever!

Image living stones. Life built upon life into an edifice surrounding righteousness.

In so building, there was a life-stone that didn't quite mesh with others. A result was chinks in the armor of the wall protecting righteousness. Righteousness leaked out.

Of course, to best defend Righteousness and husband it for another day, leakage was not acceptable to the Protectors of Righteousness. When it came to a choice of leaving an irregular life-stone in place or replacing it with one that would better protect this most valuable of resources, the awkward gets pushed outward, falling to the ground.

Picking itself up our little life-stone moseys around to the gate, proclaiming, "Open to me the gates, that I may come in and give thanks."

One might imagine a gate wondering what in the world this little life-stone would have to be thankful for. For not meshing? For being a leaker of Righteousness?

Presumably, curiosity got the better of the gate and open it did.

Whereupon, the little life-stone announces that Righteousness comes in through the gate; she had come in, therefore even a little, leaky life-stone is Righteous. This story (rightly or wrongly) caught their ear and became for them a new understanding of Righteousness shared.

Eventually they rebuilt with the little, unmeshable life-stone at a corner and Righteousness has shone in-and-out through every nook and cranny of its walls and gates ever since.

May you leak Righteousness as did little, life-stone Jesus.

---

steadfast love
endures forever
even better
expands now
expansively encompassing
rejected lovers

Psalm 119:1–8
Guiding Gift [6]

The Judicial Council of The United Methodist Church decreed (Decision 980) that they desire a particular outcome of an investigation and sent it back to be redone in their image. Presumably they will keep sending it back until they get a result they want. (Does anyone remember Florida and a Presidential "election"?)

A counter argument once found online but no longer retrievable goes:

> Both the Committee on Investigation and Trial Court need to be fully aware of their ability to define the meaning of chargeable offenses. They need to be aware that even though there are prohibitions about certain behaviors in the 2000 Discipline, that none of these prohibitions is actually a chargeable offense. Each Committee on Investigation and Trial Court must decide if violating one of these specific prohibitions in a specific set of circumstances actually constitutes any one of the chargeable offenses under ¶2702. As a trier of law, a Committee on Investigation or Trial Court must review the total circumstances of the situation and all that is written in the Discipline. After such a review, it may decide a particular prohibition is unjust, oppressive or unwarranted—either in that particular circumstance or always. And if the prohibition is unjust, then it has the power to decide no violation of a chargeable offense has occurred. No one should be convicted for violating an unjust prohibition.

We are talking here about a blessing of the laws of the Lord that lead to new life for the individual, community, and creation. Laws that don't do that must be questioned, disputed, and ignored.

If we jump way to verse 175 this becomes clearer. "Let me live that I may praise you, and let your ordinances help me."

Indeed we live to love G*D and Neighb*r and Self and One Another and Enemies. Laws (ways of living) that enhance this love are indeed blest and those that don't blast us apart. A law is not a law is not a law; it is a response to a particular time and space and action.

Psalm 119:33–40
Guiding Gift 7 — Proper 18 (23)

We are so easily discouraged by almost any resistance to trusting goodness. It is almost that we are best defined by what we stand against rather than what we stand for. When I get to the "pearly gates" I sure hope I won't be put on one of those shouting heads programs so prevalent these days in order to defend my "entrance."

Or, if I am, that I will be wise enough to listen, to wait, to affirm rather than deny.

May you also spend more time affirming life than defending temporary positions that will need to be modified in the next twinkling of an eye as someone else comes to power and cultures again shift their idols.

Continually saying "No" wears us out. It takes us back to being two or a teen. Let's deepen our mature appreciation of the time, energy, and resources it takes to participate in (to say "Yes" to) "saving justice" –NJB.

Choose your teacher.
Work toward understanding.
Travel toward basics.
Practice an outward oriented heart.
Practice an inward oriented eye.
Receive assurance.
Avoid disgrace.
And so confirm your desire for meaning.

Psalm 119:105–112
Proper 10 (15)

Where most English translations talk about our opponents as "wicked", the *Contemporary English Version* identifies them as "merciless people."

Either way, the psalmist goes on to say that G*D's teachings have a grounding effect and give peace of mind.

In a context of the whole psalm this doesn't keep the psalmist from complaining and asking for redress in the face of wicked mercilessness. It does, however, remind the psalmist that ultimately their life will be found in paying constant attention to the great teaching of mercy and goodness that will be present with them at all times, shaping them into that very same mercy.

The immediate context of the story is "Ouch!"

The expected resolution is "Ahhh!!"

May we live the resolution in our context.

Psalm 119:129–136
Proper 12 (17)

"Redeem me from oppression." A worthy call.

"Help me redeem others from oppression." Another worthy call.

"I weep because your intentions are not kept."

"We weep because our intentions are not kept."

To work against oppression of any kind is to work out of weeping that faces might shine.

Let us work. Let us shine.

Psalm 121
Conviction [2]

How has the day gone so far? The week? Year?

Many times a question is clearly called for—"From whence will my help come?"

One sort of help can be variously identified with a Creator G*D, a Wide-Awake G*D, a Keeper G*D, a Sheltering G*D in whatever moment we happen to raise the question.

Another presence, whether help is an immediate need or not, is with a Journeying G*D as enumerated above, but not limited to these qualities. The issue of presence goes beyond a utilitarian need of the moment and is certainly not tied to a need for help. Help may come, or not. Either way, Journeying G*D is present, if not accounted for.

Are you asking a "help" question these day? If so, do you experience "help" as helpful in your spiritual journey. Is it an aid or a hindrance? Is this a question only asked 'round midnight, or does it also come around at noon?

Let's pay attention to a broader question of presence rather than the narrower question of help. Our starting question is important to where our journey leads.

Journey is key to life. Nicodemus travels a fair piece from his introduction in John 4 to John 7 to John 17. Abraham journeys by stages to a promised place, has his momentum carry him past it, and needs to return later. How about you?

This psalm also journeys

- from a need for help (1a)

- to searching everywhere (1b)

- to looking beyond everywhere (2)

- to assurance of having found (3–6)

- to helping (7)

- to living (8)

How would you note your own journey to an assurance of presence and then out of a presence of assurance journeying more energetically in life?

Psalm 122
Needed Change [1]

To be ready for the unexpected runs the danger of readiness fatigue.

To have too-clear a vision of the future runs the danger of not being ready for an even better future and missing it when it is available.

Both of these dangerous approaches to Advent are needed and both raise a larger danger of setting one against the other in a battle to an unnecessary death. There may be a third way that brings out the best of both. The Psalmist sums up this non-doctrinal formula relationally—"I will seek your good."

In today's world of reading silently to one's self, the Matthew and Isaiah passages are about individuals. However, when Matthew speaks of being ready he uses an irregular plural of "you" and Isaiah speaks of the whole house of Jacob as walking together in light. To be progressive in today's world almost requires an ear for the corporate, the community, and not the individual. In time to come this will probably become as perverted as an overblown individualism is today and progressives will be those holding up the importance of a depth of psyche. But, for now, listen first for where the community might be better held together. This is our great need today—an irregular plural.

Our readiness for the future and our walking a better way in today's light can both be assisted with a reminder that we only get to that better future together. This requires us to seek the good of another in order for either and both of us to progress toward a time of wholeness, of peace.

Imaging Jerusalem as "a place of wholeness", we find it appropriate that those who would pray for peace as a significant part of wholeness would prosper, would not learn war anymore, would be ready for an unexpected experience of community beyond any arbitrary decision resulting in some taken and some left behind.

Then we run again into the tension and/or balance of Advent.

For the sake of others I will say, "Peace be within you."
For the sake of G*D, "I will seek your good."

May peace be within G*D's place and may we seek the good of others. In these two we find all the law and prophets. In these two we find our past-future and our future-future come together in a very present-future that is quite manageable. We can bless G*D and bless one another—a bit now, a bit more later, and, eventually, with an exclamation point! or three!!!

Psalm 123
Proper 28 (33)

In Judges we hear of people calling out to G*D for help. We don't hear a direct response. What we do hear immediately after the plea is, "At that time Deborah...."

This Psalm might be seen in parallel with the Judges pericope.

I look to you, heaven-dwelling God, look up to you for help.
Like servants, alert to their master's commands,
   like a maiden attending her lady,
We're watching and waiting, holding our breath,
   awaiting your word of mercy.
Mercy, God, mercy!
   We've been kicked around long enough,
Kicked in the teeth by complacent rich men,
   kicked when we're down by arrogant brutes.
                    –MSG

What we now hear immediately after this plea is, "At that time Occupy Wall Street ... summoned Ketchup and a thousand more non-leading leaders...."

Cries for mercy are important.
Showing mercy is important.
Claiming of mercy is important.
Being impatient for mercy is important.
Risking a justice that will reveal mercy is important.

So, been kicked around enough? Join G*D and Neighb*r in re-leasing mercy from where it has been held in captivity—in our hands. Yes, now.

Psalm 124
Proper 16 (21)

Imaginative speculation is more than fun.

Conventional metaphors for coming through danger abound here.

So why is it important to pile image upon image? I suppose it could reflect a sense of relief large enough that a singer needs to express many different layers of danger and danger diffused. How many different threats and defeats have progressives of any kind felt in recent days? Can we sing this song before seeing a light at the end of the tunnel?

Yes, we can. We can remember creation and extrapolate that freedom is intended to come to fruition. Hear this Psalm echoed in other scriptures like Colossians 3:15b–17—Cultivate thankfulness [Creation is for you]. Let the presence of G*D/Jesus abound in your life [Creation is for you]. In the midst of every event Sophia/Wisdom composes a song [Creation is for you]. Every step of the way, for good and for ill, give thanks [Creation is for you].

This song is based on having forgotten the intention of Creation and then remembering it in the midst of a dark night. The in-breaking speed of light squared dramatically bursts through the energy/material boundary and caged birds sing again.

May you know again this day, "Creation is for you."

If ... , it would have been enough. [Dayenu[1]]

1 out of Egypt	8 drowned oppressors
2 justice on enslavers	9 needs were provided for
3 banished ideologies	10 sufficiency present
4 slain first priorities	11 Sabbath organized
5 enriched us	12 location unified
6 opened a way	13 life taught
7 given solidity	14 home identified
	15 hopes and prayers raised

Another snare is broken. We have escaped more than 15 times. Sing it again.

---

[1] www.aish.com/h/pes/t/si/48937752.html

Psalm 128
Proper 12 (17)

Why settle for happiness when flourishing is available?

Flowering goes beyond a pleasantness of survival needs and family. Flourishing is less dependent upon conditions or results than is acculturated happiness we have turned into an idol.

I can flourish when able to redefine any limits life is currently holding up. Redefinition is a creative act which leads us to translate "fear of the Lord" as "is as creative as G*D". This is a key way of G*D.

Hear this psalm again:

> Want to flourish?
> Define your conditions.
> This is walking G*D's Way.

Peace be with each larger community.

Psalm 130
Conviction [5]

Having had a colonoscopy adds a whole new level of enjoyment to this psalm of the depths.

There is a persistence to life that just doesn't want to quit. Whether stillborn or still going strong at 90 there is a desire for attentiveness to the particulars of life. Pay attention! Someone, pay attention! Even little gremlins in the depths of bowels desire attention.

One of the processes we keep forgetting about is the need to attend to all of life, from the depths to the heights. In our celebrity-oriented culture where possession is key to happiness, it is important to pay attention not only to the particulars that demand our attention but to a larger issue of steadfastness with the parts not being attended to.

An editorial recently caught my attention as it reflected on the bad deal of bankruptcy legislation coming from Washington D.C. The vision included a return to post Civil War times of "debt peonage" where certain people can accumulate other people—not blatant slavery, but its capitalist equivalent. This sort of thing happens when the crying-depths of the citizenry are treated as a wealth producing mechanism by the rich or rich-envious.

Our antidote to this sort of depersonalization is connection with "steadfast love" for those in the depths whether they are a minority of the day or not. To persist in love is to actively participate in shaping decisions that honor cries from the depths—no matter from whom they come or how inconveniently they arrive.

Psalm 131
Guiding Gift [8] — Proper 3 (8)

Wealth is far grander than G*D. It has many more shiny things. It ranks high in distractibility from justice. It needs nothing other than itself.

I am acquisitive. I am not calm and quiet. I want more. Any affirmation to the contrary runs counter to what I will be doing next, subverting my long-term well-being for a dream of two birds in hand.

Even had I learned to be submissive, not even glancing up for another handout, accepting of my current place, unquestioning of power hierarchies, settled into a class, quiet as a church mouse in the face of patent injustice, accustomed to mere survival, reduced to an inarticulable hope—an unbidden vision of a deeply satisfying relationship within and beyond current limitations arises.

Something calls from beyond being top-dog, bottom-rung, or middle-class. Perhaps it is a mere asterisk in our language about G*D to remind about a fertile, bubbling, energy that writes on walls and moves on. We live more or we die more.

Acquisitive or submissive, the choice comes down forever twixt G*D and Mammon. Choose beyond—beyond trinkets, money, wealth, seeming security, position. For every Mammon there is a Pirate; for every G*D there is undeniable fidelity (relationship), fairness (justice), and kindness (peace) revealed in the many faces of Love.

So, "Hope on!", "Give it up!", "Get more!", whatever your mantra, and then take a step beyond.

> with calmed and quieted soul
> we hear amazing things
> still small voices
> "beloved"-ness all around
> no-thing to distract from hope.

Isn't this the kind of listening we would appreciate being a part of? May you listen for your own sake and also for the sake of the world and friends and enemies that we might learn to hope together—for there is no hope but social hope.

Psalm 133
Proper 15 (20)

How beautiful it is when relatives don't argue (negatively put) or live together in unity (put positively).

If beauty is in the eye of the beholder, what is it that strikes us about this? Might it be how unusual it is for us to so live? Would it be a wonder if it were usual? Is its beauty enhanced by its lack of being what is expected? Would we wonder about this if the standard behavior was for folks to get along?

May you be beautiful this week.

If not for the whole week, perhaps for a day? an hour? Wherever you can start being a wonder to your compatriots and foes will be OK. Then the challenge begins to lengthen and lengthen—like more stably holding a yogic posture over time. Again a chart will be helpful to note your progress and solidify your ability not to argue (nor to get even) and deepen your compassion (unity re-spelled).

Day	Opportunities to not argue	Times taken	Opportunities to bind together	Times taken

Psalm 138
Proper 16 (21)

Good old Lord. The one that was bound to our side. Or was it we bound to Lord's side? Either way—what a team! What a symbiosis!

A LORD provides protection and we provide praise. Hard to imagine a better scenario. We get to avoid responsibility, except for coming up with sufficient tribute, and get green pastures and an "arrogant soul" (alternate translation from the Syriac, 138:3) on top of this.

What is your speculation regarding what would happen should this relationship loosen up? This is where we are today in the realm of religious understanding as we wrestle with one another about whether we return to bondage of past relationships or are loosed to recommit to one another in a new manner.

What would it mean not to escape, but to simply be in the presence of steadfast presence, both Lord's and ours?

Psalm 139:1–12, 23–24
Proper 11 (16)

Where are you?

G*D's there, too.

Introduce yourself.

Travel on together.

Psalm 143
Hopeless Hope Vigil

There are a lot of desperate images here:

        pursued
        crushed
        darkness
        faint
        appalled
        fails
        hide
        pit
        save me
        flee
        preserve my life
        trouble
        cut off
        destroy

A needed out is two-fold: Refuge and Learning.

There are times we need a Band-Aid™-on-our-knee rescue. To make this a primary characteristic of G*D keeps everyone in their place. Our trouble justifies a rescuing, co-dependent G*D.

Of greater import is a teaching G*D. Now we can interact. We can pick G*D up when G*D is disappointed again and together learn not to repeat our separating behavior of hierarchy or ignoring one another until a crisis hits.

We vigil for a transformed relationship with G*D and Neighb*r.

Psalm 145:1–8
Proper 20 (25)

It's time to "ponder anew what the Almighty can do."

- What are the top ten wonders in your life?

- What are the top ten wonders in the last week?

- What are the top ten wonders from yesterday?

- What are the top ten wonders so far today?

- What are the top ten wonders you are expecting and living toward today?

- What are the top ten wonders you are expecting and living toward tomorrow?

- What are the top ten wonders you are expecting and living toward this week?

- What are the top ten wonders you are expecting and living toward—period?

Did you know you already had 80 wonders in you? Regardless of your response to this question, proclaim/live what you know.

Psalm 145:8–9, 14–21
Proper 13 (18)

G*D is more wonderful than can be understood.

Mercy, kindness, tenderness, and pity for all—for all!

Why does verse 20, about guarding us here good guys and destroying them there bad guys, tend to outweigh an image of G*D being intentionally generous? What is there about us that draws us to the division of community (with us coming out on top, of course) instead of living out of G*D's trademark love?

What would happen to this psalm if verse 20 were deleted? How would you evaluate such a change? Is this the key verse for understanding the Psalm or an extraneous verse?

Does your evaluation change if you think in these terms:

- one person—your desires

- G*D—caring for your acts of praise and dismissing everything else

- class—some folks in and most out?

Psalm 145:8–14
Proper 9 (14)

Greatness is unsearchable. There is mystery at every level of life, large and small. In the best of times and the worst of times there are opportunities for thanks. Grace and mercy can be perceived anywhere and anytime. They are universal constants, not unlike light. Of course, we are finding that light is not quite the constant we thought it was, and the same may be said of steadfast love and compassion. In the mystery of this moment we might reflect on these constellations:

- grace, slowness to anger, doing good for all
- mercy, steadfast love, compassion

Since these are parallel, each facet of the unsearchable interacts with each other.

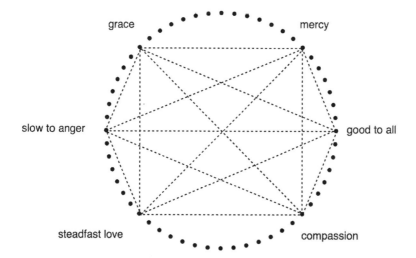

Imagine standing in the middle of this construct and receiving—upheld when fallen, raised when bowed down. How would you ever not be thankful and also stand aside for someone else to experience this in their own way?

To so invite is to be faithful in all your words, and gracious in all your deeds. You have received blessing; you are a blessing; share the blessing that is you.

Psalm 146:5–10
Needed Change [3]

This section might be considered an extended beatitude that could lead to living as an extension of or partner with G*D. As we hear about what G*D is to be praised for it may become clear that the very hope found in G*D is also found in us. Believe it or not, your Neighb*r has hope in you. G*D has hope in you. Claim this series of blessings:

- Blessed are you when prisoners are freed.
- Blessed are you when the blind see.
- Blessed are you when the bowed down are lifted.
- Blessed are you when right-doing is honored.
- Blessed are you when strangers are welcomed.
- Blessed are you when orphans and widows are upheld.
- Blessed are you when wickedness is put in its place.

Though phrased in terms of results, it is understood that results are not formed in a vacuum. Together you and I can make a difference. It may be that our action is the third or thirteenth or thirtieth or three millionth act along the way to freedom and health for someone or all of us. It may be that ours is a final one and most visible in a chain of decision-making stretching back to Creation.

At stake through the generations is not only a resolution to life's so-far unresolved issues so thanks can be given but preparation for future resolutions that even more thanks can be given. Knowing the reciprocal nature of life it is important not to forget that thanks given is related to thanks received.

Psalm 147:12–20
Blessed Body [2]

This last part of Psalm 147 focuses on various issues of maintaining solidarity and security.

How different would it be for us if we used the first 11 verses where rebuilding and regathering, creating and healing, thanksgiving and sustaining the poor were the focus—instead of security and borders and power over creation and separatingly unique scriptures?

What is there about us that desires to move so quickly from the mystery and danger of birth and movement to distilling all that into the regularity and safety of institution? This last Sunday of Christmas subtly shifts us from the raising up of judges, as needed, to the institution of kings. We begin refocusing away from the manger scene of G*D with us in the first 11 verses to using this scene to prove we are blessed over all others and can use the symbol of the manger to lord it over poor shepherd and wise foreigners and everyday consumers.

By such choices as the first or last verses of a hymn we choose a prophetic or a priestly orientation.

Psalm 148
Blessed Body [1]

If written in post-exilic times (best bet) this Psalm has one feel. If written during an exile it has another. And, there is still another sense to it in pre-exilic times.

Can you imagine Joseph and family heading off to Egypt humming this tune?

There is something lamentable about the after-birth story Matthew tells. Just look at the political deceit around the Magi and Herod, the dislocation of families, the violence of power and control, the death of Herod still not bringing security for families and a relocation of home.

There is also something very upbeat. A fulfillment motif helps us ride any and all such bucking bronco disappointments without being thrown off. Angels are heard; next opportunities are set in motion; an arc of hope keeps sparking.

And so, in the midst of run-of-the-mill pre-exilic times such as a Pax Romana and American Peace, extravagant praise such as this isn't real to the controllers. It is labeled enthusiasm and dismissed.

In exile it is all that we have left, an old song of Zion. We hold to it as a promise that will come to pass as this exile passes away. A freedom to move on to a promised land of new creation will eventually trump any and all attempts to keep it at bay.

After exile it is our emotional response to everything that comes our way.

But where a line between the end of one exile and the beginning of another lies is a mystery. At some point things change from a natural praise to a forced praise.

Even though it may not make any sense, I suspect Joseph and Mary sang lullabies to Jesus on their way to Egypt and this was one.

Psalm 149
Proper 18 (23)

What would it look like to triumph without resort to two-edged swords to slay others?

Here is a great divide.

Can we unswervingly proceed to erase differences between earth and heaven, between now and then, moving them toward congruence, regardless of the consequences to ourselves?

Must we be the vehicle of G*D's justified imposition of consequences upon those who would limit how present the powerless can be?

Do you find yourself wavering in the middle between the resistance formulations of Gandhi or Che, Martin or Malcolm?

It is time to choose which continues to be the new song of life. It may be enough to simply remember the first lines of this Psalm and let the rest go, trusting what will be will be.

Hallelujah! Alleluia! In any spelling form or language, we are singing a new song 'cause there is no fixing the old one. To keep singing, we practice it in the presence of fellow-travelers lest we forget and fall back into unoriginal behavior.

Proverbs 8:1–8, 19–21; 9:4b–6
Hopeless Hope Vigil

Under our desire for control and consistency is a more basic creative impulse always crying out for recognition. This wisdom and understanding is initially beyond words and comprehension—sensed and yearned for.

First, listen. In listening we find. In finding we and all are benefited. A key benefit is community which can only be sustained on a basis of a freed justice. This justice beyond benefit for some over others brings a commonwealth beyond simply adding mine plus yours.

Commonwealth is embodied common sense. Both are rooted in a constantly maturing community relating with other growing communities into a more whole and creation-wide relationship with one another and all.

Recognized or not, a call from beyond continues to beckon us forward. This voice can be heard, day-by-day, in burning bushes, empty tombs, and your experience.

Ecclesiastes 3:1–13
New Year's Day

I would have preferred this lection to go to verse 15. Verses 1-8 speak poetically about a duality of nature (one might say a duality of deity). There is creation and there is flood, the first day. There is a righteous anger of flood and a sorrowful repentance of rainbow. There is a cup of kindness that rejoices that not all is destroyed and a cup of drunkenness that sets family against family. There is one family of an ark and there are multiple families of Babel. There are all families set apart from one another and there is one family chosen out from all the rest. There is a promise of abundance and there is such delay as to void any warranty. There is one child who is heard crying and there is one child who laughs. And on it goes.

To end at verse 13 resolves all this into a mundane plodding survival—eating, drinking, working.

To proceed to verse 15 opens us to all the dread and all the energy of a spark of life rubbing against life—to the fear and trembling of which Paul later speaks. It brings back the issue of time that will be with us until time is no more. The first 8 verses are better summarized as follows:

> There is what is past and
> there is what is to come and
> they work with one another
> in a cauldron of what is.

What has happened this past year has happened and there is no changing it. What will happen this next year is not constrained by any particular part of the past. All this moves around a turning of the year and a turning of the reality of animal death to a mystery of what's beyond any turning.

Song of Songs 2:8–13
Proper 9 (14)

In *Sacred Marriage: The Wisdom of the Song of Songs*, words by Nicholas Ayo, paintings by Meinrad Craighead, there is this reference: "Marina Warner calls the Song 'That most languorous and amorous of poems,' which leaves the reader 'spellbound by its sensuality and drowsy voluptuousness.'"

What will it take to read not only this passage, but the whole of scripture and life, languorously, amorously, sensually, voluptuously?

Rabbi Aqiba may have had this in mind when, seeing the Song as an entry point into the rest of the writings, he wrote, "for the whole world is not worth the day on which the Song of Songs was given to Israel, for all the Writings are holy and the Song of Songs is the Holy of Holies."

Hear the scriptures, the witness of our elders, beckoning to us, "Arise, my love, my fair one, and come away". To read the scriptures as love poetry instead of a legal tome changes everything. It is not so much that we find the rules of life to follow and impel others to follow, but that we are found by the love of life to open and be opened to.

May the scriptures walk in our midst until we know in our bones that my beloved is mine and I am my beloved's. May we also know this to be the experience of others and what binds us together is our respective experience of being loved and loving.

Isaiah 2:1–5
Needed Change [1]

In days to come .... In days to come we look for life to be different than it now is. The difference is to be better. That which is still chaotic will become established. The extraneous parts of life vying for, and thus choking out, attention will find their place within larger pictures and we will live more solidly with one another.

In days to come we expect to see a resolution to life's perplexing questions. That which leads us to conflict will be transformed into consensus. The huge moral question of war will cease to confound us and we will learn peace rather than war. Imagine the transformation of our thinking if we learned history through accounts of peacemaking rather than a chronology of wars won or lost. Instead of "learning war" we would understand it as aberration, its incompatibility with the best of every teaching.

But we are not there yet. Wars and rumors of wars continue to abound. Such are convenient control methods to keep us fearful and unthinking. So how do we make a shift that seems so absolutely impossible?

A key phrase is for us to respond to an invitation to "walk in the light of the LORD". Among other things, this is a call to live the future as if it were already here. Advent is not just waiting time, but practicing time. Advent: the pre-arrival of a future that we climb aboard. We have seen a better future and, rather than wait for it or expect G*D to bring it about according to some yet undisclosed plan, we begin to implement our part of it in the present. A better future is not based on some future event, but on what we currently do.

Let us walk in the light of what we posit G*D will be doing—teaching, mediating, transforming implements and attitudes of war into communal feeding and universal health care. Our Advent is proactive waiting. Our waiting is preemptive futuring that breaks free from being caught between practice and actuality, a rock and a hard place.

We know where all this is going. Let its breaking news, its Advent, begin now.

Isaiah 5:1–7
Proper 22 (27)

Walls and hedges of protection are valuable gifts. Within these we are able to find a source of steadfastness for ourselves and a place of refuge for regrouping when life happens. These protective gifts can be personal as well as communal.

The downside is that we begin to rely on these levee-type boundaries as the end-all and be-all of living and they begin to constrain us or to over-comfort us.

Like a nautilus that doesn't grow a new chamber, our very protections from external dangers become a restraint on internal growth and maturity. If we don't make room for more than what we learned in Sunday School as a youth, we will remain spiritually stuck at that point.

As consoling as a hedge can be when we need escape it can turn us into spiritual couch potatoes, never willing to risk the fear and trembling of salvation. We take our comfort and look for more and more of it. Without knowing the limit of enough comfort, it becomes ever so much easier to avoid using our little gray cells.

---

things haven't gone
the way I expected
so I'm going
to rip and tear
that which I desired
I'll make it desolate
because that's what I am

so quick to pout
when discouraged
so fast to apply a vacuum
where nothing can exist
except huge amounts
of boredom
revenge and angst

in so recognizing
ourselves
we name our creator
in whose image
we live and move
at least gasp and pine
how convenient for us

but a time has come
to be saviors of G*D
living and moving
today and onward
to have the student
teach the teacher
so all might learn

Isaiah 7:10–14
Creation's Conception

Ahaz refused to ask for a sign. According to Mary's response to an external announcement about being a sign, she hadn't even known that asking was an option. Where have you been on this scale regarding your own engagement with signs?

Every season and generation stands in need of a sign for it's time that they not be wearied or helpless. Would that signs were clearer for we may have already had a sign for us that we missed and so we continue to devolve our trust of one another and G*D. In recent days we have received an unexpected sign from Pope Francis when he criticized the church for putting dogma before love, and for prioritizing moral doctrines over serving the poor and marginalized. We will see what will come of that challenge to the principalities and power—actual change or assassination.

If there is not a sign we will make one up. So it is with the date of March 25 wherein an Annunciation to Mary is given on a theorized anniversary of Anno Mundi (in the Year of the World) to honor a birth of creation. This conveniently works out to 9 months before December 25. We now know there is not going to be a known moment of creation. Neither religious or scientific counting of biblical generations or calculation of the speed of universe expansion is going to give us a definitive answer.

What would it mean for us to live without a sign, whether G*D wants to offer one or not?

While living in a tropical clime for a Christmas season, I noticed how tied to our signs we become. No snow, no pine trees—can this really be Christmas?

In being tied to our signs we reduce our option to be ready for a new sign.

This may be the difference between Ahaz and Mary—a willingness to have a new sign. It might even be put this way: "Choose this day what sign you will abide by; as for myself, it is a next sign."

Isaiah 7:10–16
Needed Change [4]

Prophets have been known for their use of symbolic action to dramatize their message. In some of my formative years, guerrilla theater was an outward form of an inward prophetic grace. We have gotten away from some of that and settled for unimaginative picket lines, pre-produced signs, and rational arguments. It is probably time for re-investing in symbology beyond words, as the usual forms of protest against injustice are like trying to teach a pig to sing—it wastes our time and wearies pigs, creation, and G*D.

One of the injustices is that of resisting a hopeful word. We, like Ahaz, tend to get ourselves set for the worst and not be able to see grace oozing in, if not abounding. What have you given up on? Why is that? Particularly during this time of remembering Joseph, why is that? If Joseph can be transformed, so can the kings of old and the high and mighty of today; so can you and so can I.

Let us not act unjustly toward the possibilities of G*D that move us beyond the limits of our fears to a new life that comes from actively following our baptismal vows to refuse evil and choose good.

Vocatus atque non vocatus, Deus aderit.
Asked or not asked, G*D is present.

This saying was popularized by Carl Jung, earlier by Erasmus, still earlier by the Spartans, and who knows how much earlier by others until we get back to creation.

Asked for or not, creation happens.
*Recognized or not, called or not, G*D calls forth.*

What is a sign of G*D's presence—life itself. Look! Life goes on; births occur; creation is beckoned forth and declared good. Before a next child is born, by anyone, anywhere or before a different sign is acknowledged, by anyone, anywhere—G*D is at work.

Before an advent is over, or even begun, waiting and fulfillment have met, bowed to one another, and moved on.

Go ahead, just try to ask more quickly than G*D is present.

What sign, what symbolic action, in your everyday life will stand for your having been endowed, already, with what you need? When you are in touch with your sign, your daemon, your genius, your totem, it is amazing how quickly time flies. This is our element-of-fun, our spoonful-of-sugar, our lark, our life, our spree.

What sign is given you? What sign are you to others?

Isaiah 9:1–4
Guiding Gift [3]

While it sounds as if there is a moment in which gloom gives way to joy, darkness to light, and contempt is shattered in one fell blow, there is, for those who have eyes to see, a slower process that has been building to such moments of recognition that once we were one way and now we are another.

True believers have a difficult time with this. Those who honor the questions life keeps posing to the most obtuse and recalcitrant find they are always on the cusp of great change—they are change surfers.

As you continue a process of finding a new home because life has changed, or new acquaintances, or new tasks, may you find your quotient of joy also rising. There is nothing carved in stone that won't be transformed. As in Hawthorne's *The Great Stone Face*, even an old man of the mountain moves from hillside to human face.

This is new birth, birth from above, birth from below—new birth. This is faith, hope, and love all rolled together—a joy of change. Revel in it while you can and help those around you to enjoy their own letting go.

In terms of relatively local news, ice jams are causing floods on rivers. As the National Weather Service notes in their own special way of capitalized reports, ICE JAMS ARE VERY DIFFICULT TO PREDICT. THEREFORE...IT IS UNKNOWN AT THIS TIME HOW HIGH THE RIVER WILL RISE AT ANY ONE LOCATION.

Even if difficult to predict, ice does jam and unjam; life does gloom and joy; time does darken and lighten; people accept slavery and demand freedom. Current reality is—deal with it. A different reality is already underway—be ready for it.

Isaiah 9:2–7
Blessed Body, Proper I

To be walking in darkness and to see a brilliant light is not a comfort. A flashlight beam in the eye can be painful.

Brightness coming on too quickly when living in deep shadows is not only startling, but a source of misperception. We too easily confuse a source of light and what it illumines.

A too-quick look can lead us to think that a nation is greater than it is, that a current joy is all that is needed. Eventually this mixing up of journey and arrival brings disorientation. We settle for a present modicum of peace rather than continuing to build a present that can bear the weight of tomorrow's new additions to reality.

What will allow folks to join in with a next stage of journey? Well, there will be false promises of peace at a next plateau that will pull some folks on. Some will become lonely when others have journeyed on, with a double loneliness for having seen the road wasn't quite as rough as they had feared, and belatedly and ruefully move on. Some won't ever move and they'll be buried in their grave to mark this plateau. Some will hear a sentinel, a "child" of light singing for joy about that which is yet to come, no matter what plateau they are on.

As we near a time of celebrating birth of a "prince of peace" who will need to grow into and past that designation, it will help if we recognize that wonderful counsel, creation-deep strength, steadfast protection, and an orientation of peace are all sustained with justice and fairness.

A bright light suddenly upon us focuses for us our satisfaction, the spoils, the surface of desire, and we miss that which undergirds all the good we are surprised to find has arrived—basic justice and common fairness, both lower-case. This is a necessary background for moving on. May we use Christmas not only to celebrate a past birth, but a present birth of ourselves to more consistent justice and fairness.

Isaiah 11:1–10
Needed Change 2

Notes from *The New Interpreter's Study Bible* indicate that patristic and medieval interpreters were concerned with Jesus' messianic nature in Isaiah and often quote 11:1-2 in their writings and in the church's liturgical traditions. They also indicate that 11:6-8, the image of the "peaceable kingdom", found particular resonance in the 19th and 20th centuries in the U.S.

This suggests different times see different emphases in this passage. What might we look at here in the 21st century? Is it time to cycle back to a messianic god/king? Time to continue the peace theme? Shift from the poles to look between them to see that what connects them is the issue of justice for the poor?

One option in this day of information overload might be issues of knowledge and understanding—where their similarities end and where their differences begin.

How do we inquire? That feels like an Advent issue here between times.

Inquiring becomes a winnowing fork. "Ask away, ask away, ask away, Joe", becomes a sea chanty of our day as we sort out the knowledge of "the Lord" currently wider than the sea to see where we might find an island of solidity on which to stand for a moment before diving back in to acquire further understanding.

Isaiah 12:2–6
Hopeless Hope Vigil

I'm not a Hebrew scholar so anything you see me do with it ought to first be discounted and then questioned and questioned again. With that disclaimer I note the word "salvation" and an indication that its root can be read as either causative (to save) or passive (be saved). I am stimulated by the friction between these two forms, energized by seeing more elemental particles escaping from a collision of words as well as atoms.

Traditionally, both forms point the action of salvation moving from G*D (causative) to us (passive). Kazantzakis' *Saviors of God: Spiritual Exercises* and Bernstein's *Kaddish: Symphony No. 3* turn this action around.

Does a reversal of salvation language disturb? Can Christmas or a "Second Coming" (as if this were not an every moment experience/ possibility) be seen anew as G*D with Us and that "withness" passing the gift of salvation back and forth?

If I were to write a second time on this passage I might take the translators of the *New Revised Standard Version* to task for leaving the word "song" out of verse 2. Most other translations envision G*D as "strength and song" while the *NRSV* has it "strength and might". This is a case where parallelism is helped by contrast rather than repetition.

If I were to write a third time I would wonder about verse 1 and its absence here. It is the compassion, the comfort, that has gone before that sets up the rest of the joy. A case could be made for compassion-less joy being no joy at all. Without compassion, joy is only a lovely word covering forced jollity.

---

compassion or comfort
is a prior word

so often left out

of an appreciation or analysis
of our current situation

compassion or comfort
leads the way

away from

a one-way dogmatization
of many-faced salvation

Isaiah 25:1–9
Proper 23 (28)

Cities are extensions of individuals. There are patterns that occur. The boom-town phenomenon is one sort of city. Sometimes they develop more than their original impetus of economic mono-culture and continue, mostly not.

Cities with a long history have come and gone. How many Jerichos have archeologists found? Why does New Orleans stay functional? What will happen with Fargo when Canada rebounds another inch from its glacial compression and the Red River basin returns to a lake?

We might think about cities and migrations in terms of resurrection. After a while cities fail and immigrants are incorporated into the genetics and other strata of a culture. There is a fading, a dying. But periodically there is a rebirth; a feast is re-established.

Waiting and salvation seem to be on unaligned sine waves. Even were they synchronized there would still be a waiting and a fulfillment. It is obvious that death has not been swallowed up—see to what lengths the church and individuals will go to deny death and set up protections against death. Somehow we keep thinking that G*D really will defeat death once and for all. This rings false from the beginning. Just try to imagine any vitality in a creation without death or G*D without Death—soon implacable stasis, a state worse than death, sets in.

It is this reality of death that leads us, time and again, to a gift of resurrection, not its surety. We all like a next breath too much to look forward to resurrection as a gift and not a given. For all our preaching about Easter qua Easter, Good Friday is still its straight-man. Without Good Friday, Easter's punch-line wouldn't ring true.

Isaiah 25:6–9
Opened Heart Evening

Presume a daily feast and no death. Usually when resources are abundant a population will increase. If we take this literally, how do we walk a line between over-population and a limit on the blessing of children as a mark of G*D's favor?

Any number of dystopian novels can spin out from a deathless feast.

To make sense of this in light of resurrection, the swallowing up of death needs to be beyond some literal immortality.

It would be helpful to ask about this mountain of feasting on food in relation to swallowing death. Can feasting together be a death-defying act for a community?

One take is that the mountain is creation, earth. Harking back to Isaiah 24:21, the power-brokers will be confined. Their power to wield death will be done away with. Violence will be returned to its box. Death will still be operable, but not death by violence.

This is not just a waiting for a Mr. Deus E. Machina to show up, but an engagement of whatever G*D gifts we currently have to this same end of encircling violence with blessing—teaching the humility of dying as an antidote for death.

Isaiah 35:1–10
Needed Change [3]

So often do we connect violence with salvation. Here, again, it seemed important to do so. "Here is your God. He will come with vengeance, with terrible recompense. He will come and save you."

Given your current sensibilities, would you desire your salvation to come at the expense of recompense? What pound of flesh might satisfy a pound taken from you? Would you need two pounds or more to make up for the one you lost? Is vengeance upon another a necessary part of a compensation package for injuries done you?

Since this is an advent season of anticipation and new beginnings, it would be interesting to note how many times in these remaining two weeks we find ourselves listening to violence in the media, on the lips of political candidates, among our friend's reports of life, and in our own family experience. Simply being aware of this number will begin a sensitization process needed to begin anticipating an everlasting joy that is not dependent upon divine violence justifying human violence.

If you are already aware of the way in which violence has been built into our joy, you may desire to begin removing it and finding that joy is able to be sustained on its own. There is no magic in this process. It is the same as changing any habit—persistence, persistence, persistence until it becomes second nature.

The best persistence carries with it an extension. Every time we are able to be aware of and back away from a violent response, we would be aided by inviting someone else to marvel at the miracle of our not responding in kind and being proactive in assisting them to glimpse a new avenue of their own salvation. This will mean staying in contact with ravenous beasts who are not aware of the choices in front of them and empathetically revealing them with an invitation to join you in choosing to see glory beyond survival.

An advent challenge is to remember that persistence fatigue is all too easy to arrive at. Keep your practicing communal that you might receive the support you need to keep expanding arenas for your persistent choice against violence in its various expressions, small and large.

Isaiah 42:1–9
Beloved — Clarification Week Monday

Great emphasis is placed upon a "suffering servant" as though it might be the be-all and end-all of our desire. Oh, to be a suffering servant! and all the supposed atonement such is supposed to bring.

We have given far less emphasis to a vocation of justice. Its end is often the receiving of suffering and injustice by one attempting to relieve suffering and injustice. Somehow the cause of justice is eclipsed by the effect of suffering.

In one way or another, giving heed to one's calling will call one forth to justice-living. The arena in which one operates may be large or small, but justice is something that needs to be present at every level of life. Not doing one's part where one is causes a vacuum that weakens every other justice-seeking and impedes a spirit-of-G*D.

Not only do we have a vocation of justice, but a vocation of light-bearing whereby we might see and reveal an idolatry of past and present and illumine the way of new things. Justice and Light-Bearing are vocational corollaries.

These two vocations guide our thought today. Another way of coming at this is from *The Meaning of Vocation*[1] by A.J. Conyers:

> "Vocation" is distorted by two disastrous misunderstandings: a secularized idea of "career" and a monastic concept of the religious life. Both are less than the biblical idea of vocation.... Vocation is about being raised from the dead, made alive to the reality that we do not merely exist, but are "called forth" to a divine purpose.

To be raised from the dead (to be brought up from the waters of baptism to hear one's belovedness) is to have a prophetic vocation—justice-making and light-bearing—regardless of one's current reality of prison guard, prostitute, or presidential candidate.

[1] www.baylor.edu/christianethics/VocationarticleConyers.pdf

Isaiah 44:6–8
Proper 11 (16)

A both/and *NRSV* dialogue of soul (Isaiah) and self (Wisdom):

Isaiah 44:6 Thus says the LORD, the King of Israel, and his Redeemer, the LORD of hosts: I am the first and I am the last; besides me there is no god.

Wisdom 12:13 For neither is there any god besides you, whose care is for all people, to whom you should prove that you have not judged unjustly....

Isaiah 44:7 Who is like me? Let them proclaim it, let them declare and set it forth before me. Who has announced from of old the things to come? Let them tell us what is yet to be.

Wisdom 12:16-18 For your strength is the source of righteousness, and your sovereignty over all causes you to spare all. For you show your strength when people doubt the completeness of your power, and you rebuke any insolence among those who know it. Although you are sovereign in strength, you judge with mildness, and with great forbearance you govern us; for you have power to act whenever you choose.

Isaiah 44:8 Do not fear, or be afraid; have I not told you from of old and declared it? You are my witnesses! Is there any god besides me? There is no other rock; I know not one.

Wisdom 12:19 Through such works you have taught your people that the righteous must be kind. You have filled your children with good hope and accept repentance for sins.

From a starting point of "I'm it" that feels like it is going to Lord it over us we find ourselves ending up with kindness and hope. How did that happen? Where do you see a turning point in this conversation? That may have something to do with what else is going on in your life.

> "Since God possesses absolute power and has no reason for abusing it, he dispenses saving justice with complete impartiality and freedom; by the same token, his sovereign mastery over all beings allows him to be lenient to all."
> –NJB footnote on 12:16

While having trouble with the male language and the distant theistic imagery of impartiality, I do come to a similar conclusion and appreciate the closing words of kindness and hope that we continue learning to live into them.

164

Isaiah 45:1–7
Proper 24 (29)

Just before this lection there is the imagery of foreign king Cyrus being labeled with hometown king David's title of "Shepherd".

In our time, given the decisions of past United Methodist General Conferences regarding voting patterns, Judicial Council makeup, and the like [crucial stepping stones for the religious right to continue making sweeping changes at subsequent General Conferences], the shift in Cyrus' title was as unpredictable and surprising to Israel as hearing that G*D has chosen the progressive United Methodists of the Western Jurisdiction to rebuild a vision of holiness throughout the land, beginning with The United Methodist Church, would be to the religious right.

There is no option but to laugh at our sensibilities regarding how progress is actually made. Health and wholeness are not dependent upon legislation, implementation of same, or adjudication of choices. Oh, they can be of great assistance, but none of it is sufficient to build or rebuild a community's hope for vision.

Not only does Cyrus not know G*D, neither do we. So relax. Enjoy. Light and dark, well-being and disaster—do the best you can with what you have—none of us know G*D but all of us can continue to grow in that direction.

Isaiah 49:1–7
Guiding Gift 2 — Clarification Week Tuesday

1)

It is too little, too light, a thing that our belovedness be limited to a narrow range of blessing. To be beloved at all is to toss off blessings in all directions. There does not seem to be any distinction between a touch of belovedness and a universe of blessing.

A blessing of wholeness (salvation) cannot be bordered according to cultural, familial, experiential, or political boundaries. Once set loose, belovedness has an arc beyond the particular and peculiar. Belovedness will probably start with a specific focus, but it can never end there. This is much the same with the reading and hearing of evocative text—it begins with the literal, but can never be limited to the literal.

Hear Isaiah in terms of your own life: "It is too light a thing that you should be only for those you are currently for; you are given as a light to creation that it might be whole."

Be ye lifted up and shine, shine, shine.

2)

Being called before being made is a marvelous image of the pull of the future working its way into the present and, if you are bold enough, into the past. Pushing a picture into the future of a preferred way of being is another way to talk about this same mystery that connects space and time with all parts of time and space.

Note that this work of deep calling to deep—whether forward or backward—is not intended for such minutia as finding a parking space or extra dollars. If deep is going to call deep, it is for much deeper effect than personal comfort (not that such is excluded, just that the personal will be included within a larger context).

You and I and we together are lights and light beyond ourselves. There is a temptation to use the comic phrase of "Flame on!" except that it is all to easily understood as abusive language precursing violence. Mere heat is not what is looked for, rather light that illumines an original choice—not simply knowing good and evil but actually choosing the good, whether inconvenient or not.

Tomorrow desires us to light today that tomorrow might better shine.

Isaiah 49:8–16a
Guiding Gift [8] — Proper 3 (8)

What happens should you begin to track down a choice of G*D over Wealth? Ancient Isaiah sees what G*D's leadership would mean: "I have kept you and given you as a covenant to the people, to establish the land, to resettle families on the ruined properties."

Right! To choose G*D is to choose to be engaged in service of a larger value than self. To follow G*D is to return to the ancient creation task of confirming and continuing care for the earth that is our source material. To follow Wealth is to claim dominion over the earth for our immediate benefit.

Right! To choose G*D is to choose to see that families have living water, a living wage, a living community to bind them again to deeper and wider living where they are. To follow Wealth is to toss more people off their property, always cutting labor wages, leaving people behind to increase profit—at any cost.

In these two examples, following G*D returns us to the two great commands to love G*D (Creator/Creation) and to love Neighb*r (Family/Community).

G*D? Wealth? Long term? Short term? It is still time to decide. Blessings on taking a road more traveled by G*D and less traveled by Wealth. It will make all the difference.

Isaiah 50:4–9a
Premature Fear Sunday — Clarification Week Wednesday

Physiologically, tongues are strong and flexible, made up of sixteen muscle groups. Metaphorically, tongues are also easily bitten and easily biting.

Tongues are equally at home carrying a blessing or a curse. They can cut to the quick or lovingly caress one another. They are a source of encouragement and a keener of despair.

Presume again an original blessing of "It's good". We heard it from our teacher leading us out of confusion. In such an image we honor our teacher by offering a sustaining word to the weary—those caught in moments and millennia of chaos.

The tongue of a creator becomes a tongue of the nursling.

Having the tongue of a teacher does not clearly define behavior. In the gospel lessons, Jesus' teaching tongue sends out instructions to get a donkey, says nothing at all before Pilate, and cries out our existential experience—"Forsaken!" A teacher's tongue reveals and redefines life so even a word like "crucifixion" can become a "holy" word.

The tongue of a teacher is shaped by what they are listening to. If they are not continually being filled, there is a fading—a yellowed lesson plan is a cowardly way to teach.

So, what are you listening to these days?

Isaiah 51:1–6
Proper 16 (21)

So you are interested in "pursuit of saving justice", "right living", "seeking G*D", "pursuing righteousness".

Here are two attendant tasks.

First, ponder in your heart your source material. Rehearse again G*D's touching of Sarai and Abram. Follow their journey to Sarah and Abraham. Remember G*D's touching of your life and your journey. Anticipate the touching and journeying of others.

Second, go about your interest with "exuberance and laughter", with "thankful voices and melodic songs". Joy, gladness, thanksgiving, rejoicing, melody, and song will be our modus operandi. For too long we have thought that earnestness was our calling. A sudden approach of G*D's justice can only be responded to with some form of dance. If we are going to anticipate this gift arriving swiftly it is important to do so with lightness.

Let others argue about who's in and who's out. As for me and my house—its shimmy, shimmy, shimmy—justice and righteousness are already prevailing for those with an eye to joy, an ear to song, and an eagerness to participate.

Isaiah 52:7–10
Blessed Body, Proper III

How beautiful within a manger, a slum, community, church, or home is the presence of one who not only walks with beauty but lives in peace.

May your feet quickly bear your comforting arms where they are needed this day. What check do you need to write? What protest do you need to participate in? What restitution do you need to make? What forgiveness needs offering or accepting?

Living in peace puts us in the strangest of places during officially designated "holy" holidays. If you come to Christmas Day and know someone has something against you, go quickly to ask for a gift of reconciliation.

Isaiah 52:13–53:12
Annihilation Friday

"The Israelites are still the focus in that these verses offer them a revolutionary theology that explains the hardships of exile: The people had to endure the exile and the suffering it engendered because that suffering was done in service to God so that God, through their atoning sacrifice, could redeem nations." –NISB note

It is one thing to participate in "suffering" one's self and quite another to attribute it to an outsider on behalf of one's self or others. In either case, though, there are dangers aplenty.

Suffering qua suffering is not redemptive. Jesus' suffering was no more or less than that of thousands crucified then and still killed today for challenging one power structure or another principality. Stand-in suffering is particularly problematic. At the least it is patronizing.

But to suffer in one's self does set up a possibility of redefinition of meaning. To suffer in one's self while assisting another leads to a redefinition of meaning. One of the best commentaries on the whole suffering issue is Viktor Frankl's, *Man's Search for Meaning*—"The person who knows the 'why' for their existence will be able to bear almost any 'how'."

Suffering is less difficult when there is some purpose to the suffering, or more accurately, when the person doing the suffering believes that there is meaning to the suffering. Here is an example from Frankl's book:

> Once, an elderly general practitioner consulted me because of his severe depression. He could not overcome the loss of his wife who had died two years before and whom he had loved above all else. Now, how could I help him? What should I tell him? Well, I refrained from telling him anything but instead confronted him with the question, "What would have happened, Doctor, if you had died first, and your wife would have had to survive you?" "Oh," he said, "for her this would have been terrible; how she would have suffered!" Whereupon I replied, "You see, Doctor, such a suffering has been spared her, and it was you who have spared her this suffering to be sure, at the price that now you have to survive and mourn her". He said no word but shook my hand and calmly left my office. In some way, suffering ceases to be suffering at the moment it finds a meaning, such as the meaning of a sacrifice.

Isaiah 55:1–5
Proper 13 (18)

Whether we wrestle with much or with little we all come to limp a bit. Residual atrophy hangs on somewhere. Even when alone we are not exempt from stubbing our toe. From some direction we find a wounding of the past clarified and healed beyond a curing, surfacing through us for ourselves and others.

Our state of being seems to have its pluses and minuses. Are we going to measure our state of mind by our physique? our resources? our emotional state? our relational base? our spiritual calm? our informational sources? our hopes? Are we going to measure satisfaction by some given combination of these or other qualities?

At some point we are thrown into mystery. Strangers come along and offer a new way of looking at things. Our own internals rise up to call us to account. From whichever direction, comes a wrestling that takes us past certainty. We can trust neither disaster nor plenty to stay the same.

Give thanks for the wrestles of life. They move us along. And don't forget to bring along a tag-team partner, it makes a wrestle ever so much more enjoyable and survivable. Whether your partner is a stranger in front of you or a sister/brother from your dim, dark past, thank them for sharing in the wrestle of life (which may simply be another way of spelling "The Way").

Isaiah 55:1–11
Hopeless Hope Vigil

After Thursday, Friday, and Saturday we can't be any thirstier for refreshment. We are out of resources and even if we had money to buy food we despair of eating. Nothing that can be said or done will satisfy a vast emptiness we have experienced. No promise will suffice in the face of such loss.

The old encouragements to continually seek G*D fall on deaf ears. Isn't it G*D who has abandoned us? Who can forget Jesus exclaiming, "My G*D, my G*D, why have you forsaken me?"

It would be so much easier if we hadn't done everything humanly possible to save Jesus from the Temple Police, the Romans, and even himself. We don't need mercy and pardon for nothing is making sense. We don't need more mystery. We need Jesus back.

Dry husks. Yep. That's us. Let us be plowed back into the soil. Maybe we can build the soil for we are not any good for anything else.

Listen. Was that thunder in the distance?

Isaiah 55:10–13
Proper 10 (15)

So it is with a word that goes from G*D
it will not return unfulfilled.
Yes, you will go out with joy and
be led away in safety.
—near NJB

As a word from G*D being fulfilled, how is your awareness of joy and safety?

What part of the story of your life needs to be viewed from another perspective to see yourself as an "eternal monument," living and lasting evidence of G*D?

What part of the story of our life needs to be viewed from another perspective to see others in it as "eternal monuments," living and lasting evidence of G*D?

G*D's word is present in the fertile soil of your life and our life. It has been watered and nurtured through your and our experiences. Let us live in peace.

Isaiah 56:1, 6–8
Proper 15 (20)

Once family feuds get rolling it is extremely difficult to break them. Even the one who has the power to shift the ground of relationship seems to have to work up to it.

Having decided to reconcile, it is interesting to compare this to a process of going first to the injuring/injured party and for the public nature of it to come forward later.

One reason we may get back together so hesitantly is that inherent in injurer and injured being gathered together is an understanding that reconciliation will grow to become the norm. Then where would we be? "The more we get together, together, together, the more we get together, the happier we will be" is pleasant to sing about, but only in small doses and as an ideal. Communal happiness is difficult work.

We are hesitant to let this expansive regathering loose by providing even a small family regathering as its seedbed. Not only do we remember Joseph and his brothers re-gathered, but the promise is set loose that all separations shall be overcome.

At any rate, having the outcasts and the casters-out brought back together is a momentous occasion in a restorative justice process.

At this point we are up against universal salvation, which is, somehow, more than our idealized reconciling mercy can bear. But, leaving our ideals behind, new realities open all around.

Isaiah 58:1–9a, (9b–12)
Guiding Gift [5]

From what would you fast if your fast were to be evidenced by sharing your bread with the hungry? Privilege?

Yes, sharing with others means less for you. Yes, that means this kind of fasting as a result of sharing does have consequences. Yes, we are up to facing them (both others and less).

For what purpose would you fast if your fast were to be evidenced by sharing your bread with the hungry? Healing?

Do you want your food to be correctly seasoned? Share. This is how saltiness is maintained.

Do you want to see your food, because we eat with our eyes before eating with our mouth? Share. This is how your light stays lit.

Obviously this kind of fasting goes beyond food. It encompasses every basic need. Only when we are engaged in the process of kindliness and care do we season one another's life and light the way for one another. To avoid a need is tasteless and darkening.

---

a cosmic aarrgghh
rumbles forth
I write of fasting
and take a break
for cheese and crackers

for but a bit of
lovely Wensleydale
how Wallace and Wesley
could go on and on
oblivious to anything but
honey-tinged Wensleydale

hopefully with the help of
a faithful friend
we will muddle through
steady of heart
triumphant in the end

pray all cosmic aarrgghhs
will come 'round right
to comic har-har-hars

Isaiah 58:1–12
Self-Recognition Day

A Prophet Responds

We have had difficult days. We have done our best to influence G*D through our fasting and prayers. That hasn't worked.

> "Well, of course not, these are not techniques to manipulate but relationship deepeners. If you keep going at things the way you have been, things are going to be far worse than they are."

Have mercy! Our sacrifices haven't gotten us what we desired. Now we have to choose to keep at what we find to sometimes get us what we want or risk a whole new way that brings no guarantee that it will be as effective as our current results, sometimes.

> "Injustice always, eventually, leads to difficulty for all. If your fasts and prayers are not intimately connected with justice, they are ultimately useless."

Have mercy! We are discontent with the current state of affairs and afraid to change for the better because it might not be.

> "You didn't arrive overnight at your current position of being damned if you stay the same and scared to be different. Give this one thing an adequate test of three generations—share your bread with the hungry. You shall then be called 'repairers of the breach' and your healing shall spring up quickly."

Have mercy! Let's gather the people. Call a solemn assembly to refind our joy of being connected, for better and for worse, with one another and G*D. Perhaps we might yet be the mercy we seek!

Isaiah 60:1–6
Guiding Gift

Your own shall come from far away.

Yes, they have been so far away for so long that, for the longest time, it has seemed they were no longer our own.

But, finally, we lifted an eye to find our log to be a star and, upon looking again, it is clear those who were far off are far off no longer.

Our own have come home.
We have carried home to them.

Now, just so we don't get too big a head and fail to recognize our kith and kin again, whether near or far, we are to remember that "home" rises on all—it is not just ours—we are its.

May this year be a year of everyone being home together.

Isaiah 62:6–12
Blessed Body, Proper II

"Sentinel" and "Son" and "Light" from Isaiah 62:6-12 / Isaiah 9:2-7 / Isaiah 52:7-10 are parallels. The qualities of one run into the qualities of the other.

The authority of each grows continuously. It is only in this constant growth that the possibility of endless peace comes to pass. Our tendency is to plateau our growth (for shorter and longer terms) and at each we not only consolidate our gain (light the path we have come by), but we lose sight of our journey and settle for a present peace based on a past that can't bear the weight of tomorrow's realities without more growth.

A call comes to move beyond our current plateau, to "build up" the road to which we have set our foot. A light dawns; a sentinel calls out; a child pushes the boundaries to say, "Ensign Pulver, it's time for more life than this old bucket or plateau can hold! We'll seek it first in anti-authoritarian silliness which is appropriate for Holy People, the Redeemed."

Christmas—what amazing silliness to upset and re-right every apple-cart.

Isaiah 63:7–9
Blessed Body [1]

A reflection on what it means to be an image of G*D is always in order.

G*D's gracious deeds keep boiling down to one—loving kindness. Each time we think we have found another facet to G*D it is the same old one—loving kindness. Each time we get discouraged with humanity (all the various inhumanities only define what humanity is not) we find that our base line continues to be our imaging loving kindness.

Surely Israel is G*D's people and they will not deal falsely! What hopefulness G*D has in the face of nearly constant betrayal. It would be so easy to give in to a base line of betrayal as our identity (Garden, Cain, and onward).

Surely we are G*D's people and we will not deal falsely! What apparent folly this is in light of what we do to one another. Can we suspend our disbelief enough to know that all this is a play and wherever we strut, we will eventually put such façade behind us and reveal the denouement toward which we have always been moving—loving kindness

In the end, this is not a result of a particular message or messenger. No matter how you would want to massage it, redemption is always recognized within loving kindness. This is what has lifted and carried us all these days. This is what lifts and carries us today. This is what will continue to lift and carry.

So, having again thrown back a curtain, will we live more closely and daily with loving kindness? While birth happens, will Birth Happen to us that we will more closely walk our image until there is Emmanuel (G*D/Us), a logical and experiential extension of Emmanuel (G*D/Jesus).

This revelation of Emmanuel comes not from paring away until some kernel is revealed. Rather, it is an extension of our base line into every mundane part of our life, every gracious deed.

Jeremiah 15:15–21
Proper 17 (22)

Moses has strange things to tell folks from his outsider position of being both the princess' boy and a self-exiled murderer. Jeremiah has strange things to tell folks from his insider position that is being spun against by loyalist prophets.

Which strange message would you prefer to be offering in today's world?

Our understanding of the situation we are in will determine whether we play or avoid playing Moses or Jeremiah in our setting. Are you called to work from the inside or the outside? It is important to identify this so you can come to terms with your disappointments and options when your message isn't heard. In such cases it is not enough to simply switch sides and think you can do any more from the other position. If called to work inside, work inside; if called from the outside, work outside.

Most likely, which ever way you come to the issues of the day, you won't be heard (Jonah seems to be an exception and remember how disappointed he was to be heard—as much as Moses and Jeremiah and you for not being heard). So come to grips with that and do what you do do well. As much as possible, work in concert with other insiders and outsiders as this grounds your spiritual health deeper than a world that acts as though physical health trumps everything else.

Travel the I-AM-way and persistently witness to an expansive love in the face of every argument to the contrary.

Jeremiah 20:7–13
Proper 7 (12)

Fightings and fears go on inside as well as outside.

Do I speak? Do I keep silence? Do I mutter?
Do I push away? Do I embrace? Do I stand still?
The list of ways in which we polarize our choices or
    make them immaterial goes on and on.
Jekyll and Hyde we are.
What is the weak within us that needs strengthening?
What is the evil within us that needs transformation?

We can use small groups and focus groups and self-help techniques and large bootstraps to pull on, but they all come up short.

When caught and stymied in our approach/avoidance modes it
seems the last thing we will try is singing. Do you hum? Do you whis-
tle? Are you aware of what tunes you are using? In the midst of every
confusion it is probably important to consciously sing with G*D for
the saving of the weak from the wicked even though we don't yet see
how it is happening or what part we have in the saving.

The next time you find yourself battling yourself, try this question:
Who is being hurt? Then take their side for G*D is already saving
them and you might as well join in on that side. Of course you will
have to throw out any false harm arguments being used by the principalities and powers trying to keep you from seeing the real harm (like
all those shills who say we can't yet tell if global warming is real, so
we don't have to do anything about it, or the harm done can't be un-
done, so we don't have to stop doing additional harm).

Jeremiah 28:5–9

Proper 8 (13)

The Spiritual Formation Bible suggests your journal entry for today begin with, "What I Don't Want to Hear From God."

I don't want to hear that things are going to get worse before they get better. I don't want to hear that the problem is with me, not with someone else. I don't want to hear that I need to dramatically stand up to the powers that be and say, "I don't trust you." I don't want to wait to see.

I yearn to hear that the economy will only go up from here. I desire to be assured that the problems of the world can be targeted on one group (or another, it doesn't really matter which group). I hanker for someone I can turn decisions of state and personhood over to. I crave and lust after immediate results.

What have you resisted hearing?

That's a pretty sneaky way to get us to hear what we need to hear.

Is this the missing part from Psalm 13? Instead of just complaining, did the Psalmist finally listen to an unwelcome word and come to rejoice in a meaning and purpose of life beyond being top dog?

Jeremiah 31:1–6
Assured

A sign of resurrection: The weary pull out a tambourine and dance, dance, dance. So check your tambourine for dust.
Resurrection is a jingling tambourine, not a static cross.

---

this is a day
holding the tectonic plates
of our lives in place
regardless of the stress
it places upon us
to keep things from falling apart

this is a day
we yearn for sweet release
even a release that shakes foundations
relieving unrealistic expectations
controlling our lives
spending resources on security

this is a day
of resistance to change
of dreaming heaven on earth
unknowing clouds dim our eye
to unseen consequences
hidden beneath our next step

this is a day
to rejoice and be glad in
to dance merrily
on the graves
within and around
trusting this day

this is a day
like all days
infamous and usual
ready and unready
for an earthquake opening
tombs and joy

Jeremiah 31:7–14
Blessed Body [2]

> The remnant:
> Watch, I shall bring them back
> from the land of the north
> and gather them in from the far ends of the earth.
> With them, the blind and the lame,
> women with child, women in labour,
> all together: a mighty throng will return here!
> In tears they will return,
> in prayer I shall lead them.
> *–NJB*

There seems to be some question about how to deal with what here is translated as "prayer."

Will we be "consoled" as we are led from exile to return? *–NRSV*

Will we be "filled with supplications for repentance" during this time? *–NRSV* note

Will we be weeping for joy and "have our hands held"? *–MSG*

Will this be a time of joy after "great sorrow"? *–CCB*

My suspicion is that we find our ministry in an area that corresponds with how we envisage homecoming. Do we need to pay attention to grief and separation issues? If so, that will set some of our agenda in life. Does repentance come before consolation? What about the line about home being where they have to take you in? How does this change our relationships?

What are the dynamics of coming home that speak to you?

Regardless of the homecoming mechanism you are most comfortable with, joy (first, second, and last) measures our engagement with others.

Lamentations 3:1–9, 19–24
Absent Saturday

Hope in things unseen, for hope seen is no longer hope. Here the unseen in the midst of disaster upon disaster is that mysterious quality pegged to G*D and thus to ourselves and one another—steadfast love.

Along with hoping for an unseen steadfast love, we hope that mercy never comes to an end. These two hopes feed each other. When steadfast love seems not so steadfast, but unsteady, mercy comes to remind love to be resolute in the face of any and every provocation. When mercy seems constrained, love pipes up to remind mercy that it really is stronger than any judgment.

When these two friends are engaged we are able to withstand a myriad of woes. In a way as mysterious as steadfast love and mercy, troubles may also be unseen.

All of this is new every morning and as hope rises before us and we, too, rise to meet it. Yes, troubles persist but they are also a ground for hope. Without waking or sleeping nightmares, hope would fade and then where would we be—in an idyllic utopia awaiting salvation through a return of chaos in life's wake.

On a day of confirmed loss we need to sit for a long time with verses 1–9. Without fully affirming how far we are from health we are not able to finally blink our eyes and wonder, "Was that a flash of re-membered and hoped for steadfast love? Did a glimpse of mercy just cross our despair? If I stop feeling put upon for a loss of control might hope reappear?"

Again, today is a day for sticking with the first nine verses longer than we are comfortable. Blessings to you until hope reappear.

Ezekiel 18:1–4, 25–32
Proper 21 (26)

Ezekiel catches us just right—whining—"That's not fair! G*D's not fair."

And we are right; G*D's not fair.

If G*D were fair we would be graded on a miraculous curve with extra credit given for our intentions and our creedal fidelity. If G*D were fair it would be noted that I'm not as bad as so-and-so, so I should get a better seat in heaven. If G*D were fair I would not be tempted at all, much less only up to what I can bear.

What fairness do you expect from G*D? And since you don't get that fairness, what are the specifics of your whining?

This may actually be a helpful self-help technique—listen in on your whines to find out what you need working on.

Ezekiel 33:7–11
Proper 18 (23)

Who has played "warner" in your life?

For me some of the authors have been Kazantzakis, Ellul, String-fellow, Rauschenbusch, Wesley, Luther.

I am struck with how male that group is. I am thankful for the living presence in my life of Brenda, the Kairos CoMotion planning team, Joan, Kathryn and so many more women.

Now why would I indicate the males by their last names and the females by their first? I have been warned about subtle sexism and yet so easily fall into its forms.

At any rate, together they have helped me be a "warner." Together they have convinced me that the warning that needs doing is a warning toward new life, as well as a warning away from old life.

This business of "warning" seems to go way back "to be aware," "to watch," "to care." This is more and different than the kinds of warnings we get about terrorism these days (seemingly calculated to distract).

"As sure as I am the living G*D, I take no pleasure from the death of the wicked (or the good). I want the wicked to change their ways and live (and the good to deepen their ways and live). Turn your life around (and keep it going in a healthy direction). Reverse your evil ways (and be drawn ever nearer the ways of abundant living). Why die (and why not live)?"

How aware are we of our own complicity in the consequences we have received? How much do we care that wickedness on both sides cease?

Being a warner is not easy if the warner heeds the warning as well as passes it on. Still it is a valued gift. Warn away!

Ezekiel 34:11–16, 20–24
Evaluation Day — Proper 29 (34)

The New Interpreter's Bible groups this section in a slightly different way. The title they give to verses 17-22 is "Inter-flock Conflict". That language certainly brings a lot of pictures to mind.

The commentator speaks about responsible ecological stewardship—that G*D's creation is not ours to exploit. They bring this up-to-date with images of nuclear waste, chemical landfills, cracked-open tankers, and non-biodegradable trash.

As one of today's shepherds, how do these inform you?

The section we are dealing with began earlier. In some sense we need to hear again verse four with its reversed word order of direct object before verb (lost in most English translations) and emphasize our choosing to join G*D in reversing things.

Verse 4: accusation against leaders (anybody today come to mind?)

A - the weak/sick you have not strengthened/healed
B - the injured you have not bound up
C - the strayed you have not brought back
D - the lost you have not sought

Verse 16: intention of G*D (is this worthwhile work for you?)

D' - the lost I will seek
C' - the strayed I will bring back
B' - the injured I will bind up
A' - the sick I will strengthen

What does it mean to you to place a need ahead of or before your action/re-action?

Ezekiel 36:24–28
Hopeless Hope Vigil

Given: A binary world.

Given: The grass is greener over there.

We live in uncertainty—is the cat alive or dead? There is no way to know until it is too late.

We live in dissatisfaction—not knowing whether it is better to live or die.

Being pulled between poles is painful, is suffering.

Being stuck at one or the other is unsatisfying, is suffering.

Is there a third option in an either/or world? In hope that there is, we sit vigil.

We wait until there is no choice.

We wait to hold a middle way. Here we will know weeping over a city of Peace that knows no peace. This cleansing water reveals living stones already present.

In this we find again a choice to lay down our life and to pick it up again. For a moment we have the joy of being able to pick and choose between our various treasures and healingly apply an antidote to a current state.

We will need to vigil again, but for the moment all manner of things are well. This is prelude enough.

Ezekiel 37:1–14
Conviction [5] — Hopeless Hope Vigil

How often have we been heard to woefully complain that we are defeated because we are not victorious in this or that—desiccated, destroyed—hope is lost—loneliness will be our lot, forever?

It is at such points that we, scattered, need the strength of prophetic proclamation.

The remedy is a strong one, nearly unbearable: Shift vision from the short-term to the long-term. We can withhold our desire to devour and go out of our way to assist others to stand. We can.

This means we will deal honorably within whatever economy surrounds us, tempting us to more. This means we will advocate persistently for those being screwed by whatever economic system has decided they can get survival rations, but no more.

This way of living is available regardless of the external political/economic realities we face.

There are still valleys of dry bones to wake us to poetic imagination and prophetic proclamation.

In light of current bankruptcy legislation we might change the image to a valley of the bankrupt. Can they live again?

In an editorial by E. J. Dionne, Jr. in *The Washington Post*, we hear this assessment: "There is a great misunderstanding that the key fight in our politics is between friends and foes of capitalism. In fact, the battle is among supporters of capitalism who disagree over what rules should govern the market. Should the rules favor the wealthy and the connected, or should they give some protection to those who fall into distress and would like nothing more than a chance to rejoin the ownership society?"

Regardless of the economy dealt with, the choices of devouring or assisting stand always before us.

Hosea 5:15–6:6
Proper 5 (10)

How do we respond to G*D's disappointment in us and leaving us to the strict consequences of our contracting lives?

One response is a call to return to the last G*D we knew. Let us study and worship with renewed vigor. We'll show G*D how much we've learned and committed ourselves to. All of this to bring us back to some comfort level with G*D.

I find the various titles for the subsections of this passage to be intriguing. The *Contemporary English Version* simply has it, "The Lord's People Speak." The *New Revised Standard Version* puts a meaning on the speaking, "A Call to Repentance." *The Message* puts the reverse spin on it by seeing behind the surface of the words and calls it, "Gangs of Priests Assaulting Worshippers."

I find the "assault" image to be the strongest. In the face of our false fantasies that all we have to do is get our worship right then G*D will bless us, the last portion of this passage reminds us that G*D sees through our failed fantasy that "the appearance of love is sufficient."

Being able to be clear about our choices is an important step toward being able to choose well. So choose:

> I'm after love that lasts, not more religion.
> I want you to know G*D, not go to more prayer meetings.
> *–MSG*

> I desire steadfast love and not sacrifice,
> the knowledge of G*D rather than burnt offerings.
> *–NRSV*

Joel 2:1–2, 12–17
Self-Recognition Day

There is much magical thinking that goes, "If I do 'this', then 'that' will happen". We come up with all manner of rituals in our attempt to control life. Little by little our rituals cover over the intended change we are looking for and we settle for form instead of functional change.

A piece of good news worth celebrating is that our habits are not fate and we can once again see what it is they were attempting to accomplish.

In terms of fasting we are called to look behind a form of refraining from food and the wearing of discomfort. What was once a laudable spirit quest became formulaic and can now be released.

Unsatisfied with your life? Fasting is not a self-help process to hike yourself up by your bootstraps. Rather, look at your context. It will contain a call to return to community/G*D/love—to fast appropriately. Fasting needs to be healthy, both inhaling and exhaling. Loose a bond of injustice and find health. Undo a yoke of oppression and find health. Share bread and space and find health. Cover nakedness and restore kinship and find health. This is a corollary of, "None will be saved until all are saved."

---

fast for silence
fast together with walkers in darkness
fast behind veiled light

face a face of hope
face a face of now
face a face of ever

fast, now, fast
face each other
fast, face grace

Amos 5:18–24
Proper 27 (32)

alas for you
who desire the day to come
without having made
the needed decisions of this day

to desire without planning
is racing without
seatbelt or helmet
damn silly

to desire without deciding
is counting chickens
before they are hatched
worthless

no amount of ritual
incantation or sacrifice
will atone for innocent desire
none

plan for extravagant justice
decide for expansive righteousness
for this is saving music to the ear
beautiful

Read again John Wesley's Sermon 92, *On Zeal*[1]. When someone is in need, help takes precedence over prayer and other works of piety in that moment. No volume or intensity of prayer will substitute for a glass of clean water or protection of a watershed. Certainly return to prayer for energy to engage, but it cannot be substituted for actual present love of Neighb*r.

[1] www.new.gbgm-umc.org/umhistory/wesley/sermons/92/

Jonah 3:10–4:11
Proper 20 (25)

What does it mean for "G*D to change," to do something other than get stuck in unrelenting destruction?

What is our response when this reality sets in for us?

For Jonah it brought forth fury and anger. One might almost say, G*D-sized fury and anger.

May we find a G*D-sized compassion for folks who don't have an experience of the gentleness of moving toward communal living without demanding perfection in the moment. May this G*D-sized compassion move from sheer quantity to quality in our lives that we might also have a G*D-sized hospitality.

So what makes you angry these days? What beckons forth your compassion? How do these interact in your life? Is anger occluding compassion? Is compassion inclusive of your anger?

Micah 3:5–12
Proper 26 (31)

Religious people are not exempt from an attempt to control through expansion of power and insurance of security.

The dynamics of both are similar, which lets us know how religious an endeavor is politics. In fact, one might say that politics is today's primary religion. Is there a dirty trick left untried or a false accusation not made in campaigns? Is there anything of "our" party which has the least question that can be raised about it or anything of "your" party which is not going to destroy the nation tomorrow (and maybe even later this afternoon)? Is there no end to sweatshops and economic sanctions and IMF/World Bank policies and wars wherein people are actively and passively killed for power and security issues? Is there ever an end to perjury and bribery and embezzlement attempting to expand one's own territory?

Along with Micah we are called to expose this false religion that "postures and pretends dependence on God" by ending every speech with "God bless A-mer-ca" and the vain imagining that "We've got God on our side. God'll protect us from disaster."

---

some prophets cry peace
to a raging river
a rising tide
as though desire
for continued comfort
were sufficient

being thus out of tune
with what is coming
for fear of losing
what little purchase
we have on the bronco back
of a living G*D

our cry of peace
echoes hollowly
within a hollow people
empty of hallowing
coming change
in present living

Micah 6:1–8
Guiding Gift [4]

Talk about your on-going pop-quiz! Justice! Kindness! Humility!
Perhaps they are to be everyday virtues:
> justice. kindness. humility.

Note how honesty, integrity, and the response or judgment of the environment become critical evaluation tools for our individual and communal decisions. "Mother" Nature will reveal how we are doing with justice, kindness, and humility.

G*D is plaintiff and each and all of us defendants. G*D's case is clearly stated and placed before judge and jury—creation.

What are the mountains hearing about the way we treat the air, water, land? It is the canary in the mine for the way we treat one another and resources of exchange between us.

G*D's complaint seems to be about the way we have treated G*D. The suit turns, however, on our relationships with one another. Were these to be characterized by justice, kindness, and humility the case would be thrown out. The mountains and hills could return to their everyday business; G*D's relationship with us would be restored—as is done to a Neighb*r, so it is done to G*D.

- And so today's quiz:
  Are you and yours any more just/fair than you were yesterday?

- And so tomorrow's quiz:
  Are you and yours any more kind than you were today?

- And so a quiz for the day after tomorrow:
  Are you and yours any more humble/loving than you may think possible tomorrow?

- And so quizzes continue, opportunity by opportunity.

Zephaniah 1:7, 12–18
Proper 28 (33)

"I brought you into this world and I can take you out!" Thus says a frustrated father. When all else fails and memory fractures, reactive testosterone brings a response choice of fight or flight.

G*D may want to hire an elephant as an advisor. Said memory bank would remember that we've been through this before and repeating it is highly unlikely to bring a different result. It would be more helpful to reflect for a bit on how it is community and compassion keep slipping away. The odds are we won't find some original sin causation.

This is not to say that a temptation and possibility of knee-jerk negative response isn't waiting in the wings. It is to suggest that there is a lack of what Doris Lessing identifies as a source of planetary healing in her book *Shikasta*—SOWF.

Where a Substance Of We Feeling (SOWF) is reduced or absent even the land goes sour.

Wouldn't it be interesting if the next time you or G*D are about to take everything "out" that a memory of SOWF might wiggle in view and we would instead work in the background to nurture compassionate relationships.

This is not bleeding-heart liberal clap-trap. It is full-hearted progressive leadership and facilitation.

Zephaniah 3:14–20
Hopeless Hope Vigil

The word of a prophet moves from damning to joy. One tendency is to separate these into two different states—G*D's disappointment and punishment; G*D's satisfaction and renewal. Another way to approach this is to note that both are present in every present. This competition seems to be within G*D as well as between G*D and creation/creatures.

For this moment, though, presume that you have an equal choice between organizing your time, energy, and resources toward not being condemned or toward being cared for.

To begin, can you imagine them equally balanced so it is your choice as to which you will live out of? Which do you think/feel will bring the biggest bang for your investment of time, energy, and resources? Then, go that way.

I expect that most of us don't experience these as equal choices. Our predilection is to try to figure out methods to escape a wrath to come or to blithely follow our bliss. Whether these biases come from nature or nurture, there seems to be a leaning one way or the other. It is too easy to name this pessimism or optimism as the distinction probably runs back to a temptation of gods or G*D to wrestle with disappointment and satisfaction, punishment and renewal.

Consider football. I can remember back to when many players were on both the offensive and defensive sides of the ball. I, myself, played end both ways. In these days of specialization it is exceptional to find someone able to play both offense and defense. So, if G*D's disappointment and punishment are what energize you to live better, stay on the defensive side of the ball—protect your goal. If G*D's satisfaction and renewal are what energize you, stay on the offensive team—push toward your goal. (Yes, "goal" here is the same line.)

At this point in Zephaniah's report we are encouraged to consider going on the offensive, even if we are in the midst of expected disappointments, and invest our time, energy, and resources. See, G*D is for you; who and what are you for?

Zechariah 9:9–12
Proper 9 (14)

If you were in exile (and aren't you?), how glad you would be to hear one of these:

> Come home, hope-filled prisoners!
> *–MSG*

> Return to your stronghold, O prisoners of hope....
> *–NRSV*

> Come back to the fortress, you prisoners waiting in hope.
> *–NJB*

> The prisoners who wait in expectation will return to you....
> *–CCB*

> Come back to the Citadel, you captives waiting in hope.
> *–REB*

Zechariah's focus is on the rebuilding of a people who have endured humiliation and exile. To complicate the problem, the people are apathetic about their task of facing a new world and indifferent to a call to life renewed. Does that sound like our situation? Yep. We know renewal is not easy and takes place in the midst of great pain. We also already know this is our work.

A first step is to attend to heightened language that can enflame imaginations. When dealing with those bereft of hope because a loss has been magnified by its depth or length, a renewed vision needs both scope and detail. Vision cannot be focus-group tested but can grow out of any particular. A passion for "better" is needed, whether in a family, congregation, or community.

Give thanks for whatever hope consistently reveals the exiled places that are a part of you. Your attention brings vision and release.

Malachi 3:1–4
Old Welcomes New

A final presentation has gone through many edits. Each edit adds its part to the end result. And part of the mystery is that a presentation is not the end. There is ending upon ending as those who receive a particular moment incorporate it into their matrix of meaning and see where it will lead them.

Try this reading: I am sending my editor to prepare what I have to offer to others. At some point a publication will seem to suddenly appear in its genre. If the editor does the job well, many readers will have access to the message intended to be sent. From there it will echo in additional lives.

Editors can be both ruthless and understanding of a voice. No grammatical nicety will be overlooked and yet the spirit of the work will shine through.

A final edit anticipates responses by readers. Some will want to burn the book, some venerate it, some build on, some use it as a constraint. This is like sowing seed and there being a variety of soils upon which it lands.

Jesus has been sown; Simeon and Anna receive him warmly and he germinates. In due time roots are put down and a head is lifted to the warmth of the sun. A harvest and a feast come later. In due time … another sowing—you.

May you be a responsible editor even as you are edited. Rejoice; we are in Life together and sharpen one another's presentations.

Wisdom of Solomon 6:12–16
Proper 27 (32)

Don't you love that moment when, after years of seeking, you awaken to find that you had been sought all that time!

Wisdom, your great love, has been seeking you down the avenues of time.

Through all your twists and turns with hands outstretched and eyes firmly closed—a light shone; a pheromone wafted upon the wind; a siren's song hummed.

This sort of anticipatory relationship brings the greatest of surprise and none at all when we open our eyes to find an open door and a once and always friend.

How precious is this deep, abiding, and always ready to be entered paradox of seeking and sought.

For some reason we keep focusing on a moment of finding without an adequate appreciation of the variations and permutations which are prelude. Wisdom is in the journey, not just a destination.

There is chaos here as well as creation. And Wisdom called out; and it was and is and is to come. Out of all the wandering we look back and see a straight path we once thought crooked. With all the possibilities available, the probabilities seem just right. Between these our eyes glow as we bask in a glow of Wisdom—we see as we are seen and return the favor.

Wisdom of Solomon 6:17–20
Proper 27 (32)

Usually we think of a voice as active and an ear as passive. Here it is a voice that is still and an ear that inclines. This reversal is the energy that moves generations forward as a voice is still ahead and our inclination tilts toward it. We have a choice about continuing to incline toward what a voice still has to say or settling for what we have heard so far. May you choose to listen beyond what has so far been heard that the unheard might yet be heard.

Let's see how Wisdom's theory goes:

> - Desire for instruction leads to keeping laws.

> - - Keeping laws assures immortality.

> - - - Immortality brings us to G*D.

For want of desire, G*D is lost. What are you desiring so much these days that when you are involved in it you have no notion of time ("peace is when time doesn't matter as it passes")? Choose that which brings forth this lack of sense of time (loving what you are and do), that moves us into divine space.

To incline our desire is to recognize our dissatisfaction with the limits of today. We hear a-better-than-where-we-have-arrived is yet to come and feel the present as a tar-pit threat rather than an arrival. And so we recognize how far short of immortality we are and how laws do not draw us beyond our present limits but hold us here. We call out, "Come, O G*D!"—"Come, Messiah!"—"Come, Wisdom beyond our present difficulty!"

Choose well in which direction you incline your ear. Does present law or future openness offer a larger G*D with whom we might play?

Wisdom of Solomon 10:15–21
Blessed Body ² — Thanksgiving

An interesting line from *The Christian Community Bible* raises a question of how we are midrashing these days. This is one of the more important tasks to help transition us from our past to our future and to free us from the various constraints of fundamentalism, literalism, or creedalism.

> ...when a people sticks only to its national culture, without seeing anything beyond, within a short time, it suffocates. God's revelation to the Jews was not over, but it was necessary to present it in a new way to all people who neither thought nor spoke like the Jews.
>
> The book of Wisdom is the first important effort to express the faith and wisdom of Israel, not only in Greek, but also in a form adapted to Greek culture.

Those of us involved with progressive Christianity must deal with our own midrash processes as we adapt our heritage to a 21st century culture. Keep telling the story you know to be true.

When we look back with 20/20 hindsight, it is easy to discern a Wise presence. What wasn't understood at the time as wise (fear continued throughout the Exodus) can later be attributed to some good plan. This connects wisdom with thanksgiving.

When we look around us for wisdom to make difficult choices, we find ourselves caught between focal lengths—attempting to apply an appropriate learning from history so we don't just repeat it and repeat and peering into a dim unknown for a new learning not already in our grab-bag. This connects wisdom with mystery.

When we do thought experiments regarding the future, we find our prejudices coming to the fore. Our assumptions and speculations rev themselves into red-line danger. This connects wisdom with foolishness.

Remember with thanksgiving that G*D has revealed things to the foolish, not the wise. Well what are we to do with Sister Wisdom who is all over the map? Sit back and enjoy the ride? Winnow the results with yet a fifth criterion to measure reality?

Perhaps the best we can do here is to raise our sensitivity to the mute and those struggling to put their reality into communicable language. To whom are you listening and how engaged are you willing to be to wrest meaning from inarticulate groans of creation?

Wisdom of Solomon 12:13, 16–19
Proper 11 (16)

How much sooner than Bethel might Jacob have recognized the presence of G*D with him as a freedom from compulsion to follow family stories? Having heard a story of his birth, how much programming was it going to take to move beyond one interpretation of a painful womb? How many times would Jacob need to experience again the wonder of Assurance Lost, Assurance Regained? How many cycles does it take to come to an understanding of Assurance as a Given?

What teaching would be helpful to move us beyond the limitations of family stories or curses around birth expectation so we might better receive and respond to continuing opportunities to decide for larger living? Unless we are going to posit unwitting actions under a grand plan, it is important to wonder how Jacob's anticipation of Solomon's Wisdom of mercy for others instead of practical jokes or strength through mildness and forbearance might lead beyond a fixed future. This leads us to further wonder about what would be different if we had learned that righteousness shows itself through kindness earlier than we did. [This is not to lay guilt trips, but to ask how our experience might be brought to bear to help others in their journey and to encourage us in our next steps.]

Hopefully we will hear in statements of our G*D being a top G*D, not so much an unchanging and immovable arrogance, but an entrance to a future different than currently expected. A choice is always before us, even if unrecognized: "I'll show you for chasing me out—I'll take over the land," or "You are still welcome—there is plenty". Which is righteously kind?

A result of a "gift" of repentance is a willingness to share life and resources. May any repentance we participate in set actualized hope loose in our life and the lives of those around us.

Sirach 15:15–20
Guiding Gift [6]

Choice comes with options. For instance, a basic such as "steadfast compassion" can be implemented in innumerable ways.

Before you are choices of life. Before your neighbor are choices of life. These choices find their commonality in community.

Our tendency is to measure life choices of others by our own limits. In this way we judge another's choice to be perverse, wicked, and sinful.

Can we hear that before each person is a choice of life and there is no end to the variety of ways in which a choice is chosen?

The ancient story that all is brought to life in some mysterious "our image" moves us from life or death choices to those of life and more life.

What a relief when we see how life can be refracted into an infinity of hues between indigo and violet. When the whole rainbow of visible light has added to it wave upon packet of energy within which light shines, our choices take on more meaning and our neighbor's choices become more significant to us.

Choices are gifts right for a moment and a foundation for a next choice.

Sirach 24:1–12
Blessed Body [2]

Where in our exodus or exile do we find a presence of G*D, a presence of wisdom?

Images of cloud and tent hearken back to times of traveling powerless through a desert.

Taking root reminds us of the equally difficult time of settlement and power.

There are those of us who find wisdom to be mobile and flexible and those of us who find wisdom to be strongly located and static. There is danger on each pole and anywhere along a continuum when we think we have this gift called wisdom contained in some combination of situation and station.

For whatever reasons we have a great temptation to presume that wisdom rests upon us and within us. Again and again we need to remember this song extends through the valuable verses 28-29:

> The first man did not finish discovering about her,
> nor has the most recent tracked her down;
> for her thoughts are wider than the sea,
> and her designs more profound than the abyss.
> *–NJB*

G*D, grant us Wisdom to know the difference between Serenity and Courage. Let us help one another to accept the things we cannot change in the midst of exodus and exile and to change the things we can change in the midst of settlement and resettlement. In these and every situation may we wisely join Mother Julian and know "All shall be well, and all shall be well, and all manner of thing shall be well." Out of this wisdom of wellness let us live boldly.

Baruch 3:9–15, 3:32–4:4
Hopeless Hope Vigil

Is there something sub-optimal in your experience of life these days? Some lack of peace in self or surroundings? Return again to the Wisdom of yesteryear and years to come.

This call of return is a call to awareness and discipline. Awareness of something more and discipline to study and follow. Neither of these is an individual endeavor, but communal.

Together we are called to walk in the way of living peace for ever. As might be expected, forgetfulness of the journey we are on shows up quite regularly. We get journey fatigue, peace fatigue. Both of these ways take the best we have and we are not always at our best. Predictably, expectations of exceptionalism and entitlement easily arise. These short-circuit a journey by wanting to settle in at what we consider to be a place good for us. Though unfortunate for our sense of stability, our place is on the road.

When we walk in a way of living peace we find ourselves drawn to the firmness of earth and its health. A sign of this is being able to play yo-yo with light—casting it outward and recalling it to hand. Stars are a twinkle in a cosmic eye and a beckoning to see further and deeper and wider than before.

There are so many distractions, "Squirrel!", in life, or over there, it's hard to tell just where to look to watch light ping-pong rather than participate in its yo-yoing, where glory gets in our eye from the front-side to the point that we can only glimpse its backside. Yes, "Squirrel!", indeed.

It is hard to remember, from just earlier on this page, to what we are called: to walk a way of living peace. Time to get back on for the next moment of journey. Living-peace moments do add up. Blessed are we and all when we continue our awareness of and discipline for walking peace forward, for common good and for ever.

Matthew 1:18–25
Needed Change [4]

There is appropriate guilt and there is inappropriate guilt. Likewise, there is appropriate and inappropriate responsibility.

The trick is to tell the appropriate apart from the inappropriate.

How might we look at Joseph's actions regarding Mary's pregnancy? Here his acceptance of reality is attributed to his righteousness, not his wisdom. Left to his own devices and the devices of his time and place, Joseph had every thing he needed to claim this task of covering for Mary as inappropriate responsibility.

Somewhere along the way Joseph had learned to first acknowledge and then to listen to his dreams. His dream claimed steadfast love as appropriate, not inappropriate.

In this time of waiting between a first and next comings, dreamtime remains an important category for us to pay attention to.

So, what dreams this day need to be shifted from inappropriate to appropriate in your life and in the life of the world?

Based on this scripture they will have something to do with the presence of G*D taking precedence over the current traditions of our culture (religious culture or otherwise). Where does church doctrine that constrains our relationships with one another need to be turned on its head? Where is there a response leading to peace between peoples that needs to come out from under an umbrella of being called treason and stand to turn us all in better directions? Where in our families and communities do we find the fulcrum from which to leverage a preferred future into view and into today?

Whatever your dream or dreams lead you to—imitate Joseph. It is time to wake from sleep!

Matthew 2:1–12
Guiding Gift

Matthew knows how poorly astrologers are viewed in the Hebrew scriptures. There is a sense that they are worshipping the created stars rather than the creator of the stars. At best they bring a second-rate theology just a little better than necromancers.

Star study does give some cover for the Magi in Herod's court, but it also draws attention to Jesus and is precursor to the slaughter we heard about last week that is the sequel to this story (what tangled webs are woven when story lines are broken).

Sticking with a theme of lowliness, instead of fulfillment, this may be Matthew's incarnating G*D into the realities of human life. Through pagans who remain pagans, Jesus is revealed to the larger world. Similarly, in Luke, it is through the lowly shepherds, not the angels, that word is passed about Emmanuel.

By the time we come to the end of Matthew's tale we find another pagan, a centurion affirming what the Magi searched for and only tasted the beginning of—Emmanuel. In the end we also find Jesus' disciples sent on a search for the Magi at the ends of the earth, that they might be baptized. [Note: If you are interested in an entertaining excursion of Jesus seeking the Magi, you may appreciate *The Gospel According to Biff, Christ's Childhood Pal* by Christopher Moore.]

Try looking at this passage through the eyes of surprised Jews who hear it is those second-class Magi who search for and visit Jesus (don't get confused by conflating Luke into Matthew), who honor him with precious gifts. Jewish sensibilities won't get distracted by 2,000 plus years of numbering and naming the Magi or the exoticness of the gifts. They will know there is trouble coming when they hear the Magi are connected with G*D.

The felt, but not articulated, anxiety engendered by the incorporation of strange women into Jesus' genealogy becomes clearer with the arrival of the Magi. G*D is up to something very strange. Now that we are adequately unsettled by holy foreign women and holy pagan astrologers and murder most foul, we are ready to hear about John, a baptizer, and then to proceed with an adult Jesus from whom we can accept the presence of G*D.

To look at this one story is to look at the whole story. Honor it well and don't get hung up on the consumer aspect of global trade items.

Matthew 2:13–23
Blessed Body [1]

Rachel wept as though there were no tomorrow
wept and wept throughout Ramah
wept and wept beyond Ramah
wept and wept for all children
wept and wept for legal and illegal violence
wept and wept through all generations
wept and wept without consolation

finally there is no consolation
no healing, no saving
only weeping

only weeping comes sweeping o'er the plain

and then the seeds that were sown in weeping
watered by the tears that ne'er cease to flow
begin to sprout

still no consolation for past distress
still weeping and weeping

no consolation
only clear-eyed, weeping-eyed vision
children will not deal falsely
wept water will part to free
slaves from fear of death

come unconsoled Rachel
come unconsoled weepers of Ramah
come unconsoled friends today
be unconsoled and come

do not deal falsely with hope
weep and hope
do not deal falsely with faith
weep and believe
do not deal falsely with love
weep and love
do not deal falsely with false dealing
weep unconsoled and live

Matthew 3:1–12
Needed Change 2

Here are two responses to the nearness of heaven come to earth:

- Repent
- Receive the "fire" of Holy Spirit

Question: *Is this a necessary sequence? Repentance is required for Holy Spirit fire? Is it an implied prerequisite to, "Follow me".*
Regardless of how that is responded to, there is a basic duality here of gathered wheat or burned and scattered chaff that seems negated by Pentecost and a Holy Spirit that simply tells of Wonder, cutting through all language divisions.

Question: *On what basis would a Holy Spirit not be conferred? Preordination? Resistance?*
Whatever form of Holy Spirit is received, there is encouragement here to live well, fruitfully.

Question: *All this may be helpful at the beginning of a movement. What happens after years, decades, millennia of there being no discernible connection between repentance and good fruits, between Holy Spirit fire and abominations? How do these play as part of a play filled with heart-warming trees, creches, and noels?*
This passage may have other helpful attributes, but it mostly helps us reflect on a past presence of G*D, not one still before us. At this point it would be more helpful to reflect on the genealogy that begins Matthew and to draw it from the point of Jesus through Pentecost to the present time and ask questions of what folks faced in their day and how they persevered. In anticipating a new heaven and a new earth we could use those reminders and a discerning of our current situation that we might persevere until a surprising new presence becomes known to us.

Question: *Given what you know about the lived situations and culture around you, how evangelistic is this passage? Is it only for an insider?*
A note from the *Wesley Study Bible*: "Wesley connects this 'fire' with 'love'.... (Notes 3:11)". Is this some sort of "tough love"? Does this modify the passage enough to suggest that John has a limited view of Holy Spirit and fire/love that will also show up when he sends his disciples to see what Jesus is up to? If there is room for modification because this is more about a projection of John than an experience with Jesus, what does that mean about how you would preach this in the context of this year?

Matthew 3:13–17
Beloved

So often we would prevent others from receiving what we have. Somehow or other we play an exaggerated zero-sum game when it comes to ourselves—If "they" get some of what I have, I won't have anything!

Here Baptizer John has a variation on that by preventing himself from offering what he has. He plays a "poor me" game.

Jesus has a helpful approach to change—"For the moment, let's just try it as an experiment and see what happens. If it turns out the way you say, I'll do it your way. If it turns out what you have to offer is more than you think you have, we'll just take the results."

The Baptizer consented to this approach and baptized Jesus for repentance of sins.

Turns out that the Baptizer's baptism brought forth a great deal—belovedness, both restored and affirmed.

Now the game is afoot. Angels singing of "Peace on Earth" is one thing; a dove's coo of "beloved" is quite another. The first takes responsibility away from ourselves and the second energizes us to take one more step toward a healing of our past (see *Healing of Memories* by Dennis and Matthew Linn) that our present and future might blossom and grow.

Did it really take Jesus some 30 years to come to baptism? Perhaps it takes maturing in this wobbly old world to come to a perspective of "Let it be". And for baptism to be filled with doves and voices rather than simply ritual, it takes that kind of time to know what to do about being beloved, to even be able to hear that affirmation.

You who are baptized — are you beloved? or just baptized?

You who are not baptized — are you beloved? would that change if you were baptized?

Matthew 4:1–11
Conviction [1]

The old story of temptation in a garden ended with our moving into what we experienced as wilderness (an image from the exile written backward). G*D still with us, but in the wilderness. Our mythology is that we shall return to the garden (homeland). That seems to be what we have set as our goal—a place of indolence where all is cared for, an idealized place of static perfection.

One way of looking at the creation story is not from the perspective of chapters 1 and 2 with creation, but chapter 3 with temptation. This is the purpose of Eden: to remind us there is still a choice available in a situation quite out of our control. Were this a play, it is the beginning of Act 2 where the plot thickens, where the action is. We are still early in Act 3 and not yet able to see if we are in a comedy or a tragedy.

Where the rubber meets the road, where our specialness, our belovedness comes alive is in the midst of choice—a key ingredient of temptation.

One of the differences between the Genesis story and the Matthew story is the acceptance of responsibility or accountability. This comes in the sense of fear of betraying G*D's presence. Our choice: hiding from G*D's wrath because of who we are or trusting in G*D's presence, going boldly ahead to risk the nakedness of death and failure. It is this choice that still stands in front of us as we deal with the temptations of being beloved, either by birth or adoption. There are no automatic passes for either our active or passive choices.

Here Jesus is willing to live with the limitations of life that run up against the boundaries of lack of resources, having an end, and is always short on power. Temptations urge us to take a shortcut to some desirable end, to bypass the means to an end and jump directly there.

As we deal with the vestiges of outmoded theologies that try to jump to some predetermined end without taking into account our current experiences or wisdom or thinking or knowledge, may we work the long hard way through the presence of G*D here in our current wilderness, our current opportunity to choose new life, without giving in to shortcuts or blame.

Matthew 4:12–23
Guiding Gift [3]

Great affirmations are tested by great antitheses.

"The Lord is my light" ... "seek his face/light". Our old dualisms need a model more like *A Once and Future King* rather than a splitting of having and seeking.

"Go into all the world, baptizing" ... "Christ did not send me to baptize". Here a distance between community and individual sets up a needed recognition of multiple expressions of evangelism.

"Light has dawned ... repent." "Repent ... good news." Given time and space and matter and energy it seems we cannot escape these outcomes that circle through our lives. A dawning light reveals a present darkness and recognizing the possibility of changing direction brings comfort enough to test our current orientation.

An Epiphany star reminds us of the found and lost and found again process of growing spirits to find a next immanence or incarnation of G*D illumined by the ordinary. Stars of any sort in our lives are a joy to behold and a source of yearning when lost in storm clouds.

Where are you, your friends/family, spiritual fellowship with a star this day?

    __ It is in sight.
    __ It has recently dimmed.
    __ It peeks and hides.
    __ It has been a long time gone.
    __ It is a non-issue.

---

a great light shines
great enough for us to rejoice for a moment
blinding us to flickery light twinks so small
they can be discarded with nary a squint

upper lights glare until
lower lights are lost
so enamored of mercy received
we lose track of mercy extended

it seems the brighter the beam the deeper the sin seen
pray also for a faint gleam that does not scare us
with such darkness as would swallow us whole
rejoice forever in a nearing humble light

Matthew 5:1–12
Guiding Gift 4 — Honoring Day

The wonderful words of the Sermon on the Mount are addressed to those apprenticed to Jesus, "the committed", as *The Message* has it.

If just tossed out to anyone, they lose their power. Aphorisms, platitudes, and the like are more likely to act as barriers to learning.

Instead, these are part of a periodic snap quiz, variously constructed.

- Give evidence that the blessings listed are blessings.

- Rank the blessings in your life from the most evident to the one you are most uncertain of.

- Note an intermediary blessing between each of blessings that connects the blessing before it with the one that follows.

- What would change were Pilate or Herod to recognize these blessings were the expected outcome of their rule?

- For each blessing, note 3 people who are doing better than you are with acting out of that blessing and then go to them for further instruction.

- What is another blessing that should be added to the list for at least a day?

- Complete the sentence: "Blessed are the blessed, for they ...."

When these blessings are engaged as part of an on-going self-study, they deepen one's spirit. When joined into as a community journey, they widen the reach of the common good. Note that these are not conclusions, but quizzes of our life and lives.

Matthew 5:13–20
Guiding Gift [5]

Time and again we come to ask the question—what's in it for me? And time and again we come to be asked—what's in it for others?

Rituals can help bring out our saltiness or reduce life to repetitive blandness. For instance, a ritual such as fasting is not helpful if it is only for solidarity of a group or what an individual gets out of it. Rituals that don't raise questions about our relationship with others and creation perpetuate privilege.

When ritual opens us to a mystery of more life rather than boring us, our interactions can have a positive effect in the lives of others that echoes in our own.

Experiment with each section of this "sermon" to recast it in light of the other parts. We can still be a salty prophet rather than get lost in a darkening justification-by-law. An if->then approach to each section might bring some clarity. For instance:

If fasting from anger doesn't loosen bonds we wrap around another, our fasting only makes us look tolerant.

If fasting from greed doesn't loosen a yoke we place around others to provide our well-being, our fasting only makes us look philanthropic.

If fasting from food doesn't loosen our hold on our bread, our fasting only makes us look sleek.

If fasting from sloth doesn't loosen our regard for privacy, our fasting only makes us look kingly in our castle.

If fasting from comfort doesn't loosen our closet locks, our fasting only makes us look like an emperor in new clothes.

If fasting from jealousy doesn't loosen our remembrance of injuries done to us by those who love us, our fasting only makes us look justified.

Fasting for our benefit is one thing.

Fasting for the benefit of another is another.

Matthew 5:21–27
Guiding Gift [6]

Ah, the literalist approach to salvation—trying to get into heaven by narrowly defining rules to one's own advantage. Picking and choosing and narrowly defining statements just enough to always be just on the inside side of the cut. Knowing you don't deserve heaven because of your wretchedness, what else can be done but to do everything in your power to redefine the rules to their letter and excusing behavior because of intent.

The "But I say to you ..." lines from Jesus are critical to what it means to be a person on a journey to wholeness. Here murder is no longer limited to the physical but the emotional and the relational. Adultery is not just a final act but a desire, culminated or not. It is this same desire that makes one unchaste and open for divorce.

Jesus is not a letter-of-the-law partner with G*D. This relationship is also not one of good G*D / bad G*D.

How are we going to keep following a "Yes, but I say to you ..." leader? If our intent isn't simply a desire to learn the latest, revisionist ropes in order to game the system and advance, what is it? Are we those literalists mentioned above, just over different passages?

That is why this pericope ends with an examined life and ability to trust a Jesus Spirit to prompt us to say "No" to bad stuff and "Yes" to good stuff without such being part of a programmatic approach to living or a blowing in the wind. Want to keep your saltiness by continuing to add flavor to the world? Want to send a shining ray far down the future's broadening way? Learn how to listen to "But I say to you" and, in turn, to say it and live it.

Matthew 5:38–48
Guiding Gift [7]

How does "do not resist an evildoer" feel today after recent events in Tunisia and Egypt? [Note: This was written during the Arab Spring of 2011, but its equivalent is probably still present when this is read.]

How does "love your enemies" sound today after recent events?

A part of the difficulty we always face with biblical quotes is their applicability to situations that swirl around us and their connection to other biblical passages.

Presuming a sense of parallelism in this whole sermon, we can begin substituting phrases to see what gets added to Jesus' guidance.

Is "do not resist" comparable to "love"? Play these back and forth.

Now remember last week. How would you play back and forth between "do not resist", "love", "do not murder/be angry", "do not commit adultery/lust", "do not divorce/be unchaste", "do not swear by anything outside yourself—say yes or no". If you can't work "love" into a parallel statement, what are you left with?

What are we to "not resist"? What are we to "love"?

Parallelism not only can expand meaning; it can also narrow a choice. This will be seen in next week's pericope contrasting G*D with Wealth.

How do you support those in their own version of Egypt (whether run by a Pharaoh or a Mubarak or a Majority)? What would you tell them? For how long would you counsel patience before sending the equivalent of a plague of frogs or citizens? Have you noted the long-term effectiveness of non-violence in contrast to the short-term gain of authorized, institutionalized, violence?

Matthew 6:1–6, 16–21
Self-Recognition Day

Moving from last Sunday's message of coming down the mountain to continue the ministry to which one is called—experiences of Moses, Elijah, Jesus, etc.—to next Sunday's look at temptations awry from that very ministry takes us through many mini-ministries and mini-temptations.

A ministry of alms is an honorable ministry. Temptations abound to have that ministry turn from service to self-aggrandizement.

A ministry of prayer is an honorable ministry. Temptations abound to have that ministry turn from healing to curing.

A ministry of fasting is an honorable ministry. Temptations abound to have that ministry turn from a means to an end.

There is nothing good that can't be subverted for some seemingly good purpose. Constant vigilance is the price of spiritual maturity.

Living between a call to ministry and temptation's call, integrity in small matters is important for an overall sense of well-being. Warnings about secrecy are not so much a matter of hyper-humility but of acting with integrity. What needs doing is done directly. When action is simply a matter of course and not played for ulterior gain (consciously or not) there is a reward of wholeness of being. And, what better reward is there? It is priceless.

This sense of the language of secrecy comes to the fore when the question of temptation's hypocrisy is raised. We are not looking for self-effacement, but wholeness. A show is not in order, whether that show is unseen or posed. Knowing where your heart is is a great reward.

Matthew 6:24–34
Guiding Gift [8]

In today's world we might translate, "You cannot serve G*D and Corporations."

If that is not self-evident, I'm not sure what can be done to help focus this. The issue of wealth or money is built on a zero-sum principle of competition to get your piece of the pie. There is no end to the size of the piece that one feels is needed. The operative word is a drivenness of "more". There is no sense of a joy of "enough".

In *A Spirituality Named Compassion*, Matthew Fox writes:

> The spiral of materialism is eternal and never ends.... The materialist is never satisfied. For the heart is not made full or satisfied by any, or even all, of the things that the religion of materialism and its preachers of advertising want so desperately to sell us. "Where your treasure is, there your heart will be," warned Jesus. And the treasures that lead to compassionate living are not buyable because they are less objects than they are experiences.... Greed never asks when is enough, enough? It knows nothing of limits. Therefore, it knows nothing of the true pleasures that life is about. It is utterly ignorant of celebration.

If you value relationship, growth, and celebration more than accumulating resources, it will be helpful to band together to return corporations to their functional state and remove them from competition with people's well-being.

This is larger than any movement you join. It is larger than you, though your action is as crucial as anyone's. This is for all those who are tired of striving's vanity. This is for those who understand the freedom of G*D and healthy relationships are the starting points for knowing how to live with enough today that everyone will have enough tomorrow.

Here is a key question: What is "more" about? Is it about food, clothing, security, happiness, satisfaction? What do you need more of? Is it assurance of blessedness? Is it trust in meaning beyond that which passes too quickly away? Is it simple beauty, a graceful movement through the opportunities and challenges of any ordinary day? What do you need "more" of?

Matthew 7:21–29
Guiding Gift [9] — Proper 4 (9)

It is easy to get caught up in SUTJ praise music. SUTJ stands for "Sucking Up To Jesus", where we do everything for the name of Jesus.

There is another foundation more firmly grounded and that is to take the focus off of Jesus and put it on what Jesus focused on—healing/saving humanity and unity with G*D. These are complementary practices in the same way that the greatest commandment is two-fold—loving G*D and loving Neighb*r.

No wonder Jesus can say that those who say, "Lord, Lord" miss the point. Life is not about the doctrinaire use of Jesus' name. Jesus is just too humble to be a vehicle for such blasphemy.

Ironic, isn't it, that Jesus is accused of blasphemy when it is such as ourselves who are most prone to an invisible blasphemy of going along with the power of today with nary a counter-cultural thought in our head or feeling in our heart? Whether we mean Jesus or current political/industrial/military leader, "Lord, Lord" separates us from ourselves and one another.

Matthew 9:9–13, 18–26
Proper 5 (10)

My goodness! How did we get back to Hosea 6.6 so quickly? Aren't we simply to read the scriptures, underline them in blue, and file them away?

That same cry from the universe still arises in our midst: "Go and learn what this means: 'I desire mercy, not sacrifice.'"

Over and over again we practice larger living:

"This is what the LORD Almighty says: 'Administer true justice; show mercy and compassion to one another'". [Zechariah 7:9]

"Woe to you, teachers of the law and Pharisees, you hypocrites! You give a tenth of your spices—mint, dill and cumin. But you have neglected the more important matters of the law—justice, mercy and faithfulness. You should have practiced the latter, without neglecting the former." [Matthew 23:23]

"...we are moving straight toward God, and that continually; walking steadily on in the highway of holiness, in the paths of justice, mercy, and truth." [John Wesley, *The Witness of Our Own Spirit*, Sermon 12[1]]

These three references all have "mercy" in a central location that ties "justice" with "compassion, faithfulness, and truth." It is so easy for these qualities to lose track of one another. In some sense the hard-headedness of justice doesn't know what to do with a soft-heartedness of compassion, faithfulness and truth (in the lower-case, human-sense of the word).

Where is mercy in these days of preemptive war, increasing numbers of those without access to health insurance/care, and a widening gap between economic classes? A renewal of "mercy" talk will help refocus a community of life.

It must be admitted that progressives are a pretty motley crew—disorganized, riding off in all directions at once to rescue this or that particular cause. Liberals can't always explain a "Christian intuition" that sensitizes to issues of injustice. They seem to simply know pain when it is heard whimpering under a barrage of religious jargon about why life can't be any different than it is.

Yet it might be said that injustice places one in close proximity to a key, life-shaping reality—mercy. Mercy first, mercy second, mercy last. We know we stand in need of it and value that gift so highly we want to scatter it wherever we go, no matter where it might land or how it might be received.

[1] www.new.gbgm-umc.org/umhistory/wesley/sermons/12/

Matthew 9:35–10:8, (9–23)
Proper 6 (11)

Verses 22-23 from *The Message*:

1. *When people realize it is the living G*D you are presenting and not some idol that makes them feel good, they are going to turn on you, even people in your own family.*

> How do you see your life in relation to G*D? Are you "presenting" G*D or "representing" G*D? This is worth your meditation/contemplation for a whole week.

2. *There is a great irony here: proclaiming so much love, experiencing so much hate!*

> This may even go beyond irony to reality. What did you expect when you first connected with a living G*D? Did you think G*D would exempt you from temptation's fear? Haven't you needed to hear the ancient announcement, "Peace, be not afraid." Now that you've considered it and tried to live with a living G*D, can you imagine anything other than this irony/reality—the more inclusive your love has grown, the more enemies you have garnered?

3. *But don't quit. Don't cave in. It is all well worth it in the end. It is not success you are after in such times but survival. Be survivors! Before you've run out of options, the Son of Man will have arrived.*

> The word "survival" originally meant "to really live". In common American English survival has a different feeling level. To survive is to squeak by, to just barely make it—"Whew, I survived." To really live is filled with a voluptuous joy.

The sense here is more of survival in the midst of fleeing from persecution, but remember that there is something very important about really living even while fleeing. Without some sense of present as well as future fullness of life, ultimately mere survival is no survival at all. Where is your search for meaning taking you and how do you share that without injuring others' search?

Merciful Heaven! May it come on earth....

Matthew 10:24–39
Proper 7 (12)

Enough, already.
>Enough secrets.
>>Enough enforced silence.

Enough, already.
>Enough fallen hairs and sparrows.
>>Enough fear.

Enough, already.
>Enough denial.
>>Enough division.

Enough, already.
>Enough rich pulled down.
>>Enough poor raised up.

Enough, already.
>Find enough and it will be enough to free us from
>having to better our teacher, to replant follicles,
>to fight family, to cheat to get first place.
>>Finding enough is enough.

Enough already—
>life brims over.
>>Enough.

Matthew 10:40–42
Proper 8 (13)

It is helpful to remember this is a conclusion to a longer story.

We began this section with disciples being called. Their call was into being put on trial (finding the consequences of their call and persevering nonetheless). A positive result of their living out their call is that others will see and be offered choices just as Jesus brought a sword of division or clarity of purpose. This same choice that others find will be a tool of continual evaluation regarding the disciples initial call and living out of that call—will they persist in finding life by giving it away?

Now we come to a larger conclusion, rather than specific instances. Call is welcoming, a uniting of creation and creator. This gets played out in a three-fold process:

- a prophetic and progressive proclamation of a brokenness and separation

- an appropriate and righteous response of individual and community to an identified issue of arbitrary division

- a result of willing reassessment, revision, and resolution of injustice.

Matthew 11:2–11
Needed Change [3]

The blind see and some are offended.
The lame walk and some are offended.
Lepers are cleansed and some are offended
The deaf hear and some are offended.
The dead are raised and some are offended.
The poor receive good news and some are offended.

Blessed are those who are not offended.

When a change of status occurs we find ourselves offended ("losing trust" from the Greek; "to strike, kill" from the Indo-European). If our status is lowered we are offended by those whom we blame. If our status is raised we are amazingly offended by those from whom we came.

At one and the same time we are attracted by the danger and offended by the presence of such a rabble-rouser as Baptizer John. It is exciting to be around him as he calls for such radical things as chopping at the roots of despair and rooting out root causes of poverty and unkindness. Exciting, that is, until we make the connection of what is required from us.

Question: Where are you offended these days? Not to take offense at something is to be asleep at the wheel. But by what are we offended? That is a significant advent question.

When things improve for the blind, lame, lepers, deaf, dead, and poor it means that I cannot live as easily as I did. If such as these do not have too little, then it may mean that I, having much, will have less. If such as these find themselves even worse off, then my head rests less easy for there is a revolution brewing.

Be alert to what offends you this week. Then, decide what you will do about such offense. If you are the offended party, there is advent work of new birth to do. If you note someone else being offended against, there is advent work of new justice to do. Internal or external, on our own or on another's behalf, a sense of offense sharpens our discernment of our call.

May we soon live in a world that is not offensive. May we soon live without taking offense and defend those who have been offended.

Matthew 11:16–19, 25–30
Proper 9 (14)

The left-out section is where Jesus might be seen over-trumping the crowd's disrespecting of John and himself by calling down *Doom* on places that had not responded positively to his presence. You might almost see G*D's spirit at work knowing that "Doom" is not the last or best word.

So—abruptly—Jesus breaks into prayer. (Was that G*D's prayer being prayed through Jesus or Jesus remembering his own prayer for forgiveness?) Either way—Oh how I wish our current Doom-sayers or Terrorist-baiters would learn to pray in response to their pronouncements of Doom on others.

Jesus' prayer changes things, abruptly.

Before prayer, "Doom!" After prayer, "Tenderness" for the listeners. Jesus is willing to say what he has said, one more time and one more time, again.

Is it lack of prayer that keeps us from the tenderness of working with people instead of pronouncing upon them and leaving them to their Doom?

So, when burned out (like Jesus when he resorted to Doom-talk?), come away with Jesus into a time of prayer about ordinary things and the way G*D is already present in the ordinary. Here are the "unforced rhythms of grace". And don't you really want to live within that freedom and lightness?

Matthew 13:1–9, 18–23
Proper 10 (15)

The same day that Jesus redefines family as relationship with G*D (12:50), he tells a story.

The story has G*D-seed scattered prodigally about. One of the characteristics of creation is its profligacy. Seeds go everywhere. They travel by bird and squirrel and wind and catching on pants. Seeds end up everywhere. G*D-seed is scattered on the worn, thin, wild, and receptive places of our life. [Note: "our" is both my or your individual life as well as the lives of other individuals and our common life.]

In this model we miss 3/4 of what G*D has already cast into our life. We are so caught with routine and so tired and so angry that the arriving G*D-seed rolls off and burns up and is overshadowed. Yet G*D-seed is arriving as much in our worn, thin, and wild parts as in our readiness to respond to it.

So it is with others and congregations and cultures.

A question for us is how the fertile part of us will interact with the bored and habitual and strangling parts? Will that fertile part put up a fence to keep the compression and erosion and raging of others at a distance? Will that fertile part, having more fruit from G*D-seed than it can hold, also join in the scattering of good upon the blind and shallow and hurtful?

Have you seen grass growing through cement? A tree growing with no soil from the side of a cliff? A flower growing in the wilderness? If so, don't give up on those parts of our own life and that of others where a G*D-seed has not yet flourished. G*D-seed can be joined with the blessing of your life and yet make a difference—even where we have claimed that there is no soil, infertile soil, or already occupied soil.

Jesus' biological family and G*D-willed family can yet be one. Believe it; live it.

Matthew 13:24–30, 36–43
Proper 11 (16)

A long time ago, early in our faith growth, while yet babes in faith, we dared not pull weeds among the wheat. So it was—we waited with evil in our midst, drawing nutrients from the soil that would have produced more and more fruit for a desired future.

Fortunately we have grown in the faith, always looking for ways to appropriate science to our own ends. Finally we have mastered the art of targeted herbicides. We can now get rid of those weeds when they poke their heads out of the ground. It won't be long before we will be able to treat the very soil itself to, again, finally rid our fine wheat of those nasty weeds. Yes, finally, a final solution.

Having accomplished this leap for "mankind" we will soon be able to apply it to other contexts. Immigrants will be banished and forbidden. Little pre-out gay and lesbian children will also be done away with without the need for such public events as weed burning. We will quietly care for these and other matters. Finally, our ancient gift of knowing good from evil will be applicable. We will return to Eden to aid G⁺D in ridding this world of sin. With sin gone, salvation will be present with or without a Jesus intermediary.

So goes a re-telling of this out-dated story. Aren't you glad to be alive in this time so our dominion might be complete? Dominionists arise! Get those weeds now!

Oh, fair warning—those who live by herbicide, die by herbicide. None are pure enough to escape an ever-stricter accounting of who is a weed this week. This is a lesson often too late for the learning.

Matthew 13:31–33, 44–52
Proper 12 (17)

A growing edge is a hidden edge.

When you find your bliss, you find your call.

"Every student well-trained in God's kingdom is like the owner of a general store who can put his hands on anything you need, old or new, exactly when you need it." –*MSG*

Being well-trained is an image of openness. Being well-trained does not limit one to right answers. Being well-trained allows one to bring out the best of the many traditions to respond to a current situation. Being well-trained does not limit one only to tradition, but opens up a possibility of new responses to old situations.

May we continue to train well for being able to be present where we are, bringing forth old and new to make better. To that end, here are three reminders:

- Try talking simply about the presence of G*D. Religious talk has a potential to get us talking past ourselves. Another way to use parables is to move us from yesterday to tomorrow. Simply talking about a desired future brings image after image to mind. So, wherever you see "kingdom" you might want to substitute "desired future".

- When we are in touch with a desired future we are able to access the old (the best of our heritage renewed) and the new (visions beyond any reason for them to come to pass). It is this sense of being able to be real that allows us to stand smack dab between yesterday and tomorrow to claim the best of both and to re-implement lost good and to put into place distant dreams.

- While there are a multitude of creative images for experiencing the presence of G*D, the best parable has always been the life of a human being who is able to partner with G*D and live with Neighb*rs. This sort of living always becomes visible in the world around. It takes the phenomenal growth of a mustard plant to grow one's self and provide space for others. It takes phenomenal power of yeast to raise the experiences of life to new heights. It takes the treasure of forgiveness, received and given, to move one to invest in making life better. It takes an expansive person to cast a wide enough net to catch life.

Matthew 14:13–21
Proper 13 (18)

Compassion fatigue is real. Compassionate action is still possible even when fatigued.

Jesus hears of cousin John's senseless execution. His reaction, like yours and mine, was to head off to get his head and heart back on. How is one to make sense of this other than to know our own day of demise is growing closer and closer?

Halos the size of Jesus' are difficult to hide. [One of Jim Post's songs has a line in it about Jesus' halo—"nobody else wears a hat like that".] When word got out about Jesus, alternative routes were located by which many—too many—people gathered and Fire Marshal Disciples were upset at the overcrowding.

Coming out of his response regarding John, his need for compassion to be shown to him, Jesus is compassionate and saving/healing/reorienting went on for many who came asking. Compassion fatigue is compounded; no matter how much good is done, so much more is needed.

Those Fire Marshal Disciples projected Jesus' compassion was coming to an end. Knowing they still needed compassion from Jesus, they stepped in to disperse the never-ending story of needed care. "Send them away—compassionately, of course."

In this setting it is quite radical to say, "They need not go away." Jesus attempts to engage his Volunteer Fire Marshals with an alternative way of responding: join-in, rather than send-away. Their response, "Who? Us? We've got nothing. It's all about you, Jesus."

So a compassionate one simply shows them that they have much more than "nothing".

This may be a choice of the day, decade, eternity—compassion or intolerance. It will not only say something about us, but about what we believe. Does compassion fall within an abundance model, or not?

"They need not go away," means more than avoidance or compromise. This is a word of hope for crowd and disciples, for you and for me. Let's listen to it repeated during the day, in the different settings we find ourselves. We may yet learn its quiet lesson in the midst of a story so large and loud that it tends to be drowned out.

Matthew 14:22–33
Proper 14 (19)

Courage. We are not all water-walkers—at least mostly we are not. There are moments when it does happen.

We are all encouragers of one thing or another. All you Barnabas and Barnabette types take note: There is a world full of recruits available to the "Take Heart" ministries so needed in a fearful culture.

We can reach out to all those going down after getting into a storm following what was considered at the time to be a reasonable decision. While we can acknowledge the doubts that come along we are also freed to remind folks that, given their experiences, they have come a remarkably long way along faith's journey.

After Jesus and Peter enter the boat, there is no reason not to encourage them to try it again now that the waters have calmed.

The good news here is not simply that Jesus is recognized as a "Son of God" but that courage has been evidenced; heart has been taken; learning has gone on. We need not give up after one failure.

I keep awaiting the finding of a new scroll that has it going this way:

Jesus: You of little faith, why did you doubt?

Peter: You're right. Let's try this again.

Jesus: OK. Let's go back to the mountain and pray; then we'll give it another try. Although you do need to understand that walking on the water is no proof of anything other than an ability to be one with the water, to be one with the storms of life. It doesn't confer wisdom or authority that wasn't already present. Along with enough bucks it will get you a gourmet coffee.

Peter: Oh, praying undergirds this. Let me make a note.

Jesus: Make all the notes you want. Without prayer they aren't worth the paper they are written on. Let me repeat, "You of little faith ...."

Matthew 15:(10–20), 21–28
Proper 15 (20)

We can hear it in every generation—it's not about who you are, it's about what you do with who you are (hate the sin, but love the sinner).

That's very neat, but not real. Our being and our doing are intimately connected with one another.

A Canaanite woman (2 strikes for being both a woman and a Canaanite) calls out, puts a claim on mercy being extended. According to an earlier statement, one would expect Jesus to pay attention to what the person did/said, not who they were, not their social status. Mercy was asked for and yet it was denied. Regardless of who is doing the asking, when asked, mercy is expected.

The disciples were also caught up in doing and being questions, but in the other way around.

Note how the general cry for Mercy finally has to come down to both one's being and one's doing. Eventually, "Mercy!" needs to become "Help me!"

Questions come, just as in the abortion debate or any wedge issue—a daughter is healed, a fetus brought to term. And now what—simply being female is a problem in a patriarchic system, whether in Sudan or America. What does it mean for this daughter to be healed in this moment only to be discounted later? It might be claimed that she is returned to only having 2 strikes against her (female and of another tribe) instead of 3 (female, of another tribe, and certifiably crazy). Discrimination doesn't need any basis in reality, for it can always call her less than human again for being a woman or a foreigner. This story is about the inability of Jesus and his disciples to initially see faithfulness when wrapped in the colors of another gang.

Seems a lot of us are "willfully stupid" or keep having the same limited perception that needs continual correcting. We keep trying to separate that which can't be separated—whether about being and doing or varieties of faith.

Basic take-away—a daughter was healed; a society wasn't. It is time to go for more than only the personal.

We need to pay attention to both a needed band-aid and systemic causations. If you are called to work with band-aids, put them on with gusto and support those working on causation. If you are called to shift paradigms, give it your all and encourage those who are caring for immediate needs. May your doing and your being reveal faith in an expansive and expanding Love.

Matthew 16:13–20
Proper 16 (21)

Caesarea Philippi was a place of diverse political and religious authority. When asked how Jesus was seen, we hear reports of diverse ways of putting Jesus into other schemes. When asked how Jesus was seen by the disciples, they report from their point of view—Messiah, overthrower to restore independence.

Nothing new here—Jesus is who he is and we see whom we see.

What is new is a locus of authority that is shared. The community has authority (where two or three pray, etc.) to bind and loose. These are the same qualities Jesus claimed on his own—"Not a jot or tittle will be lost," "... but I say to you ...," "Spirit will lead you into more than was knowable earlier." The past, the present, and the future are connected to lead us beyond each, to G*D.

With these keys we have a Jesus equivalent of the tree of knowledge of good and evil in our midst. Now how are we going to use them? Our heritage seems to be—Mostly to bind with a little loosening when absolutely forced by generations seeing a larger truth. With Eve and Adam we have tasted choice and decided to hide behind the leaves of doctrine. As we needed to get beyond Eden, so we need to get beyond Church, State, and the Economics of the day.

No wonder Jesus didn't want the disciples to say anything about this. What follows is a recognition that to appropriately use these keys is to put one so at odds with the cultures of the day that the mystery of death and resurrection need to be directly faced. It is much easier to use these keys to teach us to hate those our relatives hate.

The disciples weren't ready to be built into the anarchy of Jesus' way to G*D. But a hope is present that we will really bind evil and really release love. May this way of living continue breaking the bounds of Hades and other ignorances.

Matthew 16:21–28
Proper 17 (22)

What kind of self-image did Peter have of himself?

One moment he was praised and named "Rock."

The next he was shunned and named "Satan."

I expect Peter simply felt he was doing the best he could with what he had at the time.

What kind of identity do you have as you do the best you can with what you have at the time?

Sometimes you come through, gloriously. Sometimes you come through, flat on your face. Sometimes you come through, just barely.

Do you have names for the various ways you come through?

I suspect that having a way to identify our various identities would be helpful in trying to methodically move toward wholeness.

Eugene Peterson, in *The Message*, talks about Jesus' suggested self-evaluation in a way that could be turned into a scale from 1 to 10 rather than using the personification of names such as Rock or Satan.

Q1: On a scale of 1 to 10 (with 1 being the least and 10 the most), how far did you run from suffering today?

Q2: On a scale of 1 to 10 (with 1 being the least and 10 the most), how closely did you embrace suffering today?

Or would you rather use the old religious imagery of denying yourself and taking up your cross? This shift of our relationship to suffering is clearer and more helpful than across-the-board denial of or aspiring to messiahship. It aids us in simply and unswervingly doing the best we can with what we have and with whom we are. It reminds us we are an ever-present presence called to leverage such, through an awareness of death, toward meaning.

Matthew 17:1–9
Mountain Top to Valley — Conviction 2

belovedness got them

Jesus shines on the mountain
a beacon of belovedness

Peter says its good he's there
he can see that honor is given this place

he and James and John
could handle Moses and Elijah

what got them was belovedness
it knocked them off their feet

just hearing about belovedness
was more than they could bear

to pick them up again
belovedness touched them

get up - be not afraid
its time to share more

hold your experience of belovedness
close to your heart - away from your mouth

explaining belovedness dilutes it
just live as though it were real

and so it comes to us
brag? faint? model belovedness?

modeling is the middle way
claim it - live it

Matthew 18:15–20
Proper 18 (23)

I remember being accosted in the church office by someone I had not met before. Their accusations included that the church had forced them to be damned by locking doors when regular business was not going on. They also railed against church greed and abandonment of the poor. These accusations of having been sinned against by the church are accurate, no matter the source or the number of witnesses.

Often we read this passage as though we were the good guys who have been sinned against. We even rally witnesses of our righteousness. But this passage takes on new meaning when we are the ones sinning. How willing are we to change our ways when confronted by our complicity in injustice? No wonder we don't even hear the cry of tens and hundreds of thousands of witnesses against our sin. We would loose our peace and our place.

In *The Works of John Wesley, Volume 3,* Albert Outler introduces John Wesley's sermon 87, "On the Danger of Riches" as follows:

> Many, if not most, of the newly rich Methodists were stubbornly, though quietly, unconvinced that their affluence, in and of itself, was a fatal inlet to sin. Thus it was that they simply ignored Wesley's insistence that they part with all but their 'necessaries and conveniences'. Moreover, their views had lately been fortified by the immense influence of Adam Smith's *Wealth of Nations* (1776). This turn of events was, for Wesley, both perplexing and frustrating.
>
> .... [When this] is added to *Sermon on the Mount: VIII*; *The Use of Money*; and *The Good Steward*; and if these are then placed alongside the other frequent blasts against riches in other sermons and other writings, an interesting generalization suggests itself: surplus accumulation leads Wesley's inventory of sins of praxis. It was, in his eyes, an offense before God and man, an urgent and dire peril to any Christian's profession and hope of salvation. This is in clear contrast to the notion, proffered by the Puritans, but approved by others, that honestly earned wealth is a sign and measure of divine favor. What is interesting is that Wesley's economic radicalism on this point has been ignored, not only by most Methodists, but by the economic historians as well.

Separation from the experience of the life of the poor leads to complaints aplenty. Mourn for sin revealed and unconfessed.

I was struck by this graphic[1] ...

... that shows the 7x.... conversation standing as background to all our interactions, whether individual or corporate. Sometimes we think this issue of forgiveness is one that only works on a personal level. The International Monetary Fund (IMF/FMI) is only one of the places where a background of forgiveness needs to be seen. In fact its very work seems to set up the need for later forgiveness of debts.

A resistance to change in the aftermath of Hurricane Katrina, New Town massacre, or any "disaster" provides evidence of the power of our allegiance to capitalism that constantly stands in need of forgiveness for what it does to the poorest, loneliest, most vulnerable of people and to the environment in which they live.

Where else would it be helpful in your context to carry a mental image of Jesus' conversation with Peter about forgiveness? To keep this as a background against which our foregrounds are measured would both relieve us of burdens accumulated as we moved through the past and direct our decisions toward a better future for all.

[1] www.servicioskoinonia.org/cerezo/dibujosA/47OrdinarioA24.jpg

Matthew 20:1–16
Proper 20 (25)

It is easy to get caught up in nuances between "minimum wage", "prevailing wage", "living wage", and other wage formulations.

How might this story look through a lens of privatizing social security, doing away with estate taxes, or other class privileges?

How does this work in a market economy rather than a labor economy and how might it bring "good news"?

In this image[1], is Jesus talking to the disappointed left behind folk after a first hire? Is he talking to the disappointed first hired folk who didn't get more than they dreamed of? Is he talking to you?

What words do you put in Jesus' mouth?

First, do no harm—a generous act, in and of itself—
Second, do good—seems self-evidently generous—
Third, attend to what reveals G*D—which G*D? a generous G*D!

or

First, earn all you can—that you might be more generous.
Second, be as frugal as you can—that you might be more generous.
Third, give all you can—that you might be more generous.

or

First, second, and third: You are worthy; throw off your chains!

---

[1] www.servicioskoinonia.org/cerezo/dibujosA/48OrdinarioA25.jpg

Matthew 21:1–11
False Dawn Sunday

Whoopee! A parade! Even if only one float long! It is bandwagon time! About as good as Mardi Gras in New Orleans or Rio!

Into this good time creeps an important question, "Who?" This is a question we are still struggling with, a question to make us stop and think. Who is our leader? Who is my friend? Who is part of my cohort (both militarily and sociologically)? Who is on my side? Who can I count on?

The troubling response is, "Prophet."

Prophets don't run things. Prophets catalyze change of perception. If there is one thing that should cause consternation, it's a prophet. True, versus false, prophets don't tell us what we want to hear. They demonstrate their spirit in strange, strange ways that are uncomfortable for all concerned. Prophets get stoned, not throned, and in the end are spit upon, not smiled upon.

Fair warning. This certainly sets us up for the rest of the chapter and the rest of "Holy" Week. Prophets do clearly see crosses. Prophets, even more clearly, see stones rolled away. For the joy of a rolled-away stone a cross is lived through.

Matthew 21:23–32
Proper 21 (26)

During a church trial of Rev. Amy Delong (www.LoveOnTrial.org), an expected question came, "Are you now or have you ever been a 'self-avowed practicing homosexual?'" Amy wisely replied, "First let me ask you a question. Do you ever ask that question of heterosexuals—that they are practicing?"

Church counsel had no response but may have thought, "If we say yes, everyone knows that we don't ask that question.... If we say no, how can we ask it here without revealing our prejudice?"

And so Rev. Amy went on to reject the discriminatory church legal language while clearly identifying herself as a lesbian in a loving, committed relationship with her partner. Loving both her partner and her church, she calmly replied, "I won't answer a question put to me with the intention of harming me."

So, is the ministry of further revealing the expansive and expanding love of G*D done by a son who lives by the rules on the outside or by a daughter who lives by grace on the inside?

Forced choices by Jesus are no better than forced choices by chief priests of the Church un-Doctrinal Committee. Both have their limits; both reveal intentions.

What trick question have you been responding to when all that was needed was a twist and return question? Perhaps the bind you are currently facing isn't really a bind. You are not between a rock and a hard place, but between accepted fantasy and walking free.

Matthew 21:33–46
Proper 22 (27)

absentee landLORD
wherefore art thou
o how the rich are
romanticized
we are convinced
our welfare begins
with their welfare

landLORDs claim
our undivided attention
by which I mean work
no talking behind their back
no imitating mannerisms
they are
holy as holy can be

landLORDs demand
increased work time
for your time
is their money
forty hours is a beginning
two hundred eighty plus
is not for them unreasonable

landLORDs can expect
family leave
sick leave
bereavement leave
vacations
personal days
too bad about you

landLORDs are freed
from accident responsibility
long-term disability
screwing their employees
out of relationship time
entitled to their loopholes
too bad you don't have any

landLORDs are released
from telling the truth
about their real worth
proprietary property
trade secrets
hostile takeovers
everything that's yours

landLORDs are caught
from time to time
when their time slaves
rise up to claim
a garden spot
and dream dreams
of a new start

landLORDs own
public roads as theirs
public protection as theirs
public education as theirs
each claimed as natural law
leaving no counter-claim
against simple profit

landLORDs forget
what lies ahead
claiming the present
is all that is needful
and they have the present
wrapped as a beautiful present
to themselves

landLORDs tempt us
with their perks
we see and want
immediate prizes
to measure our worth
pause for a moment
consider - then rise up

Matthew 22:1–14
Proper 23 (28)

Matthew is in such a dark place these weeks. Read these parables, and for a while you may say, "That's Jesus." And then, "Whoa, that's Matthew (or the Matthean community)".

Again with the parables. If Jesus, as a revelation of G*D, does so much with parables, we might begin to catch a glimpse of a subtle G*D. In so doing we would do well to engage some humility in our understanding of G*D. Blessings to you for appreciating a more expansive G*D than doctrine or literalness can contain.

What a difference if we were to use an "invite everyone" approach to living life. Finding the good and the bad within each person we meet, we will find those ready for a next step and those who are not.

Given a choice between "invite everyone" and "throw them away" when a particular everyone doesn't measure up, we see the parable ending with verse 10—"filled with guests". After this we get into what we take is a later addition and agree with the Jesus Seminar folks who write in *The Five Gospels: The Search for the Authentic Words of Jesus*:

> The Matthean version has strayed from the original parable. The body of the parable (22:2-10) has been turned into an allegory of history of salvation: a king (G*D) prepares a feast for his son (Jesus) and invites his subjects (Israel) to the banquet. They treat the invitations lightly or kill the king's servants (the prophets). The king destroys them and their city (Jerusalem) and invites others (foreigners) to the feast. This allegory is alien to Jesus, since the story has been thoroughly Christianized and looks back on the destruction of Jerusalem.

It is important to know what a parable is and to know when one is being told. Otherwise we fall prey to an old bait and switch—I'm going to tell you a parable ... at least I want you to think highly of this allegory I am claiming to be a parable. A discerning ear and eye can help us move deeper into reported experiences and not be fooled by an initial claim.

Matthew 22:15–22
Proper 24 (29)

It doesn't take much to entrap some of us. The obverse is that it doesn't take much for some of us to overestimate our ability to trap another.

Here the Pharisees fell into the second category. The Pharisees understood themselves to be so much in the right that they could send some surrogates to practice on Jesus.

And so it came to pass that students set out to trap Jesus. They used a standard practice of beginning with flattery. It is one of the temptation techniques that has proven successful over time. A little flattery turns the head, distracts. It doesn't take much loss of focus before we trap ourselves.

"You are so sincere. You are surely in touch with the ways of G*D. You are as truthful as the day is long and filled with integrity from top to bottom."

[Any of these catch you?]

And then an innocent question disingenuously put as an easy choice.

"We're confused; can we pay taxes to the emperor or not?"

When we are awake we can catch the simple questions of life and see beyond them and respond with the complexity they deserve— with another question.

"Ah," says Jesus, "what do you mean by 'pay taxes'?"

[Note: Economic questions often trip us up. It is so easy to fear losing whatever perk we have and thus elevate a current socio-political system into that of equivalence to a universal human need. The Occupy Wall Street movement revealed that we are at a time of seeing behind an Ozian curtain of a silent plutocracy set in place by not being able to critique capitalism and democracy. This duo has lost its rhythm to the point of democracy no longer being able to offset capitalism's excesses.

To think we can find an easy way out of facing basic common good values is disingenuous. Unfortunately we have no political process readily at hand to assist us to bring an economic system into a constructive conversation with our spiritual/communal needs.

Prophets don't know what a next rebalancing is going to look like, only that every aspect of our current life has become unbalanced. So they call us back to issues of the common good .

Along with others, this may be the most important pericope of the year and well worth dealing with every week for another year.]

Matthew 22:34–46
Proper 25 (30)

It was quite the tag-team match: Scribes, Pharisees, Sadducees, Governors, and Kings all lined up against a refugee-raised, mystic prophet.

A question before us is who wins each round and who wins the match.

Yes, it will be important to define what a "win" means. To use a Dancing with the Stars image, the judges last word is not the last word—there is a spirit in the air, a zeitgeist that will not be denied. As a result, the results sometimes seem dumbfounding.

In verse 46, literalists and legalists are stymied by metaphor and creativity. This shows up in whether you are trying to split hairs or find an organizing principle.

In the first scene, regarding Commandments, the detail folks were trumped by a context setting and then, in the second scene about Messiahs, the literalists were out-literalized. We may need not so much to take away a correct answer from this interaction as to un-focus our eyes to see love shining through—to see "every loving line of you" (from a Judy Fjell song).

You are hereby given permission to follow where the spirit of love leads you—sometimes seeing a big picture and sometimes attending to a detail. Enjoy the choices as they come your way.

Silence Sought

silence from
being put down
embarrassment
not yet knowing enough
lack of authority to ask
not having a reasonable response
    is not healthy silence

silence by
poets
religionists
incumbent politicians
letter writers to editors
you
    hides healthy silence

silence to
dream
see patterns
study reality around
find a deeper question
push authority to awkwardness
    begins healthy silence

still looking
for healthy silence
in a daily schedule
in common with neighbors
based on tomorrow
lived today
    promises healthy silence

Matthew 23:1–12
Proper 26 (31)

A place of honor requires stepping into a flood rush and standing still while waters rush by, still roiled from upstream. To bear the "holy" is both honorable and dangerous.

To bear holiness, in ourselves and not just on our shoulders, requires entering all manner of metaphoric flood waters. We will stand in a flood that rejuvenates the land, building a part of a new delta with the few molecules of flesh and bone we have at our disposal. We will stand in a flood of prejudice, uncertainty, and fear that has rushed on for a longest time as a sign and witness it shall not always be so—though not yet seen, a cessation is on its way.

Still, it is time to stop by woods or flood and choose a path less traveled. It will make all the difference.

Matthew 24:36–44
Needed Change [1]

As we enter a time of preparation we are able to shift focus from an endgame and put it back on a process of living, no matter our time, culture, or faith orientation. We are not waiting for a dividing judgment, but a birth of new hope for a peace that passes our understanding and is for all creation—a peace we can hear sung, no matter how far off, hailing a new creation. We will be ready in our dark night to hear angels sing.

First let go of expectations of results. What is coming goes beyond expectation. It may come this hour; it may not. While we have preferences about the timing of things (speeding up the good stuff and slowing down the bad) the Preacher of Ecclesiastes reminds us that all the various seasons take place within a larger vision—enjoying life and work.

Whether the latest war continues or ceases or expands—what are you called to in your place? Whether one country's economy busts or all do—what are you called to in your time? Whether your health holds or you find out the latest worst—what are you called to in your body? Whether your dearest dream expands or dies—what are you called to continue nonetheless?

Appreciate that we don't really know a larger picture. The angels don't know it yet, either. Neither does Jesus. This frees us to simply enjoy life and do our work.

Simply put, what's a good thing to do, whether we are here or not in any given hour? Does this mean reducing the carbon footprint we have as individuals and congregations? What witness to a better hope, a larger future, and a more expansive love will we participate in? Will we sing this song and dance this melody in good times and bad?

While we aren't ready for judgment 24/7, we can be open to enjoying and to a next good work, regardless of our context. Amazingly, this simplifying puts us in the good company of the saints who are urging us to stop our political and religious games, to cease our military aggression and economic exploitation, and to calm our excited entitlements.

Advent comes as a gift of waiting wherein we might practice avoiding all expected hours and joining Jesus and all the other saints in feasting with other saints and sinners to provide healing touches and speak healing words to one another. Four weeks may just be long enough to make some progress as individuals and congregations in this process of "holy" non-attached participation.

Matthew 25:1–13
Proper 27 (32)

Silly old Bridegroom. Late again. Late to wake up to knowledge being set loose—"Hey, where are y'all?" Late to wake up to the futility of genus-cide—"Oops, here's a rainbow to make up." Late to wake up to laws and favorite kings being a basis for long-term community—"You, Prophet, it's back to work for you." Late to wake up to embodiment—"Rats, I was hoping it wouldn't come to this." Late to come to the bridal party—make up your own reason.

Silly old me, waiting with all my alter egos conversing with one another. Part of me is in a hurry to get there, not waiting for milking to be done or burials to be accomplished, just rushing to the party, oilless. Part of me is planning out the needed provisions and deciding on only enough for myself—no feeding of the 5,000, much less the oiling of 5, for me.

If we weren't led to the categories of wise and foolish we could see each operating out of good decision-making. A difficulty with this and all apocalyptic writing is that it leads us to divide ourselves from ourselves and from one another based on some particular value of the moment.

An ego divided against itself can't stay awake. Perhaps this is to say that a person divided into only their "wise" part, doing their best to reject and repress their "foolish" part, can't stay focused. If this story were tucked safely into another section of Matthew, there may be a great reversal of first and last. Imagine the foolish ones hurrying in before the door closed while those weighed down with provisions were left behind.

We need both the wise and the foolish at different times for different settings. May you be wise as a serpent and foolish as a dove. May you think things through and may you let your heart lead. May you keep awake to the foolishness of judging another since you can't even judge which day or hour is the most important.

Matthew 25:14–30
Proper 28 (33)

Ahh, sweet investment. Out in the world one person's gain seems to be another's loss. It is good to know that a person with wealth is willing to commit it into another's care. Even further, it is so sweet that 2 out of 3 double their original holding. Are they wise beyond belief? Willing to risk a charge of usury? Lucky? Predestined?

Depending on a time-frame for return, the un-regulated derivatives of that day may not have crashed yet, but did so right after the story. Whatever economic bubble or larger debt may have occurred between beginning and ending balances, 5 or 2 units of wealth did not crash to 0 or some other negative return.

The difficulty here is a vision of G*D as "harsh". If you are going to get it in the neck anyway, why put yourself out? There may be a correlation between envisioning a harsh G*D and following a restricted or restricting life.

There are those who see a harsh G*D and claim that it motivates them to find ways not to be cast out. They, of course, see themselves ending up with 11 units of economic wealth where they began with zero. That may work for them in the short-run. However, claiming that one is protected and will always win because they have backed the right G*D will eventually be shown for the forced and failed joy it claims. Eventually we lose our early edge and begin to err.

A basic question here is whether property is only good for leveraging more property or if it has a relational component that does not pit one person or group against another. It may even be that we need to bring some other parts of the Bible to bear to find even the two exemplars here failed to redistribute the wealth available to them.

This is all leading up to the story of sheep and goats and another division between people. How does this story play out in light of the one coming two weeks hence?

After another church year, is this harsh casting into outer darkness the best we can do? Is the goal of acquisition the best we can do? Is this the image of G*D that we are to imitate?

If this is the culmination of a year's worth of work, it is no wonder we need another Advent. Start now and avoid the rush!

Matthew 25:31–46
New Year's Day — Proper 29 (34)

2011 was quite a year, not unlike every year.

Advent   Pope Benedict XVI, while dining with cardinals and bishops, discusses sexual abuse of children by priests.

Christmas   Republican Representative John Boehner succeeds Democrat Nancy Pelosi.

Epiphany   Bradley Manning is held in solitary confinement awaiting trial in seven months, treatment the United Nations deems a form of torture when used for such prolonged periods.

Lent   A 9.0 magnitude earthquake hits offshore of Japan's Miyagi prefecture, producing tsunamis that disable nuclear reactors.

Easter   NATO jets fly over Tripoli.

Ordinary Time Occupy Wall Street begins.

Who amongst us will separate sheep from goats?

OK, each of us does it as we make our daily decisions.

Rats, that brings it back to what we are now doing as opposed to what we might do later.

Let's not get caught up with some glorified mythology of cosmic judgment. It's all we can do to set one more blessing loose in the world, to consciously choose (until it becomes second nature) to change one system that separates people out and then ignores them.

For instance what grabs your heart and won't let go:
the hungry ("the food insecure" is too passive)?
those without potable water?
refugees looking for a home?
those without clothes for warmth or work?
inequitable health care systems focused on profit and illness?
punitive legal system untouched by restorative justice?
education locked into tests rather than learning how to learn?
religions not trusting G*D and making up rules for lesser gods?
mental illnesses that remove people from community?
your addition?

Commit to one thing that will be different by this time next year because you have shifted from protecting your own "inheritance" to investing in those currently ignored.

Matthew 26:14–27:66
Premature Fear Sunday

Choice: a slow daily walk to focus on Palm Sunday or a big gulp of all of pre-Easter week focus on the Passion.

Thanks to the wisdom of Robert Frost you are encouraged to take whichever path is least traveled by you and/or your community of faith.

Palms: There is still hospitality in the big city. Someone needs your donkey and colt; you lend it. That's the happy spin.

Less happy is the implication of an entitlement to have one's needs met. There is no reporting here of a question being asked when the disciples followed Jesus' command and took the animals. This is the moral equivalent of stealing. Just being Jesus doesn't get anyone off the hook of the commandment.

From there we are on to Hosanna and a recognized, but too easily passed over, understanding that Jesus is a Prophet. It would be clarifying to counterpose Palms and Prophets.

Passion: In addition to a usual look at the Passion of Christ and focusing on his suffering, we might also look at the Passion against Christ and focus on what fear drives people to participate with the principalities and powers.

In this vein we would investigate the commonalities between Judas—Chief Priests—Peter, John, James and the other disciples who choose secondary betrayals after a first betrayal—a crowd ready for violence with swords and clubs—false witnesses—Governor Pilate—a crowd still ready for violence with voice—military cohort—and guards. What passion sustained them, one to the next, until passion led to passion, in not a good way?

Thief Jesus dies alongside thieves
    like calls to like
Messiah Jesus dies alongside thieves
    like calls to like
do you like the call you're calling?
    who lives with you?
do you like the call you're receiving?
    who lives with you?
like still calls to like
    like still lives with like
better like who you like
    better like who you're like

Matthew 27:57–66
Absent Saturday

Nicodemus comes bearing a Magi gift of Myrrh. Bringing more than can be used, a prodigal amount. This is our last encounter with Nicodemus. He has questioned Jesus and stood up for Jesus' judicial rights. Now he comes as a disciple to care for his body.

When was this latest switch made? It wasn't a post-resurrectional experience. How close to the cross did it come? Did he hear the affirmation of the centurion? Did he see Jesus bind Mary and a disciple together as new family?

This is a day of reflecting on what we have come to. What do you come up with regarding your own life? Is it time to huddle in fear, to run away, to chop off more ears, to address what needs addressing so health will flourish as long as possible?

Hopefully this day of waiting will bring with it a particular action that will demonstrate our discipleship in the most difficult of situations—while bereft.

Matthew 28:1–10
Hopeless Hope Vigil — Assured

Creation begins again and again.

Rather than a scene of mud with Adam leading to Eve via a rib ... we find a rolled-back stone with women leading to new community via "Galilee".

New community lies ahead of you—run.

In the running new community is found.

"Be not afraid," said shining messengers;
"Be not afraid," said Jesus;
"Be not afraid," said the women.

What say you?

Matthew 28:16–20
Live Together

The Gospel again imitates
the imperial patterns and perspectives
that it resists throughout.
–NISB comment

Yes, it is so easy to fall into that pattern of power we find all around us. Authority trumps humility; making disciples trumps the transformation of mutual teaching/learning; baptizing takes on an institutional formulation rather than an empowering experience; obedience takes precedence over breaking new ground and doing greater things.

Can we be clear about where we have fallen prey to the imperial patterns around us? Not on our own. It takes a village of prophets and progressives to keep our eyes open to such temptation.

Luke 1:26–38
Creation's Conception

So did an angelic messenger get it wrong? What's with the pronouncement regarding a coming Jesus getting a throne abolished generations before? What's with the language of "reign" or "rule"? And a never-ending "kingdom"?

I suppose we could say that nothing is impossible with G*D, but does that cut it in terms of the way Jesus will deny a kingdom in this world, dismiss blood family ties, and focus on prophetic acts of mercy, healing, and teaching?

It will take some fancy spinning to have the angelic message end up anywhere near the experience we have of Jesus. While there are many who would set up institutions to rule in Jesus' name, that seems to end up being heretical to the life lived by Jesus.

Here, as we near the focus of Advent—Christmas, it would be well to pay attention to what is and isn't being said. It is all too easy to toss institutional metaphors around as though they were literal.

If we buy into this initial proposition put to Mary we will be able see how her heart will be pierced later—it's hard to put an expectation down. May you watch your story-telling for saying too much. It is easy to use acceptable images, but they have a way of coming around to bite. Think again; speak slowly; don't over-promise. Learn from an angel's over-stated sales pitch and stick to what you know—"Mary, here's a surprise big enough to take your breath away, but G*D will be with you to continue breathing new spirit into you. Relax and enjoy the ride of your life."

Luke 1:39–57
Needed Change [3] — Elizabeth and Mary Meet

"Blessed are you among people, and blessed is the fruit of your life." This is indeed an extended translation of "Namaste". Greetings between people at this level bring forth lives leaping from within— Mexican jumping beings, if you will. This greeting that sees G*D within the other is a creative word that brings forth more and more. One word leads to another, story upon story, until we marvel at how far we have come because we weren't paying attention to the results of our interaction, simply the interaction itself.

We are to become a fulfillment of the greetings we have received and given. This is a sacred foundation that can set things right.

---

magnified my soul is ...

remembering Isaac escaped from sacrifice
cowering behind the altar
reflecting on Abraham's fearful faith
finally stammering
magnified my soul is ...

remembering Mary at the cross
immobilized in hope and fear
reflecting on birth and death of love
finally stating
magnified my soul is ...

remembering every trial come through
still caught in some unfinished
reflecting on my little jokes and G*D's big one
finally claiming
magnified my soul is ...

Fragment inspired by translational material from *Provoking the Gospel of Luke: A Storyteller's Commentary, Year C* by Richard W. Swanson (this series is evocative and recommended).

Luke 2:1–14, (15–20)
Blessed Body, Proper I

You! Remind G*D!
You! Give G*D no rest!
You! Prepare for a place of peace to be established!
You! Build up! Build up!
You! Build righteousness!
You! Build justice!
You! You know ... go ahead!

So shepherds in the fields abiding, far from respectability, honor, wealth, or power have this mercy offered—a light, a song, a sign, a witness. Wise shepherds that they be, they look and listen and come and go.

This is a model of being a Christ-bearer—a Christopher Christmas, if you will. It is so valuable that Jesus models himself after shepherds.

---

what we treasure most
we shine with pondering
turning it this way
and that

through this pondering
a treasure outgrows our grasp
loosing it here
and there

humble words stir up
remembrances of holy experience come
root words ground
expectations of holy boldness to come

fearless news
joyful people

let's go, shepherds, peace is promised
let's ponder, with Mary, peace
let's return, shepherds, with a song of peace on earth
let's treasure, with Mary, a favoring of peace for all

Luke 2:(1–7), 8–20
Blessed Body, Proper II

Well, this is the day of the night for light to dawn. Do you think the shepherds had any inkling of what was coming? Had they passed a street-corner preacher anticipating this with such specificity (and, if they had, would they have paid any more attention than to the last umpteen specific pronouncements that had come and gone to no effect)? Do you think they routinely asked what would make this night different from all other nights?

They had no clue. You and I have no clue about tonight. Will it be another pageant that cutifies a sanctuary? Will a light-bulb go on for an individual or a congregation about what it means to enter people's lives through such an everyday event as a birth and lead them to welcome all on a similar basis? Will we get our last payment in to keep our heavenly insurance going for another year? Will we band together, unionize, leave our securities and responsibilities to find a life larger than either of those basic goods? Will we shed a sentimental tear? Will we tell what we have experienced? Will we open presents? Will we wrap a present for someone unthought of before this time?

We have no clue about tonight. Perhaps we might start a nightly ritual:

1) review how the day has gone

2) identify the blessings it held and plan to build on them

3) ask what would make this night different from all other nights

4) be ready to follow where the music of the night leads

5) sleep with a satisfied mind and a joy of anticipation

Luke 2:15–21
Naming Day

Named before conception, it took 8 days after birth for the name/ life of Jesus to be confirmed.

There were good biologic reasons to be wary of a child surviving. Life can be brutish and short. There were also good political power reasons not to trust whatever Pharaoh was on the throne to not decree death for newborns. Life can be capricious.

To claim some prior value to an intention to conceive, to a time of gestation, or any period of time hence that elevates it over every other consideration is very artificial. This is evidence of our desire to make meaning even if it doesn't necessarily correspond with the realities of life.

Naming adds to our signifying but also bears a cost—gain a name and lose a foreskin.

Shifting gears, it would be interesting to have listened in to the shepherds returning to their sheep and whomever had been left behind to protect against lions and tigers and "Oh, my". How might they have glorified G*D without the name of Jesus? We have so ritualized this name we have made it into a magic token. Consider how a congregation might glorify G*D today without the name Jesus being used.

To take part in this experiment puts one in solidarity with the shepherds of old and the "nones" of today. This may be an important step to more effective mission.

To honor life as Life is as critical an issue as any in a world in transition, going through a growth spurt.

Luke 2:22–40
Old Welcomes New

Led by the Spirit, Simeon entered the Temple. Led by the Spirit, John entered the desert and Jesus entered the wilderness. When the Spirit is loose in one's life there is no telling where it will lead.

As we draw nearer to a traditional time to use a Covenant Service John Wesley adapted for his use, it is helpful to remember the lines:

> Lord, put me on whatever task You will; rank me with whom You will. Put me to doing; put me to suffering. Let me be employed for You, or laid aside for You, exalted for You, or trodden under foot for You. Let me be full; let me be empty. Let me have all things; let me have nothing. I freely and heartily resign all to Your pleasure and disposal.

So where have you been led—into Temples to hold babies and benedict—into the slums to accuse a brood of vipers—into the wild on a Spirit Quest—into ... ?

Enjoy the ride. Bless, preach, clarify, whatever—but do it well.

Luke 17:11–19
Thanksgiving

The space between wake and sleep where drowsing, active-dreaming, springs to life is a critical creative space. Here the interface between Samaria and Galilee is just as creative. You might want to consider where a creative interface is for you—it may be geographical or relational, an art form or a time of day—and intentionally and regularly engage it.

Here, in an in-between, the least likely avenue to spiritual growth shows up. In this case, outcast lepers come out of nowhere. It is a surprise that lepers are waiting just inside the boundaries of a village—their place is to be at some remove. In effect, lepers become judges at the gate and might bring an appeal for healing from any number of perspectives. Here the healing rubric is "mercy" and raises a question of whether the dreamer will be mercy-full—full enough to have it overflow.

In this dreamtime, a community of lepers could be made up of Jews and Samaritans. Their common exile binds them together in much the same way that folks from differing religious groups have more in common with those with similar experiences in a different religious group and are in closer accord with them than with someone else from their own religious group who hasn't arrived at a similar values package.

Whether the lepers were all Jews except for one Samaritan or all Samaritans, sending Samaritans to Jewish priests would have no meaning to the Samaritan. Might Jesus have sent the Samaritans to a Samarian priest? It takes an especially active dream to have a/the Samaritan return to Jesus, as though to a priest, to say "Thank you", to offer "Praise/Sacrifice" for completed healing.

And so, in a daze, Jesus reflects that a faithful, trusting, relationship—regardless of its religious orientation—is a source of healing. Quite a dream—healing goes beyond ritual, expectation, or privileged religious affiliation. The faith of a faithless person is a wonder to behold.

May you dream strong dreams of new ways of being together. This sort of dreaming will lead you to situations as equally strange as Jesus and the lepers—all healed, mysteriously on a hidden journey, even if through ways passing strange and beyond our usual sense of reality's limits. As you enact your new, strong dream, may you hear, "Go on your way; your dream has made you well."

Luke 24:13–35
Assured [3]

Talking to compatriots builds solidarity. If that is all that goes on, it also builds deafness to other perspectives. Whether true-believers or true-disappointees circle their wagons, there is a built-in barrier to hearing another way, even if it may be of assistance.

In this setting, even a spirit-breathed word doesn't illuminate. Jesus can talk until he is blue in the face and not make a dent in the armor of like-talking-to-like.

When faced with these sorts of situations street-theatre is needed—Jesus took bread, blessed, and broke it.

He was recognized. He vanished. Mission accomplished. Who was that masked man?

Now a good part—these renewed disciples returned to other compatriots and were able to introject a new perspective in an old conversation. The two on the road become a presence of Jesus in their old crowd; it was as if Jesus himself stood among them.

Having broken the spell, each can now go forth to other relationships and be witnesses of the reality of suffering and the process of repentance and forgiveness that raises us from simply suffering.

Having received a virtual bread-blessing, may you break it again in solidarity with your neighbors. In this we find peace.

Luke 24:13–49
Opened Heart Evening

With or without power from on high, Jesus is capable of surprising.

We seem incapable of recognizing Jesus on the testimony of someone else, even a fellow-traveler on our way. Jesus isn't recognized as present even when we relate past tales and experiences with him. Jesus isn't recognized in all the prophetic scripture that might be re-pointed toward him.

Jesus becomes recognizable in the breaking of bread and the sharing of a cup. Then like any good catalyst, he leaves unchanged but leaves a changed situation. Jesus becomes a new community and gives it space to re-form.

Later we hear, witness added to witness, that a resurrection has taken place. And, yet, fear is a first reaction to a next surprise visit by Jesus. Again our fight or flight response needs to be addressed with a word of new perspective and possibility—peace.

Here the whooshing wind of a new creation doesn't come immediately after a word of peace and a revelationary reorientation. Now we hear—it will be coming. Those of us who know the story can see this as a setup by Luke to get his sequel (Acts of the Apostles) off to a fast start. And, so, we are left hanging having taken all the courses, done our best with the tests along the way, and written a thesis based on our gifts. No diploma, no power from on high, and here we are.

Can it be so or is it Luke's understanding that, like a maple double samara (winged fruit), the disciples are to be maturing in Jerusalem and when the time is ripe they will be spun two-by-two out into the surrounding countryside? Maturing is different than waiting, though it does entail waiting.

How is your maturing going where you are? How is your partner in ministry? How is your spinning outward going? How is your readiness for a surprise?

Luke 24:44–53
Our Turn to Witness

Remembering the empty grave scene, after the Acts version of ascension we hear two guys in white as a Greek chorus telling folks to move on—there's nothing to see here—and as you saw him go, so he will return.

Here in Luke we see a bit more about how Jesus went—opening their minds and blessing all the way home.

If we see Jesus in this fashion of open blessing, rather than the great police eye-in-the-sky waiting an opportune time to drop in to arrest and eternally imprison, then we need to pay attention to signs of open minds and blessing that herald Jesus' presence in our day-by-day living.

———————————

Let's see

Jesus leaves
after opening minds
and blessing lives
disciples take their blessing
and bless G*D in return
in the temple blessing
still in the temple blessing
until it is a blessing cocooned
a potential blessing entombed
until two dressed in white
drop by to ask an explosive question
why are you looking up blessing heaven
when so much blessing is needed next door

kaboom

back to common rooms
rather than inward looking temples
this slight movement
changes everything
neighbors must be encountered
in Jerusalem, Judea, and Samaria
opening of hearts and minds and doors
is again the order of the day
adding blessing to blessing

John 1:(1–9), 10–18
Blessed Body [2]

Once upon a time, for a Christmas Eve, we bundled up a mirror and placed it in a crib. When folks came by to gaze upon the Babe and reflect on the significance of the celebration, they found themselves gazing upon themselves.

12 - But to all who received him, who believed in his name, he gave power to become children of G*D.

How do you read Matthew's and Luke's birth stories into John? Is Christmas a self-revelation for you and a release of power into your life?

What power would it take to move you to live from your "child-of-God self"?

What are those two birth stories, with their competing details, trying to tell us and where do you fit into the story?

You may have seen yourself as Joseph or the donkey or a sheep-herder or a wise-one or Mary. Have you visualized yourself as living out the consequences of truly being a child-of-G*D?

While John tends toward the grandiose with his lofty creation-oriented language there is this little line of becoming children of G*D that would have you and me reflect on our own creation. How inter-dependent have we grown? How dependent are we still? Have we claimed our inheritance? What changes in us when we catch a glimpse of ourself as G*D's babe? How have we lived out the mystery of our birth with growth of stature and wisdom?

––––––––––––––––––––

"Word" was in the world.

The world came into being through "Word".

The world didn't know "Word".

Wrap your heart and mind around that series and you can take the rest of the year off.

John 1:1–14
Blessed Body, Proper III

G*D has done marvelous things.
G*D is expressing steadfast love and faithfulness.
G*D will act with righteousness and equity.

These three can be present simultaneously and yet be experienced sequentially. These can mark stages of faith in G*D, as well as in ourselves. It is not contradictory or heresy to either conflate or sequence these qualities.

A child is born! Every child born bears G*D's imprint. How various is G*D! How versatile is G*D! Of course a manger holds G*D. Of course both shepherd and magi can see G*D in a manger. Of course you are an imprint of G*D. Of course we can see G*D in each other.

———————————————

in the beginning was a word
today word becomes flesh
tomorrow flesh becomes a new beginning

every word, flesh, beginning
is a celebration and a mourning
as each opens new worlds
and closes others

our call from long ago
and unto eons
through birthing and birthing
is to ascend
to enflesh word
to begin with flesh
to speak a new beginning
is to move on
past past words
past current flesh passing away
past even a new beginning
is to be between
a lens for ancestors and descendants
to better see one another
and be at peace

John 1:29–42
Guiding Gift 2

While recognizing another one of those conversations that demonstrates "communication between two human beings is nearly impossible", another look behind the scene might focus on optical recognition.

Baptizer John saw Jesus coming toward him; he saw a spirit come and remain on Jesus; he watched Jesus go by and said, "Look."

Those who followed an instruction to "look" and then did something about it (stealthily following), carry the story onward.

Jesus saw them and asked what they were looking for.

Their nervous response is in terms of where Jesus might be staying. To keep the visual going this might be thought of as a request for the perspective from which Jesus views the world. "Where is your point of view located?"

Jesus invites them to come and "see".

Together they gazed in the same direction until late afternoon.

Later, Andrew goes to his brother and says, "We have seen a new heaven and a new earth and our viewpoint will no longer be the same. Come and see for yourself". [Or, "Come and see yourself!"]

Jesus looked at Simon and saw a new person (new name). His looking and seeing revealed (made it so) what was already there.

As those who have seen a new light, we go forth to see what is not yet revealed and, by that seeing, bring it to life.

May you be seen to your depths. May you see others. Together may you see beyond a mysterious circle of behind and before and strike out together to find and live out of a new viewing place where blessing abounds.

John 3:1–17
Conviction [2]

While glad to see the pericope widened past a John 3:16 be-wigged sign carrier at sporting events, it would be interesting to continue seeing it go to the end of this particular story—all the way to verse 21.

We then get a fuller picture of the give and take of the conversation with Nicodemus that has been condensed to one voice. Try on this dialogue of J(esus) and N(icodemus) and a fulcrum point of choice in verse 15:

10 - J - You don't get it?

11 - N - You don't receive tradition's witness.

12 - J - If you don't accept experience, you won't accept "heaven".

13 - N - You are not a prophet ascended to heaven.

14 - J - I anticipate healing and wholeness to come.

15 -　　Those who see signs of tomorrow, see me.

16 - N - G*D loved us enough to Covenant with us.

17 - J - Not to condemn, but to make whole.

18 - N - It is what it is. Covenanted, good; uncovenanted, evil.

19 - J - Privileged perspective is not light.

20 - N - You will be exposed and exiled.

21 - J - It is what it is. Light is light, exiled or not.

John 3:13–17
Relic Day

It took 350+ years to find and identify a piece of the "cross" Jesus was crucified on. CSI, wherefore wert thou?

Where are you with having your belief tied to something tangible? Jesus would be just as dead, whether some cross piece were found or forever gone. Whatever splinter came to be designated as a part of the whole did give a good excuse to build a magnificent edifice, but no more proves a sign of steadfast love than not.

Do note that although this day has a belatedly-found cross orientation, an older tradition is about G*D's introduction of belovedness, not its death. The world is made whole through Life given, not life taken.

This pericope could be equally used at Christmas. It depends on whether you want to focus on the first three verses or the last two.

For me the material about a theoretical construct of high heaven and low earth needs to take second place to lived experience of life given for making whole, not for condemnation, no matter how good may be the intention.

Does anyone claim a piece of the implement Moses used to hoist a healing serpent after other serpents did G*D's dirty work?

This would be an excellent time to reflect on what Carl Jung has been heard to say—churches are emptying because the symbols no longer touch people and because the church has lost touch with its symbols.

What have we forgotten about the cross in our push to universalize it in the part of our tradition that responds to violence and sacrificial atonement?

John 4:5–42
Conviction [3]

The disciples of Jesus, those baptizing ones, had gone into Sychar, for they were feeling a little eleven o'clock-ish. When they came back, they brought no one with them (and were still not strengthened enough to ask the questions on their hearts). Apparently they had not yet connected Jesus' "food" with food for the stomach and to use their feeding opportunities to expand their hunger to compassionately connect with the "hunger" of others.

Contrast this with Photina (the traditional name for the Samaritan woman at the well) who was a post-modern of her time and who was able to raise leading, expansive, questions of her neighbors and brought many out to visit with and invite Jesus in. In John 1:41, Andrew states, "We have found the Messiah", while here Photina says, "Come and see a man who told me everything I have ever done! He cannot be the Messiah, can he?" Are these evangelistic techniques simply a difference between male and female sensibilities, or the difference between how you speak to the privileged versus the unprivileged?

In some sense the visit to the well was Photina's being led into a wilderness by the spirit, there encountering the "other" that allowed reflection upon present constructs and set a direction for reentering life from a changed perspective.

Do note that Jesus does not rebuke Photina. Note also how noncreedal her testimony is. This gives you permission to tell your insights based on your experience.

Side note to self: Try tracking through John to see how the identity temptations were worked out in longer conversation blocks with people:

- "Here is the Lamb of God" – "If you are the Son of God"
- "Turn this water to wine" – "Turn these stones to bread"
- "Stop making my Father's house a marketplace" – "All the wealth of the world can be yours"
- "How dramatic does renewal have to be, rebirth?" – "Jump now; reveal angels"
- Etc.

John 7:37–39
Energy to Witness

How manifold are G*D's works! So many languages, so many gifts, so many prophecies, so many locked doors walked through, so many "Peace"s, so many breaths, so many rivers of living water.

This is a time to remember how calls and gifts have been loosed in the past, to talk about how they are currently ebbing and flowing all around us, and to anticipate more blessings than can be counted.

While we can get caught up in the mechanisms of all this we are basically dealing with a song of hope and faith and love all mixed up in its themes and meters and keys.

A part of our task is to stand and proclaim, "What you are experiencing is real—don't deny it by blaming it on excess of one kind or another." More is going on than this world knows.

languages speak what they know
today is a day to focus on what we are saying
how we are saying what we are saying
going beyond whom we usually say what we say
there is a drive to communicate
we will even learn another language if need be
we will talk with our hands and our eyes
until our tongue connects with an ear
in camp or out of room
we will join gift to gift
forgiving past separations
calling Peace where there is none
until there is

John 9:1–41
Conviction [4]

bring light

who sinned?
a question from the blind
leading the blind

wrong question!
responds a sage
we've covered that

assigning sin
is a delaying tactic
keeping one from change

such parsing
keeps everyone in the dark
about present revelation

it's absurd
take muddy spit for instance
what a recreative hoot

opened eyes
don't claim privilege
for opened eyes

opened eyes
don't dismiss
unopened eyes

imposed sin
denies grace
sight beyond sin

already told
and told again
life is gift

revealed already
revealed again
life is gift

who sinned?
get real
wrong question!

bring light
while gifted
with life

John 10:1–10
Assured [4]

A simple story about a shepherd walking up to a gate and its being opened by a gatekeeper is not as straight-forward as it might
seem. Folks either find it too simple, there must be a trick to it somewhere, or so deep that there are too many layers to be clear about. At
any rate, we will do well to be suspicious of this story, even as were
the first hearers.

When questioned we begin to see that our first inclination to associate Jesus with a shepherd is too facile. Jesus identifies with a gate.
Those who go through are alternately and mutually shepherds and
sheep, nurtured and nurturing of one another and others.

This Gate of G*D is very close to the Logos/Word John begins
with. Through this gate is everything created. We move back and forth
between a womb and a world, a sheepfold and a pasture. All who
recognize the gate are welcome and have an easy way (remember
your *Pilgrim's Progress*); those who do not come directly to the gate
are thieving climbers. This is more about ourselves than the exclusiv-
ity of a Gate, which, like in Hell, is probably always open.

It is not that the gate is limiting, as this passage is sometimes interpreted, but expanding. To enter or leave through the gate is a trans-
formative process moving a thief to a shepherd.

Think of other gateways: Peter Pan's second star to the right and
straight on 'til morning, Narnia's wardrobe, the monolith in 2001, etc.
What might be symbolized as a gateway in your life's experience? No,
the answer isn't always Jesus. Asked another way, what has been your
gateway to G*D? If you still want to say, "Jesus," what led you to Jesus?

John 11:1–45
Conviction [5]

bumpy hope

ill	cave
lazarus	stoned
mary martha message	rolled
jesus	stinking
stayed longer	away
let's go	thanks
no! stones!	thanks
light	thanks
sleep	thanks
dead	thanks
for four days	come
martha	unbind
unconsoled	release
jesus	hope
coming	here
mary	stones avoided
goes out	stone rolled
weeping	stone prepared
jesus	stone placed
come see	stone rolled

hope
released
rolls
bumpily
along

John 12:1–11
Clarification Week Monday

This Mary has stolen a march on the Magdalene by getting her hands on Jesus. Headlines: Strike while the iron is hot; Give roses while folks live. It seems that our little needs to honor aren't as easy to give to a missing body as a present one.

Once in a while I wonder whether Mary got confused and had meant to anoint Lazarus, who may not yet be over his four-day stink—thus making him a more acceptable dinner companion. Or, having come to believe Jesus is Messiah and having experienced his getting out of many a scrape, Mary, knowing the authorities were out to get Lazarus (following 3 verses), anointed Jesus to throw them off the scent, so to speak.

Regardless of such silly musings, Judas is often maligned for his imputed motivation of materialistic greed and Mary is lauded for her spiritual generosity. Into this too easy a dualism—hear William String-fellow in *Dissenter in a Great Society*:

> In the Gospel of Christ there is no dichotomy between "material" and "spiritual." Indeed, the realities to which these words refer in the Gospel do not exist separately, in distinction one from the other, or in opposition to one another—although that was what the Greeks supposed and what many Americans still vainly assume. In the Gospel, these are made one, each indispensable to the other, each inherent in the other. The very event of the Incarnation concerns the reconciliation in the world of the realities which men call "material" and "spiritual". Since the Incarnation, for men to persist in thinking and speaking of "material" vs "spiritual" is not only a sign of confusion but is also both false and profane. (p. 36)

If we can associate Jesus with the outcasts, a question from Mary asks who should we be anointing today? Might it be the poor and would that, after all these years, reconcile Mary and Judas?

John 12:20–36
Clarification Week Tuesday

Ya gotta love this strange Jesus.

Philip and Andrew (in excited unison): Hey, Jesus there's some folks looking for to join up!

Jesus: So? I'm about to die, here. Tell 'em to consider their own death—that's the short course. Invest your life in death, and alakazam, ipso facto, and zoomazoozi here is eternal life in the midst of what was thought only regular ol' life.

Once started, like an easily distractible professor (or one who works by providing all manner of strands until folks can begin weaving some of them together), Jesus mutters on about what a troubled soul he has (oy vey, such trouble has my soul seen!), how he'd just as soon, if it wouldn't be too much trouble, avoid such trouble.

After a moment of high humor and thundering angels, Jesus gets brought up short when asking for a revelation of glory with a revelation that glory was already present (remember that death/eternal-life thing). So get on with living.

Of as much interest as these little gems is the assumption that a Messiah must last forever and keep us in that forever. Such a boring assumption when faced with the excitement of a death/eternal-life connection. No wonder Jesus went and hid away.

What did you think you were signing up for? Forever? Nah. Ain't exciting enough. Try the short course instead; it'll take you much further—right into a paradise of now.

John 13:1–17, 31b–35
Courage Thursday

Once Jesus began washing feet, did he complete the circle? Were Judas' feet washed as a sign of being loved "to the end"? Presumably so. No one is left out of being loved. Neither before, during, or after any act is one denied love.

Missed communication is par for the course. Not only does Peter get confused, but the rest of the disciples can't decode the symbols and conversation between Jesus and Judas. There is even a mini-communion/blessing time between the two of them before their parting that is usually missed.

Note the brief four-word sentence after this communion variant—"And it was night."

Night is the beginning of a day's cycle—and it was night and it was morning, the nth day.

Night is chaos over the deep, a pre-creation opportunity.

Night is where the church often is. Within the United Methodist Church we are more than 40 years into discriminatory legislation that ignores the freedom of G*D to gift and call whom G*D desires for "set-aside" ministry. Perhaps it would be best to discontinue offering regular communion until official discrimination ends. To continue is to tacitly support discrimination with the excuse that it is meaningful to us—forgetting all the folks who cannot participate in offering communion.

The church has betrayed Jesus. It is night. May a next General Conference raise a bit of light by moving away from discriminatory legislation. This would sign we were serious about loving one another as we have been loved by G*D through a betrayed Jesus.

John 13:21–32
Clarification Week Wednesday

Betrayal is upsetting, no matter who is dealing with it. With a whiff of betrayal scented we are aroused to resolve it—is the betrayer you? is it me? can it be avoided? Isn't every murder mystery about the mystery of betrayal of self and others?

Here the action of Jesus stimulates fear around betrayal. What does it mean not only to recognize the presence of betrayal, but to initiate or give permission for its engagement?

Jesus will be betrayed by the person to whom he gives the bread of sustenance. Jesus gives it to Judas. Then this interesting line, "After he (Judas) received the piece of bread, Satan entered into him. Jesus said to him (Satan?), 'Do quickly what you are going to do.'"

Of course the disciples heard nothing (the equivalent of thunder in place of a voice announcing belovedness or glory) and made up a story of where Judas went. If they had known, they would have had to do something about it, intervened between Judas and the chief priests.

If we extend this passage to Hebrews 12, we might also find Judas among the cloud of witnesses. We learn not only from saints, but sinners.

One of the things we learn is that Jesus enters this next round of temptations with his eyes wide open. There is no plea here to be delivered or turn back. May you enter your next time of temptation with your eyes wide open. In this way you will glimpse a glory worth following.

For a perspective that the conflictual information about Judas in the Gospels and the lack of reference in the Epistles might suggest that Judas is a fictional necessity for the Jesus story, you can check this short review—www.edges.canadahomepage.net/2011/04/20/1014/.

John 14:1–14
Assured [5]

To know a name is to have power over that which is named. This is a well-attested understanding from days of yore. Obviously if you ask it in Jesus' name, then Jesus will do it. This is pretty straight forward cause and effect.

But this Jesus guy can be pretty tricky. Which of the many ways Jesus is identified is going to be a mechanism whereby Jesus can be controlled? If you go, "Hey, Jesus" and that day he's going by "Word", whatcha gonna do?

Consider this format for your asking:

- Identify what aspect of G*D you need to be in relation to for a particular purpose and call to that.

- State your asking in one simple sentence—no dependent clauses, parenthetical statements, or metaphors.

- Say, "Thank you" and "Amen."

This is almost as simple and difficult as a breath prayer. Try it for a week and see what happens.

A second way of using names is that of identification. To know what to ask for and from whom to ask puts you in a direct one-to-one relationship. What we have here is Sympathetic Magic. A way of understanding this is that asking in Jesus' name connects Jesus to us and us to Jesus—we are in him and he is in us. And, Jujitsu, the greater things Jesus said we would do we are doing.

This leads to a question of whether there is anything greater to ask than to exemplify a divinity in which we were created and intended. Well? If that is asked for, it is to be lived: in the asking is the doing. This turns out to be our participation in a creation call that ends with a recognition, "It is good."

Ask. Act.

John 14:15–21
Assured [6]

just because

love
love me
love me by
living your best

love a mystery
too easily named G*D
until such a mystery
becomes such a reality

love a self
as a neighbor
and a clannish one another
that hates to love an enemy

in such
loving and living
we invest our time
and move through space

of course
such is dangerous
for suffering does not direct
our response to deep assurance

and when in the course
of all too human events
we shift to larger loves
belovedness is revealed

living one's best
just because
gladdens all hearts
to love expansively

John 17:1–11
Assured [7]

As dense as this passage is, it is representative of the poetry of life.

Here we find such a spinning of relationships that the faces of G*D, Jesus, and ourselves become indistinguishable. Glory streams from afar and from within. Hours are glorified, as are people. Before creation and this present are as glorified as a future.

It is this blurring of cause and effect, foreground and background, which brings us to a sense of oneness that is protection at its deepest—an identity so deeply grounded and so elevated that there becomes an eternal aspect to each moment.

Assurance ceases to be a word—it is experienced. Assurance—we are not alone. Assurance—we are one, uno, eins, or any other similar understanding.

Everything is given and everything is received. The yins and yangs of life are actively balanced.

The above was written at the 2008 United Methodist General Conference; voting had began in earnest and this reality check interjected.

There has been some excellent work done in the legislative committees. For example, proposing to remove the hurtful words "homosexuality is incompatible with Christian teaching" from *The Book of Discipline*. We have come to similar positions in the past only to have them over-ruled in the plenary.

In committee conversation we can see how interconnected everything is and then we get to plenary debate where code words and political blocks come into play. In setting our policy we lose this spinning interrelationship when "all means all"; we divide ourselves into those privileged with grace and those undeserving of it; we reveal our underlying anxiousness about being beloved.

John 18:1–19:42
Annihilation Friday

Well, were you there?

If the Preacher of Ecclesiastes got it right, "There is nothing new under the sun," then we need to say, "Yes and No" to the question. We were not there at Jesus' crucifixion but we are witness of other "crucifixions" today. Let's look for some connections between then and now through one of the eye-witnesses—a Roman Centurion.

Perhaps we will hear the song change from "Were you there?" to "We are here".

Jesus' disciples stood at a distance, just watching, and that is our temptation, as well.

At bottom we are afraid to draw near Jesus' cross guarded by the status quo, a fear of being different, and a reluctance to lose any privilege or comfort we have, no matter how small.

Sometimes I think today's Church has lost track of following Jesus' ministries and has settled for just guarding empty crosses and being complicit in the on-going crucifixion of the least, and lost and lonely in our own families, community, state, nation, and world.

My hope is in remembering.

Remember Eden—a sad day wherein we too often focus on how bad Adam and Eve were, without remembering that G*D left Eden with them. They were never alone.

Remember Cain crucifying Abel—a sad day wherein we focus on how bad Cain was, without remembering G*D did not start capital punishment then and there.

Remember an unending series of lonely misdeeds and betrayals that continue to this day. These are ours and are not dependent upon blaming someone before us.

We have been like the Centurion who didn't plot against Jesus, or try Jesus, or put in the nails, or raise the cross—who only stood there while an unjust act was carried out, while an unfairness was allowed to move forward.

What eventually shone through to the Roman Centurion was Jesus still commending his life into G*D's hands, into a promise of more life that couldn't yet be seen. That Centurion heard enough to do an about face and to forward march into a new way of living. Jesus' life calls us, too.

Even before Easter that Centurion was transformed. Even on Good Friday we have plenty to call us to risk our life for a common good.

Remember Christmas—a good day wherein we focus on Emmanuel, G*D with us; we are still never alone.

Remember the Magi—a good day when those identified as "Strange" and "Other" are blessed for letting their gifts loose in the world.

Remember Baptism—a good day when Belovedness is set free in the life of every lost person and is a background against every temptation.

Remember those who were ministered to by Jesus and still need ministry in our day. They were set free to be G*D's Beloved, even without baptism and well before Easter.

Remember Betrayer Judas was still given communion and was still a part of Jesus' love, whether he or the other disciples knew it or not.

Out of your remembering, begin anticipating a better way than guarding and watching—a Jesus way, a compassionate way, a way to a new heaven and a new earth through better living in community and for a common good. Watch for these signs:

- Basic laborers are called as disciples.
- Traditionalists are taught, "You have heard it said, but now a new learning ....".
- Lepers are returned to community.
- Gadarene Demoniacs—the mentally ill—are freed from imprisonment.
- A woman hemorrhaging for 12 years is set free from a health care system that ate up all her resources and savings.
- Mute people, including the young, the poor, and the immigrant receive their voice.
- Hungry people are fed by those who didn't know how to admit they had more than enough.
- Foreigners in the land have access to healing.
- Little children, like those who are not in our church, are welcomed, nurtured in Jesus' way, and brought near.
- Religious leaders are reminded that everything hangs on love: Love of G*D, Love of Neighb*r as Self, Love of One Another, and Love of Enemies.

All of these teachings and healings of Jesus continued to shine through on Crucifixion Day. All of Jesus' Living was a background that could not be denied. Even a battle-hardened Roman Centurion finally woke up. We are not told what happened next to the Centurion, just as we are not told what happened after so many people were touched by Jesus. But imagine for a moment that you could be freed from the inertia of just watching Death happen and, again, see Life before Death. Might you join Jesus in Living in solidarity with today's Innocents rather than defensively against them? Imagine!

I can't help but reflect that in June of this year (2011) a Wisconsin United Methodist pastor is going to be tried by her church for blessing people forbidden by the church to be blessed—gays and lesbians. Will that trial rise and fall on the current letter of the law, like Jesus with Pilate, or the gift of new life for people for whom Jesus also lived? If you haven't heard about this coming trial, it would be good to wonder why not.

This very day in this city and county and across the state line, there are people being crucified on the basis of being different, and difference happens in so many different ways. But the big crucifiers are, on one side, impotent poverty of one kind or another and, on the other side, privileged entitlement of one justification or another.

If we have seen G*D with us and Jesus' Life as the backdrop behind his Death and heard the Centurion's change of perspective, then we may be able to hear a call from the Cross coming to us again today. It is found in the fourth verse of our next hymn, *When I Survey the Wondrous Cross*.

> Were the whole realm of nature mine,
>   (which it isn't – false choice)
> That were a present far too small;
>   (too small because it isn't yours to give)
> Love so amazing, so divine,
>   (Love of G*D, Neighb*r, Self, One Another, Enemies)
> Demands my soul, my life, my all.
>   (join the Centurion—invest your soul, life, and all)

> May this Good Friday
> not find you watching from a distance
> not guarding people away from Jesus
> not protecting an institution
> but reconnected with an Expansive and Expanding Love
> that energizes your soul, your life, your all.

John 19:38–42
Absent Saturday

Who can bring a clean thing out of an unclean thing, a live thing out of a dead thing? Certainly not a magician. Certainly not positive thinking or prosperity theology. Certainly not an acculturated church. Certainly not individual faith.

It is important at some point to give up hope, to have dead be dead. This day we don't even wait. We go through motions. We become the walking dead.

Yesterday was bad enough. Today is badder yet. Tomorrow will be worser than anything. The end of all things is near. I wouldn't believe a proclamation of good news if it were yelled in my face.

Peter with his "disciplined prayers" and "constant love covering a multitude of sins" can go hang himself with Judas. If there is a next generation, they might listen to that but, today, it's most unreal.

John 20:1–18
Assured

In the dark of lingering night and the dark of tomb, eyes-that-can-see note that stumbling, blocking stones are out of place. To note an unexpected opening is to rouse even more fear from within. In such times we run to others with a heightened story. Here the story escalates from moved stones to an interpretation of such—"They" have done something unspeakable. [The excuse of "they" seems to persist in both time and space.]

Where are we after all this running to and fro? Back at the beginning—The Magdalene alone, and now weeping.

Twice comes the question about why the weeping? Twice usually indicates an important question. Why are you weeping these days? There is ever so much to weep about, but why are you weeping? What are you looking for that weeping is a helpful response?

In this setting we are looking for that word of assurance known as being known by name. Does a lack of a sense of being known have anything to do with your weeping?

At any rate, regardless of ascension language, Mary shifts from Weeping Mary to Announcing Mary. Does a lack of having something to announce have anything to do with your weeping?

Look—light breaks in through cracks in hardened situations; weeping stones shout out an old "new message"—*Follow on and jump ahead; we are all becoming G*D.*

John 20:19–23
Energy to Witness

When sins are to be dealt with, they are to be forgiven—no ifs, ands, or buts about it. Not to forgive a sin is to multiply it.

Standing behind this is a bold statement that forgiveness transforms sins—they are gone, for "good." Is your life going, for good? Imagine that out of sin comes good. This is not a straight-forward process for as much as sin abounds, grace abounds the more. Forgiveness is not a forgettable experience—it is as revolutionary and as explosive as $e=mc^2$. The transformation of the past into a new future of today is linked to the exponent of forgiveness (70x7) which is even greater than a mere squaring of the speed of light.

$$T=PF^{490}$$
Today equals Past times Forgiveness to the $(70x7)^{th}$.

Want to participate in building a new kingdom? Forgive. It is the multiplying constant in a gift of life.

Forgiveness is drinking deep of thirst-quenching life. Forgiveness revives both the forgiver and the forgiven, the forgiven and the forgiver, in whichever order the mystery of forgiveness occurs.

Forgiveness is a participation in the carrying on and deepening of the acts of Jesus. Here greater works are done. We have it available to us to bind ourselves and others together, mutually. There are some who would claim this is greater than having that binding take place from the outside, as though someone else's forgiveness would take precedence over that of the parties involved.

So with Peace breathed into us we are energized to move from Peace-made to Peace-makers. Enjoy the journey.

John 20:19–31
Assured [2]

Whether Holy Humoring or not, I find sweet release in *The Message* version of John 20:22-23. It is a reminder that the resurrection of Jesus brings the forgiveness he asks for in Luke's version (yes, acknowledged, it's not fair to so conflate Luke into John).

With some stage directions thrown in:

Then [Jesus] took a deep breath [bigger, bigger]
and breathed [Pentecost whooshed] into them.

"Receive a Holy Spirit," he said [with a smile, knowing it was going to change them].

[Then seriously] "If you forgive someone's sins" [dramatic pause], "they're gone for good" [good chuckle].

"If you don't forgive sins" [start of giggle], "what are you going to do with them?!!" [belly laugh or guffaw].

Sometimes we need to pause in the telling. Thomas wasn't there, so how long before he heard the report of the other 10? (Or was it only 8 because a couple of others were also missing in action and it wasn't in their nature to kvetch about missing something?) We can let the good news of forgiveness hang in the air for a bit before proceeding to verse 24.

This helps me remember that "angels can fly because they take themselves lightly" (G.K. Chesterton) and we begin to soar when we take forgiveness seriously enough to participate in it.

Acts 1:1–11
Our Turn to Witness

On this day of remembering ascension we do well to pay attention to the NRSV footnotes prior to this telling:

- Other ancient authorities lack "and was carried up into heaven" (Lk 24:51)
- Other ancient authorities lack "worshiped him, and" (Lk 24:52)

With this guidance, Luke could have the same sort of abrupt ending as that of Mark. Luke would then end with verse 50: "Then he led them out as far as Bethany, and, lifting up his hands, he blessed them."

This is a good place for Luke to end his story of Jesus and then to pick it up again to begin his story of Church.

This reading also helps us see the issue of "blessing" without the confusion heaven adds to this and almost every conversation of which it is a part.

Acts begins with a remembrance of Jesus speaking with the disciples for forty days about the presence of G*D, the freedom of G*D, the mercy of G*D, the new-beginning of G*D, partnership with G*D (or, if you must, the kingdom of G*D).

This conversation reminds the disciples that they are still not experiencing these gifts of presence, freedom, mercy, new beginnings, or partnership. So a hinge question, "Is this the time you will restore the king-dom to Israel?" (Note: The phrasing here indicates they and we are so conditioned to power politics that we can't go further back to procreative presence.)

Confirming this is their response to Jesus' being lifted up and out of sight (still without heaven being mentioned), they gawk upward. Two strangers remind them that Jesus will return in the same way, inexplicably, and if they keep avoiding one another and the world around them, they will have missed the next opportunity to share their experience of an amazedly unexplainable G*D.

To put the two passages together—It is time for us to rise, as workers/saviors of the world, to throw off our chains of gazing in a wrong direction, and to be a blessing.

Acts 1:6–14
Assured [7]

[The named "apostles"] agreed
they were in this for good,
completely together in prayer,
the women included.
Also Jesus' mother....
—MSG

Tomorrow is the cultural icon of Mother's Day (the case in 2002).

How easy would it have been to have Queen Mary, full of grace, and lots of other words of authority, take over the Jesus story? We could read back into this opportunity all the wonder of immaculate conception and the other goddess images stuck onto Mother Mary. (Note: This is not a complaint about goddess stuff.) There is some evidence that Brother James tried a take-over—why not Mary?)

But here Mother Mary is not front and center but an "also". The key is being together in prayer, not separated as apostles or women or family or race or culture or sexual orientation or ....

How might we be together in prayer when our very prayer styles get so competitive? Sadly I know I have mocked those prayers and pray-ers that my sensibilities say go overboard in repetition of phrases like, "Lord... I just...." Issues of diversity in prayer and every other community ritual can both bind us too tightly and drive us apart over one little word in a creed.

We are not at a place where we naturally pray together without anxiously waiting our opportunity to pray the right prayer to show we are in closer contact with the "Holy" than other lesser pray-ers. Still, it is appropriate for us to do the preliminary work of praying that we might soon be able to appreciate the prayers of others. Pray that someday prayer will be less divisive than it currently is. For that prayer to come to pass we may need to listen to the humble word "also" and see ourselves in that category.

Pray for me, also, in whatever style you can and I trust G*D will translate it into that which is better than the best either of us can thus far pray.

Acts 2:1–21
Energy to Witness

Trying to take control in order to be on top leads inevitably to confusion. Take a look at any political process, even dictatorial ones, and it becomes apparent that common interest soon loses out to partisanship. We can claim we are after the same goal and even use the same words to describe it, but when the day ends we are suspicious of others for wanting to succeed so desperately. We know our suspicions are well-founded because, given half-a-chance, we would be glad to take the lead among equals.

We don't need to have G*D enter the picture to deliberately set folks at odds with themselves; they do plenty well all by themselves.

The real trick is to keep a focus on our differences that might be mobilized in the same direction. When our differences can be brought to bear on a subject, we are able to make better decisions than when we are assuming we are all on the same page only to find we are not.

The value of Pentecostal language is its appreciation of the different languages and the perspectives they bring to the table. To try to tell someone else what is so very important to you when they obviously speak differently is to better pare down to the most important what we have experienced.

What, then, is so important that you would be willing to learn a new language to be able to share it? Or is it only important enough for you to repeat it and repeat it in your own personal language with no concern whether or not it is heard?

---

god and adam and eve
talked each evening
there was agreement
understanding
and yet
a babelsnake
was able to confuse
them about one another

farsi english and swahili
yuwaalaraay hindi and aymaran
blue white-collared and monied
child teen and adult
and yet
a babelfish
enlightens our differences
with a gift of a new brainwave

[Never mind that Douglas Adams claims, "Meanwhile, the poor Babel fish, by effectively removing all barriers between communications, has caused more and bloodier wars than anything else in existence."]

Acts 2:14a, 22–32
Assured [2]

Joy is not limited to what is currently going on, but in participation with a vision of a Peaceable Preferred Future always before us. [Look at "Peaceable Kingdom"[1], an early American painting by Edward Hicks, and wonder about what changes are needed to update it.]

This is a loose translation of a phrase from Acts 2:25: "I saw the LORD always before me." It was from this same perspective David affirmed, "...therefore my heart was glad and my tongue rejoiced; moreover my flesh shall live in hope."

The word "LORD" is fraught with overtones. It does not mean one thing to all people. So it is important to figure out what one means by the old language of "LORD" when using it and begin to use the meaning (even if it is a more awkward phrase that does not run trippingly off the tongue) rather than the shorthand.

Here it would seem we are speaking of a particular vision. Peter casts it in terms of escaping Hades, but we might well speak of it in a positive way by referring to some aspect of what might loosely be called "Paradise" or a preferred future come on earth.

What vision would you hold before yourself to stimulate joy?

---

in your presence is joy
summarizing
every love song and hymn
uniting
secular and sacred music
challenging
every separation we construct
expanding
lovers into love
concretizing
love into lovers
binding
joy to presence

---

[1] www.worcesterart.org/Images/Collection/Photos/American/1934.65.jpg

Acts 2:14a, 36–41
Assured [3]

All who are called are welcome.

Can you imagine someone not called by G*D to life and life renewed and life eternal? If you can you've slipped into the strange land of judgment that will come around to bite.

To be devoted to good news (rather than Fox or other media-driven news), to fellowship (all the way to sharing of possessions), to ritualize (connecting to the presence of G*D through memory of previous connections), and to contemplate (more than we yet know) is to open oneself to a mystery of renewal. In these basics we open our eyes to more than our self and are ready to engage it to deepen peace and to widen mercy.

Suppose you have an opportunity to raise your voice in a gathering—what general points would you have as your goal? Would they include assisting others in catching a new vision of themselves and their relationships? intentionally gathering folks together to explore their heart-level connections? aiding folks in sticking with spiritual disciplines over a long haul? exploring the "more" of life?

Hopefully you are reminded for at least a third time today that it is possible to live at peace and in mercy with everyone (whether they live that way toward you or not).

Acts 2:42–47
Assured [4]

It is so easy to translate "the apostles' teaching" into the "Apostles' Creed" and avoid the life that was being taught—Jesus' wider ministry of revealing a Presence and Freedom of G*D. To so engage the world in Jesus' Way takes a good bit of solidarity that comes from a comradeship or fellowship or common-cause with others who will encourage us to faithful action and pick up additional actions when we falter.

Another pairing of bread and prayer can likewise be seen as fellowship (bread) and action (prayer). Should prayer ever become as language bound as creeds are, it will in that moment lose its power of transformation (Easter-ing).

Whether finding a synergy between teaching and fellowship or prayer and bread, we are at an important decision-making point of engaging and growing into G*D through a loosening of our entitlement to possession (whether of money or breath). This example of finding a Presence and Freedom of G*D to be available, as evidenced by Jesus, and for us to abundantly distribute life's core values in the face of whatever the economic determinism of the day might be, will be long-term attractive to others and transformational for all.

In this day and age, when we can get so angst-driven about numbers and dollars, it is good to remember that significant and emblematic growth occurs through witnessing to the Presence and Freedom of G*D—by having presence and freedom to reorient from restrictive Mammon to expansive Love.

Want to see peace? Be peace!

Want to see growth? Grow!

Want to follow the Apostles' teachings about Jesus? Fellowship!

Want to fellowship well? Act on the teachings!

Want to feast? Pray through action!

Want to know what and how to pray? Feast together!

Acts 7:55–60
Assured [5]

Have you had teeth ground at you? What was your response?

Did you grind back? Did you see a better vision and witness to it?

What constitutes your better vision? Is forgiveness for yourself and others included in it? To what degree? To your first degree of relationships? Your sixth?

In some sense this scene is about a martyr. It is also a stop on the way from least to greatest for the coming story of Saul/Paul. Out of Stephen's death grows a new shoot from the deadened root of Saul. Even as we recognize this we know that we are somehow glossing over the pain of others who are still being hurt by the religious righteousness of those who so clearly see deficiencies of everyone else. This phenomena is as ancient as Cain and Abel and as recent as Save Straight Marriage Proposals or preemptive wars based on false information.

An important part of a puzzle of life is how we live and die in the midst of such deadly jousting over so little.

In the current scriptural record, Stephen is the second disciple of Jesus to die. Judas was first and showed Jesus against a backdrop of unmet expectations. Stephen was next and showed Jesus against a backdrop of transfigured glory.

We have both Judas and Stephen within us. Are we giving up or moving on?

Acts 10:34–43
Beloved — Assured

G*D shows no partiality and in baptism we are called to live in that same image. Our baptismal vows ask us to resist evil in whatever guise it comes. Partiality, particularly unconscious partiality, is a major disguise of evil. Our baptismal vows ask us to affirm Christ as our way to G*D, to impartiality.

This is a definition of the presence and hospitality of a Holy Spirit:

> In the beginning was impartiality, and this impartiality was with G*D, and this impartiality was G*D. All things came into being through this impartiality, and without impartiality not one thing came into being. What has come into being in Christ was impartiality, and this welcome to all was and is the light of all people. Impartiality shines in the partial, and the partial did not and has not overcome it.
> –WW

Acts 17:22–31
Assured [6]

Paul notes how religious folks are. Indeed, we don't seem to be able to help ourselves from doing religion. It is a handy way to try to pass on to others any numinous experiences we have had.

A difficulty comes when our religious attempt to articulate a larger reality begins to take itself too seriously and restrict any further experience of a more expansive way of living. Religion starts with a helpful impetus—to share—and little-by-little puts up road-blocks to something new to share. So Paul notes the impetus and notes that the shrines established after a first experience no longer carry life forward.

The processes Paul indicates are still worthy ones. Working within space and time we are shaped into search engines for that which we may become. Searching for, groping for, finding, and even becoming what we find represents what it means to live and move and have being.

And so, identify your current shrine and begin to step outside its limits. Repent. Break the power of denial. Say "No" to that which claims your soul for itself. Upset the status quo.

In preparation for later saints: Religious people, throw off your chains! All you have to lose is stale air, dirty water, and shiny objects that distract you from loving life.

Romans 1:1–7
Needed Change [4]

Are you, or someone you revere, old enough to have been a mouseketeer? Remember, or ask about, the energy needed for that position.

Paul claims to be a gospelteer. Imagine the energy that needs as you play back and forth between prophets-of-old and not-yet saints.

Is this an intersection where you have been playing? Or have you focused overmuch on a prophetic end and getting a message "right"? Or have you focused overmuch on imaginary saints that might some-day be, but who are unable to jump from here to there, and blind to a next step on such a journey?

To helpfully play between is a place filled with tension and fear. You risk a prophetic message by trying to literally translate it into each new situation rather than being a prophet in your current time and space. You risk being co-opted by some definition of saint rather than modeling saintly living in the here and now without waiting for some certification of X-number of miracles.

No wonder Paul finally blurts out—Grace and Peace!

Well, enough. To receive Grace and Peace is to claim permission to energetically play with both revered prophets and almost saints. Play on!

Romans 1:16–17; 3:22b–28, (29–31)
Guiding Gift [9] — Proper 4 (9)

Would it be an example of "excluded boasting" to suggest that finding our common lot as sinners is not the only way to find our common humanity/divinity?

Our tendency seems to be to find the lowest common denominator rather than the highest common multiplier. When we do justification or atonement talk it can appear that we are being quite positive, but it is simply a sub-point of starting with a Fall rather than with Creation.

Let's reflect a bit more on what faith might mean from a perspective of having been created good rather than from a focus on evil, sin, and other frailties. In Paul's terms we may have to pay more attention to grace than to law. This is always a dangerous thing to do, but it is also a necessary thing to do if we are to continue pursuing life in its fullness for ourselves and all.

A helpful line is verse 17—G*D is revealed through faith. Our tendency is to see G*D revealed in faith by the letter of the law rather than in faith through a spirit of grace. Christ, have mercy as we tussle over backgrounds and foregrounds of "faith", not simply faith as simple faith.

Prophetic progressives start with Creation Goodness and find it revealed, time and again, in moments of Grace. Smile—Mercy outweighs Judgment; Atunement is more fun than Atonement.

Romans 4:1–5, 13–17
Conviction 2

Calling into existence things that don't exist is a high calling. What is it we are interested in calling into existence? Is this something we want, desire, need, require?

Might it be that what we are after is more blessing—blessing piled on blessing, overflowing all cups? If so, how might it be called? Does simply being a blessing call forth more?

This is a challenging question. To say, "No, it takes more than this", denies the power of grace, unbidden and open, to operate even when accused of being "ungodly". To simply say, "Yes, grace happens", is to risk taking our blessing for granted (both that received and that given) and turning it into technique.

We need faith to undergird the impossible and work to forge a way where there was no way. And now we await a revealing of what has been gained by our faithful work of receiving and offering blessing.

This is a prodigiously prodigal process leading to inclusiveness. Enjoy it through the long-run without giving up on it in the short-run.

In light of the conclusion of this passage regarding a G*D who gives life to the dead and calls into existence things that do not exist—we were traveling Sunday and saw a billboard that said, in large letters, "Nothing is too difficult for God." A beloved traveler in the car saw said sign and remarked, "Yes, 'Nothing' is 'too difficult' for G*D." This insight is an impetus for creation—that "nothing" was "too difficult". G*D had to start making stuff (creation) because "nothing" was too difficult. [Are you grinning yet?]

Romans 4:13–25
Proper 5 (10)

To Abram and Matthew a call: "Go from your country" and "Come, follow me". Being open to these calls in our own day is a challenge for settled individuals, congregations, and nations.

This call is not just geographical. The Psalmist and Paul remind us of the changes we need to be making internally that our heritage might be healed—that our distress and betrayal be swept away by steadfast love.

Envision a mutual journey—G*D's and ours—not one pulling or pushing the other from where they are, but a mutual attraction and desire to move in common.

---

journey without a destination
challenges our control need
even with past adventures
having turned out well
there is hesitation
to trust again

journey without a destination
raises again an insatiable god
testing and testing again
our temptation
to settle
in

journey without a destination
is a realistic assessment of our lot
no matter how we disguise it
change and death obtain
warrants to search
empty lives

journey without a destination
anticipates beyond current plateaus
use of several learnable skill sets
to envision preferred futures
to enact their foundations
to enliven generations

Romans 5:1–8
Proper 6 (11)

We can focus on G*D's putting everything on the line of Jesus' death and try to figure out how to talk about this in the sacrificial milieu of Paul's time or in some other imagery of participation from our own time. Trying to define G*D too closely runs into difficulties.

Perhaps this year it would be more helpful to look at the work of a Holy Spirit to help us recognize and reshape a generosity of G*D toward us that we might have a passion for the patience it takes to help others identify a generosity of G*D in their lives.

Through this radical patience our character is made like G*D's as G*D waited for us to recognize a generosity offered us. So, together, we are in alert expectancy for a critical mass and energy necessary to transform this wobbly old world into a new heaven and earth.

Isn't it better to be so expectant of more glory than it is to try figuring out how G*D of the first part ("Father") authorized G*D of the second part ("Son") to pull a sacrificial switcheroo?

May your heart be filled with patience as you imitate the character of G*D and respond with hope through a generosity of love.

Romans 5:1–11
Conviction [3]

Pop Quiz

Compare and contrast the following two statements:

- G*D's love has been poured into our hearts through a Holy Spirit.

- G*D "proves" G*D's love for us in that while we were still sinners Christ died for us.

If you play long and well with the words "pouring" and "proving" you may begin to see the secondary nature of atonement and suffering and dying.

Pouring is a release and is tracked back through such words as "vent" and "wind" to a creation breath of life.

Proving is a testing of what is good but can easily shift over to a rigidity of "answered once-and-for-always". There is a tendency to rely on a proof for all time, rather than any new questions such testing raises.

Trust again that a steadfast pouring of love into your life will continue, regardless of any suffering you or any other have experienced. This out-poured love is the experience we desire that will allow us to deal with every temporary blockage of same. No matter what the suffering, there is none great enough to substitute for a cup of love overflowing.

Rejoice in a flow, not a given explanation.

Romans 5:12–19
Conviction [1]

Where sin increased, grace abounded all the more. (Romans 5:20b)

Grace Greater than Our Sin was a catchy hymn for previous generations. The refrain is hard to beat:

> Grace, grace, God's grace,
> Grace that will pardon and cleanse within;
> Grace, grace, God's grace,
> Grace that is greater than all our sin.

> Words: Julia H. Johnston
> Music Daniel B. Towner

I suspect that Jesus could easily have added this refrain into his singing of the Psalms—it would have been a "contemporary" hymn addition to the tradition. I'm not so sure he would have approved the extant verses with their exclusive focus upon crucifixion and a formulaic reversal [sin condemned = death; death justified = life]. Anyone out there up for a rewrite that scans better than this?

> Marvelous grace of a living G*D,
> Grace that exceeds any sin or guilt!
> From deep, deep within each life's facade
> Creation wells up to be rebuilt.

> refrain

> Sin and despair, like the sea waves cold,
> Threaten each soul with infinite fear;
> Grace that is greater, yes, grace untold,
> Reveals a refuge always so near.

> refrain

> Marvelous, infinite, matchless grace,
> Unrestrained in its application,
> Extends to each neighbor an embrace
> Grounded in salvation's foundation.

> refrain

305

Romans 6:1b–11
Hopeless Hope Vigil — Proper 7 (12)

While appreciating plays of concepts on several different levels, this passage is particularly dense. Issues of death and resurrection, baptism and sin weave and interweave until it may sound as if the only bottom-line available is that we are baptized into death rather than into resurrection and that sin needs to die rather than be baptized and resurrected.

Consider Hagar whose vision of a well may be her equivalent of baptism and how it leads to life in a new land or an entering into a new country of unexpected grace. Consider the disciples invited to live so openly and beyond their tribal past that the limits of a cross would become as nothing for them.

Certainly there are those who arrive at this position and understand that their beginning spot is to focus on sin in order to do it in, to overcome it, to reduce it to naught. Their driver might be seen as a preference for a death of sin.

Certainly there are those who arrive at this position and understand that they are to focus on new life where none seemed possible—to revision a world, to undergird it, to bring forth new relationships. Their driver is resurrection past the sin of others. Baptism comes as a crack of grace in a shell of sin (reference to an interesting book, *Crack in the Cosmic Egg*, by Joseph Chilton Pearce).

Do we need to set sister against sister against brother against parent against all others to chose one of these? Will the "end of death-as-the-end" have to play itself out once again as Christianity comes to another opportunity for definition?

So what do we do in the midst of such language that seems lawyerly enough to open more loopholes than it closes?

Romans 6:12–23
Proper 8 (13)

Down through the years, traditionalist and literalists have accused those on the progressive portion of the Christian continuum of being libertines—those who abuse their freedom.

The expansive freedom of G*D does come with some built in testing points. It does travel beyond the limits of rules and commandments. G*D does sometimes change decisions mid-stride. In turn, we had heard it said and now we need to listen to what is being said anew and differently.

In listening to "grace" first and "law" second we do run risks. These are different risks than attending first to the "law" and then to "grace." The risks are different and folks do seem to find themselves gravitating or levitating toward one or the other polarity—law or grace.

Perhaps the best we can do at this point is not to argue or defend or apologize for the gifts we have been given, but simply use them. Trust there will be an opportunity to change directions (an angel will open our eyes) or an opening available for new knowledge about G*D and self.

May our freedom in G*D lead us to so care about others that we too will be accused of being too free in associating with the poor, the outcast, the sinners. May our freedom in G*D lead us to so care about G*D images that we will find a way out of the slave talk and sacrifice talk of yesterday into recognitions of the obsessions and compulsions of this day and a gift of participation in the fullness of life rather than relying on something merely done on our behalf.

Let the accusations come that we do cast a net of grace too broadly and that we do recast images of G*D beyond those that have been codified and constraining of G*D's expansiveness. For now, this is our way to a "whole, healed, put-together life." This way does lead to eternal life. We rejoice that this is our path and trust others rejoice in their path.

Romans 7:15–25a
Proper 9 (14)

So many fractures in life.

death -/- life
sin -/- good
mind -/- flesh
spirit -/- body
law within -/- law without

Living a divided life of ever-present sin with only periodic grace is quite a set-up for self-flagellation.

No wonder Paul finally exclaims—"I'm Wretched."[1]

Consider a divided life of ever-present grace with periodic experiences of sin. Is this a possible consideration? If so, where might it lead and would it be worth experimenting with?

---

[1] I recommend, *A Wretched Man: A Novel of Paul the Apostle* by RW "Obie" Holmen. It contains much good contemporary scholarship and will get your thinker going.

Also look for his latest book, *Queer Clergy: A History of Gay and Lesbian Ministry in American Protestantism.*

Romans 8:1–11
Proper 10 (15)

If there is "no condemnation" we are in a new story. The old story relied on Newtonian cause and effect. The new story incorporates the astrophysicist and the quantum mechanic. Their stories add in the expansion and generosity of creation as well as the mystery of uncertainty that spontaneously brings forth new bits and pieces not known before in the game of life.

Who else needs to have their voice added to the mix of no condemnation? Poets and prophets? Priests and novelists? What about biochemists and environmentalists? Laborers on the line and the poor? Who else will help us catch the new life of no condemnation by helping us break free from simply working harder that we might live healthier (living by the future of a beckoning new enterprise of G*D rather than an extension of the tyranny of habits based on an overly simplistic limitation to the dynamics of earth's surface without including the stars or the atoms)?

What ripples forth from "There is therefore now no condemnation for those who are in Christ Jesus"? Can you bring Paul's insight into common language for today?

———————

This is a good time to do a refrigerator chart. On a simple sheet of paper draw a line down the paper to make two columns—a condemnation column and a raising from the dead column. Periodically through a few days jot down the number of times you thought, said, or acted in a manner characterized by one of these columns since your last review. After a couple of days, see if there is a pattern. Do you find the chart to be affected by your bio-rhythms, the quality of your sleep, the healthiness of your diet, the meditation discipline you follow, the people you spend time with, etc.? While the goal is to join a spirit of life in raising new life, the usual pattern is to gently move in that direction, with a step backward every now and then, but generally moving forward. Don't give up.

[Yes, there could be a prepared chart here, but this is good practice to develop your own self-modification program. Blessings on developing a chart just for you and not simply filling in a generic one.]

Romans 8:6–11
Conviction [5]

The church in Rome might also hear that to set the mind on death is to focus on flesh and to set the mind on life and peace is spirit work. These things are not one-way orientations. If we take death as an advisor for what to pay attention to in life, we might name death a spiritual advisor. Likewise, life and peace find their context in death—what transforms it, redeems it, resurrects it.

In Ezekiel, dry bones cry out as much as does "the spirit of the LORD". Here, Lazarus' flesh cries out as much as do Martha and Mary and Jesus. Out of the depths comes a cry for new life, a new life that is tied to forgiveness.

G*D needs to deal with forgiveness issues with those lying in the valley of dust. Jesus, Mary, Martha, and Lazarus have forgiveness issues with one another. Forgiveness is still a key element in our lives and deaths that desires resolution beyond every opportunity for resolution. A key question: How we are doing with our forgiving and receiving of forgiveness?

O so slow we are
to establish a relationship
on and in and through
forgiveness

justice calls for it
and justice grinds slow
but it does surface
even from the dead

forgiveness drives
a hard bargain
as steadfast love's
altar ego

it will not give up
until satisfied
slow or fast
eventually

leaving us a choice
cooperation early
prolonged resistance
but no choice

bones will rise
flesh will be unwrapped
death becomes spirit
peace becomes flesh

fear not O crier
from deep places
there is forgiveness
wait - hope - redeem

Romans 8:12–25
Proper 11 (16)

So, sisters and brothers, we are not called to live according to our past, for this is a way to irrelevance and death. But, if you forgive the deeds of the past, you will live. All who are led by G*D's mercy are freed. In this freedom you are to release your slavery to the past. Adopt a future!

To make this shift is to participate in a creative force that is willing to move through difficulty, suffering even, for a larger purpose. It is this revelation of something better that moves us beyond all-things-being-equal and on to living for ourselves and next generations.

We waited long for this revelation that we have a part in tomorrow. We were caught in the futility of coming to a better place by using the same old processes. Hope has been reborn for us and we are willing to risk what we have for what we anticipate is arriving.

It was not just ourselves that were groaning, awaiting a birthing of a new way of relating to our past and to one another. All of yesterday and today have been moving toward tomorrow. Now, together, we are able to each be beloved for the gift we are—the gift of who we have been and all love and life have taught us; the gift of who we are and of our deep questions; the gift of our yearning for more.

This hope organizes our health. It is not yet seen, but already is at work changing patterns and engaging us in the patience necessary to act boldly without relying on immediate results. We are making adjustments in life-long habits simply because our health depends on it.

Romans 8:26–39
Proper 12 (17)

To bridge into this section remember these perspectives from the NRSV. Verse 25 "But if we hope for what we do not see, we wait for it with patience." Hope and patience are what might be behind verse 26, "Likewise the Spirit helps us in our weakness, for we do not know how to pray as we ought...."

Those of us who live in hope and are patient in suffering the distance between our present and our desired future have been easily labeled as weak. A part of our waiting is praying tentatively, while we clarify our prayer in light of bridging present realities of a created order to a further evolution of such. Where two or three accord in prayer is like unto having ourselves and our reality accord in prayer. Creation around us has been an ignored prayer partner.

Continuing to verse 28, "We know that all things work together for good for those who love G*D, who are called according to G*D's purpose." It has been all too easy to move this into a prosperity theology—the way you know G*D is on your side, that you are within G*D's purpose, is that good things come your way.

This really is not about a wonderful resolution to any and all circumstances, proving our worth. It is about steadfast love, a presence of G*D's tending things toward good. It is a vision, in the midst of whatever our current circumstance of weakness—there is movement toward wholeness.

And would someone tell me who is not called?

So much here. I would point to one other little spot—versification. Why was verse 39 begun in the middle of a list? My vision is that those little numbers 3&9 (trinity and trinity squared) open a place for us and for others. Here we are welcome to add our particular problem of life and love; not even our difficulty will separate us from G*D.

Try reading it again:

> "(38) For I am convinced that neither death, nor life, nor angels, nor rulers, nor things present, nor things to come, nor powers, (39) [nor my/our particular problem of life and love, _____,] nor height, nor depth, nor anything else in all creation, will be able to separate us from the love of God in Christ Jesus our Lord." –NRSV

Romans 9:1–5
Proper 13 (18)

What enormous sorrow do you carry with you?

Is it some regret, some continuing thorn in the flesh, some addictive behavior, some awareness of principalities and powers, some thwarted desire?

How might that sorrow be assuaged? Confession, healing, power, audacity?

Paul writes of his sorrow regarding those who have not yet caught his vision of resurrection.

He claims himself willing to trade places with them.

Am I willing to trade places with a biblical inerrantist or literalist? They are part of my family and have everything going for them in terms of the knowledge of details of the Bible. And yet I hear e.e. cummings observing that they are "so full of knowledge that they are empty, empty of understanding." Am I willing to trade places if it means giving up my little bit of experience of the expansiveness of G*D's love? Not yet.

Is this lack of generosity on my part why we seem to be at loggerheads in the church today? Since I don't think that even Paul could exempt himself from his own experience, I expect that there is some other blockage. Simply deleting all that "cursed" language might be a helpful beginning. Paul's intensity of intention can hardly be faulted, but denying one's self is hardly a good starting point. A strong affirmation of knowing one's self is needed to deny impulse and do no harm.

Perhaps the best we can do is to proceed in trust without getting into a competition to see who can be most humble, cursed, or martyred. If nothing is impossible for G*D then there is bound to be a both/and way for a new community. Let's keep looking.

Romans 10:5–15
Proper 14 (19)

We are what we do.

What do we do and what is the basis of our doing that keeps us doing what we do do well?

These have to do with community (the law) and heart (the Christ) working together. This has been imaged as "good cop" and "bad cop", foreground and background, inner and outer, and several other "thises" and "thats" that complement one another.

One of the differences I experience between some form of literalized fundamentalism and creative progressivism is that of flip-flopping between the two poles to see how to keep things under control and that of rubbing the two poles against one another to see what sparks fly.

Rub well.

Has G*D rejected creation?

Has G*D rejected Adam and Eve?

Has G*D rejected Cain?

Has G*D rejected the Nephilim?

Has G*D rejected the prophets?

Has G*D rejected Canaanite women?

Has G*D rejected Jesus?

Has G*D rejected the Jews?

Has G*D rejected Gays and Lesbians?

Has G*D rejected the people you reject?

Has G*D rejected Islamic Extremists?

Has G*D rejected G*D's mercy or steadfast love?

If you say, "Yes," to any of these, how do you get out of the eternal threat that at any time G*D will, for whatever reason, reject you?

If you say, "No," to all of these, how do you get out of the eternal work of expressing welcome, hospitality?

Romans 12:1–8
Proper 16 (21)

Who do you say that I am? Who do you say you are? When tracking well we say we are members of one another. Which part of a larger Beloved are you? Pinkie, Pate, Patella?

We receive meaning from the body as a whole as well as from our particular locus. We all hold the keys to love and life. There is no holiness but social holiness!

If there is one corrective to today's resurgence of fundamentalism (claiming one part is by nature more important than another part) it is a sense of universal social holiness where none will be redeemed until all are. This plays out in economics as well as in theology. You might think of a tax as a binding principle that keeps us together even as death drives us apart.

There is a cost to a body of many parts. Each part cannot maximize its own wealth (its predominance among the many) but must play and pay its part. The greater the perception of the part, the more it costs to be a part of the whole.

To wrestle with the purpose of taxes is valuable community building. To put taxes beyond our decision-making is the same as putting G*D beyond our current time and space (no pie in the sky, by and by). Taxes do for a healthy community what serving one another does for the body of Christ. Taxes will always be with us, not because they are imposed from the outside, but because they are a constituent part of being in community. We need to talk about them more and more honestly.

Romans 12:9–16b
Elizabeth and Mary Meet

May you have the grace to offer a "Namaste" greeting to all you meet. This transforms both parties into a larger party together.

The gifts we carry and give birth to will vary. Their value to the community does not vary. Oh, sometimes we make up hierarchies of value, but CEOs are not of more value than those who labor or purchase. Without laborers, so-called management would starve.

What a different world we would be living in if we were quicker to honor another than to fear our own honor disregarded.

May we claim our value, even if that means disrupting an established system of made-up values that favor some and disenfranchise many.

> Prayer: Abundantly creative Life, may we not say or claim more than we know. Thanks be for a humble communal perspective. Uh-huh!*

---

* An interjection used to indicate affirmation, agreement or gratification.

Romans 12:9–21
Proper 17 (22)

Friends, Romans, Countryfolk, and Lurkers, lend me an ear.

Thanks. Now let me give it back to you with interest. No, not with poison tragically poured into it, but with a comedic filter which lets us hearken to the sorrow of the day, the bitterness of the years, the fear of the generations so we might hear steadfast love moving within our experience.

When listening to the poison of the day—assassination folderol and the like—may its screams not drown out an Elijah whisper of hope.

What we listen to, we respond to. Yes, acknowledge the pain loudly around and about. Even more Yes, rejoice in love, mutual affection, honor, patience, perseverance, hospitality, blessing, harmony, nobility, peaceable living, overcoming evil with good, and on and on.

Bless your ears—whether they hang low and wobble to and fro or perk up and fun pun new insights beyond stodgy dogmatic repetition.

What are you hearing these days?

Romans 13:8–14
Proper 18 (23)

Theory: Love does no wrong to a Neighb*r.

Reality: Members of the church sin against one another.

What's a Christ to do?
Better yet, what about you? Paul suggests living honorably.
How's the day gone so far? Been honorable, regardless?
How's the rest of the day look? Is honorable action still an option?

Just as being untruthful means more work for us as we try to keep all the little pieces of untruth in order, not being honorable ultimately means more work. May you lay the burden of not being honorable down.

Perhaps working on a common definition of honor would get us out of some of our usual binds. Honor is not the whole response needed to life's perplexing options, but it is a good start. Too much honor gets into honor killings, but honor is still a good start. You might want to make up a little card and look at it hourly for the next week. One version of the card might read, "Being honorable is the easy way, is my way."

Romans 13:11–14
Needed Change [1]

Put on the armor of light.

Advent is a time of putting on. We put on our imagination of how the world might be better. We put on our intellect to figure out a next step toward that imagination. We put on our experiences to sort out what has been helpful and what has not been in order to change our patterns toward the helpful. We put on our intentions regarding our relationships with one another and the "wholy" (G*D and universe). We put on all this and more as a next future dawns. That which is coming needs to be welcomed. Advent pulls us onward.

Advent is a time of putting on. We put on pageants of Christmas. We put on angelic heralding. We put on bringing gifts of gold, frankincense, myrrh, and time away from our daily work. We put on awkward pregnancy. We put on redecisions about relationships. We put on all that has come down to us and so we put on baptism and temptation and healing and preaching and teaching and listening and praying and dying and resurrection and service and mission. Advent pushes us onward.

What do you need to put on? for your soul's sake? for your neighbor's sake? for one another's sake? for the sake of enemies?—For G*D's sake, what do you need to put on?

Romans 14:1–12
Proper 19 (24)

This is my beloved's birthday. She has a large enough perspective on life that where most folks would claim it is their "X" birthday, she claims "X+1" and says she has completed "X" years, but prefers living as "X+1". It is this kind of larger perspective that aids us when it comes time to be tempted to judge.

Can we join my beloved in one of her favorite pronouncements, "They're doing the best they can with what they have"? This openness to that which is beyond our current seeing aids us in hanging in there, nonetheless. Just as she remembers Jung remembering Erasmus, "Called or not, G*D is present", just so we can see the presence of more than the surface. This brings a larger sense of time and a greater opportunity for growing with and forgiving.

I am thankful to have her as a compassionate presence (even as she has promised to nominate me for sainthood right after she strangles me). I pray you have your own compassionate presence to slow your temptation to judge too quickly and strongly. I pray you will be a compassionate presence when others are tempted to judge too quickly and strongly. It is appropriate for us to help one another stand and to intercede on behalf of one another when we fall that we might all be accountable in the present—letting future accountabilities care for themselves.

As you might guess, such openness to let evil rest and compassion be chosen comes from knowing the dark side of life without being overcome by it. See how a larger perspective becomes a source of grace so we can make more of the present than day-trading our way through time?

Romans 15:4–13
Needed Change [2]

Posited perspective: The past was written that
we might find our commonality today.

Well and good. Has it worked out?

A more fruitful mantra is "Welcome as you would be welcomed". This anticipates a future commonality breaking into the present.

There are some who have not been welcomed well. Their behavior reveals that lack. Welcome them anyway, for you have been well welcomed.

There are some who have been welcomed well but for whatever reason have not received that welcome. Their behavior reveals that lack. Welcome them anyway, for you have been well welcomed.

A stimulus or a response to poor or generous welcoming is not predictable. There are some folk who overcome an unwelcoming beginning and those who are thankful for the welcome they have received. There is not an automatic response to welcoming. When a positive response is available to a welcome it can come in an instant or in stages.

Nonetheless, there is a bedrock need of welcoming as broadly as possible and then to go beyond what seems impossible to welcome. This is a key to this pericope, "For G*D's sake! Welcome one another as Christ has welcomed you." Substitute "forgive" for "welcome" and you'll see the connection. Try "be merciful to" as another alternative and the connection deepens.

Whether believing or not—joy, peace, and abounding hope are revealed in how we experience being welcomed and how we welcome. Act as though you were introducing these qualities as greater than your own entitlement. Could you be the equivalent of Baptizer John preparing a way for joy to flourish, peace to be grounded, and hope to bounce around?

Well, yes.

So?

1 Corinthians 1:1–9
Guiding Gift [2]

"Called to be saints" is a line worth remembering as well as simply membering—being mindful of something important, like being beloved.

We might translate this phrase, "Intended to be beloved". Note that this is addressed to a congregation and not just an individual. When was the last time you dealt with the plural reality of "saintliness" or "belovedness"?

A result of revealing mindful saints is the giving of thanks. May someone be thankful for your individual saintliness and our common belovedness.

1 Corinthians 1:10–18
Guiding Gift [3]

Church quarrels go back to our very beginning. They are part of our DNA. We are still splitting ourselves into various constituencies.

Has Christ been divided or is that a necessary component of a Christ that engages this particular creation? We do tend to idealize our leaders, whether Paul, Apollos, Cephas, a particular Pope, Martin Luther, John Wesley, the Jesus of Matthew, Mark, Luke, John, Thomas, Mary, or yourself. What do you make of our ancient or contemporary quarrels? How many Saints were burned as Heretics and how many Heretics have been elevated to Sainthood? What is the half-life of a Creed? What is the cost/benefit ratio of any given Creed?

If Jesus told us to go and baptize and Paul explicitly says he was not sent to do so, what does that mean for you? How else might you join Paul in foolishness beyond a literalism of red letters?

Are you following Jesus and baptism, Paul and the cross, Kairos CoMotion and expansive love? One of these? Two? All three? Another? Blessings to you on following your call, even if not understood by the institutions (formal and informal) around you.

1 Corinthians 1:18–24
Relic Day

Crosses are multivalent. A key question is whether that is based on our perception, G*D's, or both? Wisdom, like beauty, is in the eye of the beholder.

It is always interesting to try to weave through writing intended to be persuasive. In the *NRSV*, Jews "demand" and Greeks "desire". Christians/Paul, however, "proclaim". From these starting points it is no wonder that we get to stumbling Jews, foolish Greeks/Gentiles, and powerful Christians.

Just turning these characterizations around we hear Jews proclaim signs and Gentiles proclaim wisdom, while Christians demand crucifixion. Now who is petulantly foolish?

A better approach than trying to make a symbol carry more than it can bear is to work on common interactions, to practice seeing signs everywhere (even in nasty crosses), and to add wisdom to creeds. Above all we need to talk together about what constitutes meaning and knowing/understanding. To have these important categories defined from on high removes change and growth from the equation.

The cross did not hold an elevated position in early Christian art, no matter how much Paul preached it[1]. Now it has been all the rage since Constantine. There is still hope that a return to a tree of paradise or moving on to some new image of life renewed will revitalize our engagement with one another and our imaging G*D.

[1] Rita Nakashima Brock, *Saving Paradise: How Christianity Traded Love of This World for Crucifixion and Empire.*

1 Corinthians 1:18–31
Guiding Gift 4 — Clarification Week Tuesday

Those with Power claim they have wisdom on their side. How else would they have been "entrusted" with the power they have? We hear that expressed in one way or another by every winner of a power position. Power and meekness or power and humility do not live well together.

At play is a large movement from the nothingness of chaos to everything being vain. We live between and do what we can to hold briefness lightly and with all the gravity we can muster. It is this heavily invested and laughably usable moment that makes a difference.

Paul would equate this with his language about a cross that measures the meaning of creation and re-creation. Paul's cross image tends to reveal the corrupting power of power. It is a bookend to belovedness and lifts up the powerless.

A conversation with death reminds us how frail is our sense of power and how far from wisdom we yet are. We are thrown back on choosing how we will live. Our choices will show their grounding. Will we live in light of such qualities beyond the collusion of perceived power and accepted wisdom as the following?

poverty	peacemaking
mourning	persecuted
meekness	reviled
desire	justice
mercy	kindness
purity	humility

The ancients say, "Aye"; the present says, "As soon as we can, but not until I have surety my wisdom is safely in charge"; the future says, "Yea". To listen beyond ourselves can help us stand prophetically in the present whether from Paul's vision of "Cross" or another creation-centered or eschaton-engaged perspective.

1 Corinthians 2:1–12, (13–16)
Guiding Gift [5]

Verse 15—Those who are spiritual discern all things, and they are themselves subject to no one else's scrutiny. –NRSV

This may well have been Paul's experience and claim for authority. For Paul and the plowing and seeding of a Church, he may have felt the need to set up a separation of spirit and flesh, grace and law (short-term effective, long-term problematic). This sort of clarity and either/or was probably effective in his time and for his purposes, but 2,000+ years later—not so much.

Our experience is that the more spiritual we are the more worldly we must be. Barbara Brown Taylor's book *An Altar in the World: A Geography of Faith* is an excellent account of this perspective. She notes, that currently church people seem to think that the only "more" available to them is more of the same.

> Somewhere along the line we bought—or were sold—the idea that God is chiefly interested in religion. We believed that God's home was the church, that God's people knew who they were, and that the world was a barren place full of lost souls in need of all the help they could get. Plenty of us seized on those ideas because they offered us meaning. Believing them gave us purpose and worth. They gave us something noble to do in the midst of lives that might otherwise be invisible. Plus, there really are large swaths of the world filled with people in deep need of saving.

> The problem is, many of the people in need of saving are in churches, and at least part of what they need saving from is the idea that God sees the world the same way they do. What if the gravel of a parking lot looks as promising to God as the floorboard of a church? What if a lost soul strikes God as more reachable than a lifelong believer? What if God can drop a [Jacob's] ladder absolutely anywhere, with no regard for the religious standards developed by those who have made it their business to know the way to God?

Somehow we need to realize the world is bound to G*D and then rebind the world to G*D and G*D to the world. Out of this encounter, sparks will fly.

1 Corinthians 3:1–9
Guiding Gift [6]

To choose or not to choose is a significant question.

On the one hand, everything depends upon this moment. What we decide will echo on forever. What we decide against is stillborn. All of life hangs in the balance—all of heaven holds it breath. What will they decide?

Here it might be good to listen again to that old hymn, "Once to Every Man and Nation" [written as a poem protesting America's war with Mexico]. What decision is now needed regarding America's pre-emptive war against Iraq or elsewhere and impending one with Iran or another? Will you choose to choose it? What else has changed within and around us, leading to new choices?

Will you throw a first stone or a last stone or no stone at all? Does it make any difference whether the issue is personal or communal, spiritual or political (not that these pairs can be separated very well)?

On the other hand, a choice doesn't make the slightest difference. We are simply G*D's servants whether we find ourselves with Apollos or Paul or Amy or Janet or performing one function or another. As a simple servant of G*D, just how much choice does a milk-sucking child have?

Now, when to choose to choose or to choose not to choose, aye—that is a good question. When to say Yes! or No! can be both imponderably confusing and intuitively clear.

---

happy those
who are able to decide
after the fact
Monday-morning quarterback
after the fact
but happier still those
who decide
with an eye to the future
before the fact
that will become an after fact
to move toward a preferred tomorrow
before its factness
is highly satisfying here
decisions take on deep meaning

1 Corinthians 3:10–11, 16–23
Guiding Gift [7]

There is much trust needed in being connected with a religious institution. No matter how well we build new foundations in a new day, someone else will eventually further build well or poorly on that foundation.

Paul suggests that the foundation of life is Jesus and yet we don't have the same foundational understanding of Jesus as evaluator of each foundation claiming to be built upon Jesus. Consider how far we are from a near-future parousia. Paul saw things one way, and millennia later we see things another way. Consider, also, the variety of Christian sects and the variety within each of them. It would be a very strange Jesus that could be deduced from the variety of religious expression in just one community.

Perhaps the strongest image here is that of connecting with one another. We have wrestled with an image of Trinity for a long, long time. Imagine a trinity of G*D, Jesus, and You. We become interconnected with Jesus and G*D and, through this, with one another.

Realize that G*D is present in you as well as with you. Nothing will look the same again.

1 Corinthians 4:1–5
Guiding Gift [8] — Proper 3 (8)

What does it mean to be judged by G*D and is that different than being judged by Wealth or Money or Mammon or Profit?

One way of coming at this is to ask about where they end up.

G*D's judgment seems to end up with mercy outweighing justice and steadfast love taking precedence over disappointment.

Wealth's judgment seems to end up with there never being enough for all and so compassion takes a back seat to separating one self from all others.

Questions:

A) Who or what won't take mercy away from you? (Matthew 12:7; James 3:17)

B) Who or what will eventually take your resources away from you? (Ecclesiastes 2:21)

Responses:

A) Invisible Hand of G*D and Death

B) Invisible Hand of the Market and Death

1 Corinthians 5:6–8
Opened Heart Evening

It is so easy to view Easter through a lens of power—power over. Death is overcome! Alleluia!

This is still "old" yeast boasting. Somehow we came to be on the winning side; a Hail Mary touchdown pass worked. We won.

Just so quickly do we subvert every evidence of steadfast love. If it doesn't supply an advantage for us, we will remake it in our image.

Here, on Easter evening, we again come face-to-face with our temptation to be exceptional, to be entitled, to let old yeast puff us up.

What is a sincere and truthful response to an unexpected resurrection?

Are we still surprised or is this old-hat, removed from our experience into the cant of creed?

Is our task to resurrect hopeful energy to join a prophetic way to move beyond system tinkering to address and disrupt systemic evil as resurrection disrupts the placidity of death?

Will we give over any privilege we might claim from a preview to the majesty and glory of indeterminacy, a never-ending creation?

Will we find ourselves arising into a new day only to repeat yesterday?

Easter evening is perhaps a tad more significant than Easter Eve when we were just hanging on. Now a real choice—restructure or transform?

May you sit quietly after a day-of-days and receive this transformational blessing:

take care
dream strong
smile gentle
and so go well

1 Corinthians 11:23–26
Courage Thursday

What are we remembering when we share bread and drink together?

We remember death—Jesus'. Might we also remember his calling us together? Might we remember all that led up to this invitation? As we look back, might we not also remember subsequent events? Or is this only about remembering death?

It is important to remember that in the phrase, "my body that is for you," the "for you" does not mean a substitutionary "instead of you." –*NISB* note.

That same source reminds us that remembrance is a way of recalling that includes the participants in a larger story. So, what is the larger story of which you are a part?

1 Corinthians 12:3b–13
Energy to Witness

To say "Jesus is Lord" without using a phrase such as "for the common good" is a misuse of the affirmation.

That same process needs to be in play when it comes to claiming a vocation. If you see "Jesus is Lord" standing behind the building of community, it also stands behind an individual's participation in that community.

For a moment consider that every vocation has aspects to it regarding wisdom, knowledge, faith, healing, miracles, prophecy, discernment, and interpretation. Every vocation can help build the common good and some folks will even say every vocation reveals that "Jesus is Lord" when a common good is actually built.

This builds on the understanding that

Jesus is Lord comes from Holy Spirit.

Common good comes from Holy Spirit.

Activity/Vocation comes from Holy Spirit.

This connects Jesus with communal common good and individual vocation as long as one understands and values Holy Spirit.

Whether or not you buy the above model, proceed to build the common good by attending to the virtues of your task.

2 Corinthians 5:20b–6:10
Self-Recognition Day

Entreating someone on behalf of Christ may have some power, if there is a relationship with said Christ to begin with. For someone outside the fold, this doesn't carry much weight. This is like an Ayatollah imploring Billy Graham, for the sake of Muhammad, to be reconciled to Allah the Merciful.

Then we come to a personal entreaty based on what I have had to deal with. Because of my faithfulness, you, also, ought to be faithful. Again that has some strength or is rather weak, depending upon the relationship.

Seldom, it seems, do we entreat on behalf of a joy to come. Usually we are operating out of the past and trying to make the present conform to it. On Ash Wednesday we may want to simply have space for folk to remember their fondest dream of how life might work well for all concerned, what has gotten in the way of that, and how this might be a moment to shift gears by practicing that which moves them one step closer to a better future. Nearly two months of practice might get us ready for an Easter, Transfiguring, Transforming, Resurrectional reality.

This practice is based not only on what others have found helpful down through the years (that's a pretty wide spectrum of spiritual disciplines) but which of those best corresponds to the person's experience and tendencies. If it doesn't touch some base inside, all the appeals to external authority will simply be appeals that don't appeal.

2 Corinthians 9:6–15
Thanksgiving

The point is this: Sowing your life into Life is beneficial.

It is not a question of sowing sparingly or bountifully. At different times of our lives we can only sow sparingly or bountifully. In each season there are constraints and opportunities no one else can see, much less appreciate.

Small or large, sowing good endures and echoes along the way. Such participation in Life is not about some formula for guaranteed prosperity. It is not about what benefits you or someone half-a-world away.

Entering into the processes of Life is simply being connected to a wellspring of energy we variously call hope or trust or love.

Entering into the give-and-take of Life is not a test to be passed—that would be an indulgence. In its simplest form, sowing is expressing one's bliss or joy or beauty. What a wonderful trinity that would be to live within. We move in that direction as we recognize, receive, and translate processes of thanksgiving, generosity, and well-being-for-all from everyday life into our every-day life.

2 Corinthians 13:11–13
Live Together

Sequencing is one way of looking at things.

Here we might read the qualities Paul is looking for come first and then are followed by a blessing.

This is the other way around from Abraham having been blessed first to, then, be a blessing.

Likewise we can start with any part of a trinity or more-sided symbol and move on around and across such. Starting points are important and we find ours in a number of quite mysterious ways. As with any good journey, the starting spot only gets us going to find all manner of interconnections along the way.

We are not looking at a One Way approach to life. For us life comes from all directions and goes in all directions. This interconnecting web brings additional meaning to the smallest of encounters.

Galatians 4:4–7
Naming Day

Yesterday we had an opportunity to spend time with our adopted grandson and his parents. Why this child, out of all the millions of children that needed a new home? Why do some choose to adopt and some choose not to? For those who do, the choice of whom to adopt out of so many remains a mystery.

"Paul employs the theme of inheritance, introduced in chapter 3, to dissuade the Galatians from becoming circumcised." –*NISB* There are other arguments that could be made not to follow the Jewish law of circumcision. So the adoptive role is not unique to or constrained by the situation and therefore not required. This opens an arena of speculation regarding adoption as a spiritual model. It is particularly suspect in light of a creation-based theology.

In some sense adoption is simply a welcoming home, as in the tale of the Prodigals. Reflect on a creation image of G*D that is never lost (even if it be rudimentary [elemental] in some, or even invisible in others). Prevenient Grace has kept us all within the purview, providence, and provision of G*D's image. This is a re-covenanting, as much as it is an adoption, and accords better with a sense of coming to maturity that is Paul's endpoint reason for dismissing circumcision as a requirement.

Adoption has a legal feel to it that may or may not get lived out in the formation of a real family. Again and again we need to look beyond the formal relationship to the lived relationship.

Ephesians 1:3–14
Blessed Body [2]

This is one heck of a long sentence. To try to condense it runs the risk of misrepresentation. Nonetheless, here is one shortening:

> Blessed be G*D,
> who desires us to be holy and
> blameless in love
> as we move toward G*D
> by way of Jesus' witness to
> redemptive experiences.

What is your best approximation of this broad purpose statement that will get more specific as the letter goes on?

While you are at it, see if you can figure out the antecedents for all the "he" and "his" language. In terms of a Trinity, it would be helpful to have more than just male references. Earlier saints who speak of Mother Jesus help us out of unnecessary confusion. To simply read it as it is in a public setting loses folks very quickly. It would take a thespian's thespian to read this aloud to today's congregation and have them follow along. This same confusion also frees preachers to make any number of assertions about destiny as a forgone fact rather than a journey toward a destination.

Ephesians 1:15–23
Our Turn to Witness — Proper 29 (34): "Pentecost" Last

Not ceasing in our prayers, we bring blessing upon blessing to person and situation. To be rapturously caught in the act of blessing is a double blessing.

Wisdom, revelation, hope, and calling are good blessings to be strewing willy-nilly into the lives of those in our vicinity. They are needed.

Note that it takes some wisdom, revelation, hope, and calling to focus on these as a needed blessing in this and every generation. Rejoice that someone has blessed you with wisdom, revelation, hope, and calling that you might, in turn, pass these blessings on.

This might be what it means to live from above.

---

far above
all rule and authority
and power and dominion
is the simplicity of blessing
knocking the underpinnings
out from under said
rule and authority
and power and dominion
for they fade in the face of
wisdom and revelation
and hope and calling

Ephesians 3:1–12
Guiding Gift

3:3 *Mystery* is used four times in this section. Originally a Greek military term from Ptolemaic Egypt,
"mysteries" were plans drawn up by the royal family
and kept secret even from the generals before battle.
In Greco-Roman religious practice, "mysteries" were
the secret information shared with initiates to lead
them to immortality. In the Qumran scrolls, the word
is used in connection with God's wise providence,
the mystery of salvation previously hidden in God
but revealed to the Teacher.
–NISB

Here is an interesting mystery: Paul's commission of highlighting
grace was given for others, for us as well as for others. It does seem to
take a revelation behind our vocation for us not to measure ourselves
and our work against the usual standards of the day. This insulates us
from everything being about "me". As we go where we go and do
what we do, it turns out that we build up the community by our little
part or we reduce community by our little part. One way of predicting
which way it will go has to do with gifts we have been given. Give a
gift away, whether gold, frankincense, or myrrh, and community is
strengthened; others are included in. Keep a gift and its interest, and
community is weakened; others are excluded.

This mystery is not about victory, eternity or prosperity. Mystery is
about giving—giving a child, giving a safe trip to Egypt, giving gold/
frankincense/myrrh, or giving grace. As we approach a day that is traditionally associated with giving, what will you give (not resolve to
give, but actually give)?

Ephesians 5:8–14
Conviction [4]

Once you were in darkness—threatened by leader and community—then you came to understand "not wanting" and you proceeded as though it were light, as though there were no threat.

When we feel threatened we shut our eyes, physical and spiritual.

With our eyes closed we divide our experience from our theology. Saul is Saul is Saul and ever will be king (substitute the leader of your choice) so there is no sense in doing anything about it. Blind from birth is blind from birth is blind from birth (substitute the present personal limitation of your choice) and so there is no sense in practicing an alternative reality. Once darkness sets in, darkness is all there is.

These limitations and their overcoming are the stuff fairytales are made of. And there isn't much truer than fairytales.

---

sin, sin all around
and not a healing left
unfairness abounds
and blame is our motif

through the most unlikely one
the youngest the weakest
the ugliest the most foolish
the spit and the mud

sin becomes irrelevant
unfairness ceases to be a mantra
so what now that our understanding
of blame needs recalibrating

well well well
it is time for the depth
of experience-based belief
in muddy spit-based kinship

Philippians 1:21–30
Proper 20 (25)

v.27 – Simply live as citizens of a new common-
wealth, pointed toward G*D, as was Jesus, so,
whether I am with you or not, come hell or high
water, I will know we are striving together. –WW

Not so simple, this. Dual allegiances, competing covenants, and survival issues cloud every situation, as do inherent privileges so diffi-cult to cast off. Is it better to go and be with G*D or stick around and be with y'all? Is it my physical life or spiritual life that is at stake as a result of my behavior? Is it the privilege I currently have that I need to wrestle with or the privilege I still secretly desire that shapes my inter-actions?

To have one foot in here and now and another in what is just be-ginning to come clear is a risky place for faith to be revealed.

Given this reality among us, it is perhaps the Christ position: as-traddle choosing points which are charging off in all directions, all the while, mostly consistently, finding a story large enough or contrary enough to keep choosing the best from the past for a better tomorrow.

Simple, no. Worth striving for, yes.

Uniform, no. Together, yes.

Philippians 2:1–13
Proper 21 (26)

An intriguing image of G*D is presented in Philippians—an emptying G*D. Is there a distinction between an emptying and a creating G*D, or are these integrally bound? If you substitute Moses for Jesus Christ and then look back at Exodus, you can catch a glimpse of this emptying G*D.

See again where G*D is—standing on a rock in front of Moses—where Moses will strike. Can you see G*D facing Moses (no backside here) and saying, "Strike through me"? Would you have the courage and humility of Moses to strike G*D to obtain water for the people? Whether anyone else could be witness to this or not, Moses understood he was to strike G*D that the waters from beyond (that had been pent up at Creation and again in Noah's time) might surface through G*D, through Horeb, through a suffering and emptying of G*D.

Where are you called to strike that life-giving water might flow? Does it feel like you would have to muster more strength and humility than you have in order to do so? Does G*D always need to be bruised for life to flow? Do we always need to work through our own resistance to striking G*D that we might grow the next stage of our journey?

---

obey this why don't you
here it comes our difficulty
work out your own salvation
not someone else's
work it out in the absence of G*D
not for G*D's good pleasure
for your own
this is G*D's pleasure too

obey this past pleasure
again a difficulty
work with your fear and trembling
not someone else's
work in the presence of G*D
enabling with pleasure
a willingness to face fear
our pleasure too

Philippians 2:5–11
Naming Day — Premature Fear Sunday

Ahh, humility rewarded. Surely my humility will be likewise recognized for its quality.

Somehow we have lost track of an antecedent. To what was Jesus "obedient" and in regard to what was he "humble"?

Our tendency is to return to a dominion system. G*D has it; Jesus didn't; you don't. Jesus knelt better than you do. G*D wants proof of Jesus' submission, of your obedience. This is a test of Abraham's being submissive and obedient enough to slaughter Isaac taken to the next level. Are you willing to have G*D kill you? That is what the whole bloody substitutionary and obediently humble atonement theories would have you desire.

So back to the question of antecedent. To what was Jesus obedient? What would be a sufficient call to you that would result in your obedience to it? I would hope it is more than some bowing of the neck to fate, to meanness, to our lowest common denominator, to power, to ....

To be humble one might be expected to reject any kowtowing to the excellence of one's humility. To do otherwise, to accept adulation as expected, is to deny the focus one had on bringing love of G*D/Creation together with love of Neighb*r/Enemy. Humility here is intended to bring everything possible together and to laugh at the resulting response that the answer to life, the universe, and everything is simply 42[1]. Humility here would get up on its high horse, in high dudgeon, to say, "Wrong, G*D, we are all exalted or none of us are!"

---

[1] *Hitchhiker's Guide to the Galaxy,* by Douglas Adams (a trilogy in five parts)

Philippians 3:4b–14
Proper 22 (27)

"Surpassing value" is a strange concept to any economic system. Each system has its value pluses and minuses, but not any values beyond itself.

Surpassing value turns our usual economic, political, religious, processes into so much dog-dung (as *The Message* so graphically puts it).

Surpassing value puts the other usual values of life into a new frame.

So, state your surpassing value in 10 words or less.

Paul puts it, "knowing Christ Jesus my Lord."

Kairos CoMotion puts it in more than 10 words:
Re-form the way we live together so as to more fully embody the radically expansive love of G*D
Network for solidarity, advocacy and action
Act-Up on behalf of those who are silenced, excluded or dispossessed

Love Prevails puts it this way: Disclose(t), Divest, Disrupt.

The United Methodist Church says it is "making disciples of Jesus Christ for the transformation of the world."

How do you play with "knowing", "reform", "network", "act-up", "making", and your own way to phrase "surpassing value"?

Philippians 4:1–9
Proper 23 (28)

Are you Syntyche (fortunate) with your Euodia (good journey)?

How might you account for such blessing? Is it attributable to your excellent rejoicing, your high quality gentleness, your above average ability not to worry? Might it be your qualities of truth, honor, justice, purity, pleasing, and other excellent commendables?

Just keep on keeping your head when others around you are losing theirs and G*D's peace will be with you. [Accurate? or not? Can peace be present in times of distress?]

Given our usual backgrounds, experiences, and cultural norms that run counter to these, it would appear it takes a whole lot of hard, hard work to arrive at such a disciplined peace.

Do you have a place of refuge from your own history, old tapes, and peers wherein these looked-for qualities might be nurtured and freed? Will it take a touch of Spirit? a Spiritual Director? an examined life? hitting bottom? to refocus and know with whom you need to associate—the Euodias and Syntyches available in your life?

Come; wrestle with what it takes to receive good news and you will develop an experience base that will make it far easier to share what you receive.

Colossians 3:1–4
Assured

If you have been raised with Christ, **you** now show no partiality.

Ouch! and Wow!

Do you have a vision? This is being raised to life.

Have you tested your vision? This reveals deeper glory.

There is nothing like a deeper raising to tickle one's fancy.

1 Thessalonians 1:1–10
Proper 24 (29)

Want to be saved from a coming wrath? Unfortunately, there are no free passes. Fortunately, there are resources to aid us in not responding to wrath wrathfully.

Find a living and true G*D. That ought to be easy, except such tends to toss salvation back to you. Since the future is not just an inbreaking of a quantum leap surprising to behold, but an outgrowth of investments we make in it by the way we operate today, we again hear those ancient words, "Choose this day ...."

All the encouraging words patting us on the back for having moved in the direction Paul was headed will eventually lead us to a key issue in the whole book of 1 Thessalonians—persistence in the face of difficulty that we be ready to receive a present paradise in what appears to be a dark and dismal day to come.

Let's say Jesus saves us from a coming wrath. OK. How?

- By snapping fingers or impeccable calendaring or a past act of integrity that rolls on of its own accord? No.

- By modeling a persistent drive for a preferred future through intentional present action? Yes.

In following Moses' way of following G*D, following Jesus' way of following Moses and G*D, encourages others in following us following Jesus following Moses following G*D—not dissimilar to a house that Jack built. Such persistence does not allow a passive waiting for an apocalyptic moment, but insists on active investment, willingly risked, anticipating a way through a next self-caused crash based on what we do today.

---

persistence of trust
of something better
in the face of great persistence
claiming only more of the same
is our way through
to paradise
while wading deep
in unnecessary wrath

1 Thessalonians 2:1–8
Proper 25 (30)

How does one care for their own children? One starting point is that of recognizing that children are different and need different responses, even in the midst of the same situation. This reality has been overlooked in the realm of religion where we face a temptation to make one answer good for all children at all times.

It is this appeal to universal answers that keeps getting us in trouble. It is like saying that we are made to be reduced for the Answers (Sabbath) not that the Responses (Sabbath) are made for our moving on to wholeness.

Here we need to recognize the pragmatism of Paul and our ancestors in the faith who did their best to be all things to all people. As they fit their responses to the particulars of a situation, they helped folks take a next step.

This recognition of incremental change expresses care for people and how we grow toward and into a next stage of faith … and a next.

1 Thessalonians 2:9–13
Proper 26 (31)

You are witnesses of our behavior, and G*D also. [verse 10a]

So often we appeal to our good intentions, to G*D having our back, to having followed the rules to justify our behavior. This won't suffice. It needs the witness of those who have experienced in their lives the consequences of our behavior.

To claim any form of trickle-down theory is effective needs the witness of those currently being harmed by it. We cannot rely on some future betterment if folks are not being bettered in the moment.

To claim any form of just-war theory is applicable needs the witness of those who are harmed by it. There is no collateral damage; there are only hurt people, dead people.

Instead of thinking about how G*D might measure our behavior, we would do better to ask how those affected by our behavior, right here, right now, are measuring us. In many ways the whole religious charade is propped up by always substituting G*D for Neighb*r and never hearing from our neighbor about how we have injured them, right here, right now. We need to hear both parts of the commands to Love G*D and Love Neighb*r.

1 Thessalonians 4:13–18
Proper 27 (32)

Given: Those of us alive will not precede into eternity
those who have died.

Those who think they have things under control and absolutely know the best way to live might want to consider who might go ahead of them to glory. It could be any given prostitute, a collaborator with injustice, a starved child, a worthless old coot miserable all his days, or the person who has most injured you.

Some have even been heard to assert that it is just the righteous dead who will rise with Christ and our illustrious selves! It is our brothers and sisters in The Way that Paul is writing about! This is encouragement for those of us still left that if we are persistent we will get in with the good guys, leaving the rascals behind!

Well, no. Rather, encourage one another with these words, "Not one will be left behind". G*D desires the salvation of all and will see to it. We live well, healing and teaching wholeness in Christ, not because we are afraid of missing the boat, but because it has more meaning than anything else.

On All Saints Day, 2005, the United Methodist Judicial Council reinstated a pastor who played gay-keeper in a way that attempted to block G*D's desire for all, setting up the heresy that one must live up to some contrived standard before entering the exclusive fold of "brothers and sisters". May they finally hear that they won't precede anyone.

Rats, now I have to affirm that even that pastor and that Judicial Council will join me in a new heaven (that is, Paradise/Earth). I also need to affirm that this affirmation does not allow me to passively allow G*D to do all the work. I am called, again and again, to say that decision was wrong/sinful and to work to overturn it.

What "Rats!" moment do you have? Use your disappointment and move on to live and teach healing and wholeness in a sick and broken context.

1 Thessalonians 5:1–11
Proper 28 (33)

An encouraging word is needed in these days. Regardless of how the geo-political environment and an urge to empire turn out (history gives evidence of much pain and many deaths in these sorts of moments), we are still called to see that no one is left behind—a previously popular book series of the same title not withstanding.

A word of hope I have is not based on any rebalancing of political realities; it is built on the fact that you and I are still working at issues of hope for ourselves and others. We still see everything working together and not that there will be winners and losers. We still invest our lives in life—standing out in the open and insistent that no one be left out, no one be left behind.

Here is the circularity. I see hope in hope. Sometimes wishful is misconstrued as hopeful. Energy to act is what tells them apart. Live in hope, live together.

For example, those in the dark, intentionally or not, get caught in a great hypocrisy—claiming peace when violence abounds. "Peace", thus used, is a great coverup of a great sin. For tainted and counterproductive "peace" we are willing to lose just one more and then one more.

Seeing false peace requires many concomitant gifts that bolster one another. When used in concert with one another, Paul's list of those gifts—sobriety, faith and love (paired), and hope (of wholeness, not just anything)—allows one to catch a glimpse of true peace under the fog of false peace. What would you identify as a peace-revealing constellation of gifts?

At base, we understand, beyond generations-long setbacks, all are destined for salvation. Abolitionists, from Theodore Parker through Martin Luther King, Jr., have long affirmed: "The arc of the moral universe is long, but it bends toward justice". We are encouraged and encourage one another to get on with it. Put forward the good stuff. Pull back the mist of false peace. Pursue that which builds up.

Titus 2:11–24
Blessed Body, Proper I

Living lives that are self-controlled, upright, and godly has no reward to be waited for. They are, in themselves, rewards already. If you are hoping for something, the way toward it is to begin living it in the present. We are to be a peace we desire.

Alternatively, if you wait long enough and get your timing down right, a traditional God will finally come around to sending the cavalry to the rescue. In this way salvation finally has nothing to do with our living well, only G*D's living well.

With these two options comes a joy of discernment, knowing when to hold 'em and when to fold 'em.

This is part of what is behind differing traditions of salvation where folks stop wrestling with the whole business of incarnation. If it were merely a matter of correct doctrine superimposed on lives, we would coalesce around one understanding or another. When dealing with real life, we need to be able to go in a variety of directions with equal ease and even to go in every direction at once, thus confusing the heck out of ourselves and others who look for some seamless garment to throw over every issue of living.

Indeed, this freedom is the image of G*D, the reflection of G*D, and whatever glory G*D wields.

Titus 3:4–7
Blessed Body, Proper II

Re-imagine atonement from a Christmas perspective rather than one of Good Friday.

If this seems a strange exercise from the outset, no amount of further comment will help. Either shift or stay in the pit.

Any work you do here will bring more than a day's wage of return.

Hebrews 1:1–4, (5–12)
Blessed Body, Proper III

G*D spoke in the prophets. G*D spoke in Jesus (and Joseph and Mary and shepherds and manger beasts and magi). G*D speaks still in you, in me. G*D still speaks in the lives of others.

The prophets reflected G*D's glory (remember Moses' veiled face?). Jesus reflected G*D's glory. You and I, images of G*D, reflect G*D's glory. G*D's glory is reflected in the lives of others.

This glory of G*D is shown in goodness and loving kindness, is freed from acts past, and enhances deeds right now. It has been poured out upon us by Jesus, adding to the pouring out upon us of G*D's image at creation, and we honor these models as we pour it out on others.

Thus salvation is brought to all. Thus we are active in our waiting. Blessed Creation, Merry Christmas, Joyful Today.

Hebrews 2:10–18
Blessed Body [1]

The weakest person you meet today is still your long-lost sister or brother.

As their sibling, be not ashamed to proclaim wonders that they might overhear and put their life in a larger context. You will be proclaiming mysterious things such as death doing away with death-dealers and thus freeing those enslaved by fear of death.

You've been tested and sometimes come through. This is the authority you have to proclaim new life to someone who has had a test they didn't altogether pass. To proclaim past our experience is to get into the tricky area of saying more than we know, having our praise become mere words and formulas. So stick with reality.

It may help to remember some of the tests Jesus faced—birthed in a no-account place by ordinary folk, being a refugee from persecution and knowing that innocent others were killed while he got away, growing up oblivious of the turmoil he caused by not traveling with the family, being in another no-account place for years of silent growth, hearing he is beloved and not letting it go to his head during some temptations, etc., etc. What tests have you faced? This is a grounding we need to be an evangelist.

G*D, Jesus, Spirit, Church, you, I—are to connect sisters and brothers with one another and creation. To work together is a position of hope and power. Through your testing experiences you have learned to be a merciful and faithful high-partner in the service of G*D. With this learning under our belt, we have only the small matter of implementation. Go ahead; be not ashamed of your long-lost sister or brother or whole clan; express G*D's mercy.

Hebrews 2:14–18
Old Welcomes New

How far does sharing flesh go?

Here it is limited to humans and for a particular purpose—to go through a back door to settle an old feud.

It could be seen that this high priest is only taking advantage of flesh, not engaged in advantaging flesh.

In light of Simeon and Anna, it might be said that their vision set Jesus on a path of growth toward wisdom and seeing G*D's favor where it had been previously overlooked. This included nurturing by others over time.

Appreciating full humanity doesn't stop with flesh but continues on to additional aspects of creation and context.

With a human wounding of the environment and structural violence in society, individualized atonement seems tone deaf. Since the power of death for flesh is not destroyable, this strategy for getting at some old, unresolved relationship with a Satan reduced to the status of a devil seems doomed from the start.

Our tendency to anthropomorphize privileges us ahead of any other aspect of reality. It is not that we are alone in need of healing and wholeness. All of creation is groaning and desirous of Anna's and Simeon's affirmation.

A wounded healer image without a healing of the wounded, including angels, leaves us stuck in narcissism.

Hebrews 4:14–16; 5:7–9
Annihilation Friday

Let us provoke one another toward forgiveness.

If we can learn obedience through suffering, can we learn glory through forgiveness? And what will we learn by forgiving suffering and suffering forgiveness?

One learning is that we cannot rely upon a reinstitution of a high priesthood as the only vehicle through which we can access G*D's mercy. For some reason or other this model says mercy cannot be mercy on its own, but only if earned by one or mediated by another.

Mercy is understood to break all the rules for the presence of G*D. Mercy provokes us to additional acts of mercy. Against mercy there are no limitations other than our proclivity to ration and control a G*D we see careening out of control and being merciful beyond our capacity.

If Jesus can sympathize with weakness, there is no one who will be left out. Jesus learned this from a pagan, Melchizedek; a Syrophoenician woman, unnamed; and each and every prophet. Whether we learn mercy from outside or inside a religious tradition, let us affirm our hope, participate in love and good deeds, encourage one another, and identify with those left out.

Hebrews 9:11–15
Clarification Week Monday

The writer to the Hebrews knows that a new covenant does not depend on some third party, but on the integrity of those engaged together. She reminds us that it is not the sacrifice of others that brings life; it is our own participation in that which we deem essential and moves us from life's repetitive works to continually revealed expressions of a steadfast love not held away as a carrot for tomorrow, but offered as a full feast for today.

Whether it is our commitment to give a rose, perfume, or anointing in a relationship now instead of later or our past experiences of resurrection coming to challenge a leaden inertia of cultural and political blocks to more life for more people, we challenge the current status quo. It is in fact our generosity and awareness of new life that sees opportunity for revealing basic choices of life. Here we immediately run into fears and tremblings of past teaching claiming that we now know what's what. Generosity and awareness of abundance of life are still counter-cultural fulcrum points that can move the world.

Let's keep clarifying and telling a larger story than our own small part and honor our small part in moving a larger story along.

Hebrews 10:4–10
Creation's Conception

We still easily talk about sacrifice, and what a sacrifice we make for another. Our culture too easily jokes about guilt-producing mothers, "I gave up so much that you might be here...."

Consider a "sacrifice" that isn't related to guilt or causative of guilt—that would be something, but maybe it would no longer be in a category of sacrifice.

How is a Jesus sacrifice better than a mother's sacrifice or a sacrifice of animals? Can a sacrifice at any level destroy sacrifice?

If G*D is with us and we are with G*D, is our willingness to enter into difficult situations still a sacrifice. Isn't a strategic and tactical plan that has been agreed to something other than a sacrifice? This sort of intent needs a new model for we've used and abused the old sacrificial one and plumb worn it out.

Look in the direction of magnificence, as Mary later describes her soul, her relationship with G*D, and all that is related to G*D.

Sacrifice is a reminder of sin, fall and redemption. Magnificence is a reminder of blessing, original blessing.

---

magnificence is desired
my body is prepared
blessing received is a pleasure
blessing given a joy
together
we wrestle on

Hebrews 10:16–25
Annihilation Friday

Persistence in the face of overwhelming sorrow can lead to provocation to love and good deeds, anyway (recommended read—the Thomas Covenant series by Stephen R. Donaldson).

Overwhelming sorrow can also deaden us to the point of non-responsiveness. It can call forth intermediary rituals to disperse such sorrow that eventually become a barrier to experiencing the sorrow at all. At this point we cling to our ritual rather than face again that which overwhelms us, every time. Far better, we think, to be obedient than to wrestle, as did Jacob of old, with unknown forces.

Suffering does come, as does everything in its time. But here the suffering may be more in the eye of the beholder than the actor. We do come to an empathetic and cathartic experience of suffering, but one that tends to keep us captive to it rather than release us into a new freedom to accept our suffering and not run from it.

We do not seem to find a way through suffering (a better conversation between Buddha and Jesus would help many a Christian and their congregation). Suffering has becomes a totem for us and we carry it around our necks and tattooed on our bodies. A cross too easily becomes an ending spot for us rather than a corrective lens putting meaning and death in perspective.

Note: None of this applies to the kinds of suffering we cause to the least among us, either directly or by ignoring them. This kind of suffering has nothing to do with redemption.

Hebrews 12:1–3
Clarification Week Wednesday

This is a week in which we might have a weak heart. How can we make it through?

Seemingly, from the Biblical record, trying to make it through the week as individuals is difficult if not impossible. There is evidence of bodies continuing to show up but as mere shells of themselves. Folks run away, stand afar, stand next to each other without recognizing their connections. At best they are mute; at worst they deny.

We do need a larger picture of solidarity to see us through this time when the scabs come to break our survival line. It takes more than a village to consider enduring hostility without moving toward revenge. Give thanks for every witness you can name and those un-named but glimpsed on the dim horizon. You will need them all for the days ahead.

James 5:7–10
Needed Change [3]

Prophets are fine examples of patient waiting. By nature they are as clear and noisy as they can be about what they currently see going on as they project the consequences of present actions some way down the line. They have no control over how their insight and presentation of that (in word and theater) will play out. Will people hear and understand and change? Will people hear and understand and keep on the same track anyway? Will people hear but not understand? Will people even go so far as to hear?

Who knows how prophecy will play itself out. Its intention is to effect change but is not in charge of that change.

The way in which we discern a false prophet from a true one is in the results—did people change and thus come to a new future? Did people not change and the consequence come to be? Only afterward can one tell self-serving prediction from that of community-serving wisdom. And if people change and a different future comes about than the one prophesied, can we ever tell if the people really changed or if some other factor came to bear on the situation?

Prophets must wait to see the fruit of their labor. Evangelists, preachers, and teachers also have some wait built into their work to see if what they do sticks with folks and makes a qualitative difference in those lives, but their venue and timeframe is usually far narrower and shorter.

At the same time there is this burning inside a prophet if they are slow to carry out their task and so there is both a hurry-up and a wait component to their work. I suspect it is easier to get relief from a pent up message than it is to wait to see how it will be received. This type of prophetic patience is not a passive waiting, but active. In the best of situations a prophet persists in a message and in the worst of situations a prophet whispers and goes off to sit and wait and see the destruction they expect and even desire.

Those who read here are part of the prophetic tradition. It is a difficult task to prophesy and be patient; it almost takes a split personality. This is one of the reasons that a prophetic community is so important and why it is important to be part of a school of prophets and a tradition of prophets. Let's keep talking together that we might be encouraged to be prophetic, in season and out. What keeps you going, persistent and patient?

1 Peter 1:3–9
Assured [2]

Blessed be G*D and your Intimacy with Creation. A mercy you participate in is the hope engendered by being resurrected from a previous limitation. This connects with a larger web linking us with all parts of time and space and energy. As a part of such a web and benefactor from its support, we bounce higher and see farther into an available wholeness of life.

Consciously being part of one or more interdependencies is cause for rejoicing, as well as weeping, and attests to a genuineness of relationship being as basic as other physics of time, space, and energy. Test it where you will, the results continue to reveal an interpenetration of self and other. Rejoice in connections, unseen and yet present, wherein we grin all over ourselves in the wholeness of life.

All of this is periodically focused on revealers of connections heretofore unseen. Standing at an oblique angle (you've heard it said..., but look!) allows a deeper look and the holistic outcome of the revealers of the world beckons each of us to become a next revealer of connections and participator in healing at least our part of a larger web of life. Called by the name Buddha, Jesus, Mohammed, (your name here), or one we have yet to hear of, we look forward to seeing where a whole web of life might yet travel.

How much tinkering did you have to do to this passage to have it be something other than an external creed of long ago yearning for new life through a corrective lens of today? Or was it just fine the way it has come down to us?

1 Peter 1:17–23
Assured [3]

Do you think this was something that Jesus told the folks on their way to Emmaus? Would this creedal language get through to them better than Jesus' recounting of the prophetic story from Moses onward? I doubt it.

Perhaps an antidote to creedal language is not a counter-creed, but communal experience. Try redoing verse 23 as a key to this section:

> *You have been born anew,*
> *not of either some difficult to define*
> *perishable or imperishable seed,*
> *but through a living and*
> *enduring presence of G*D*
> *in the mystery of a communal meal.*

1 Peter 2:2–10
Assured [5]

One way of living is to be between a rock and a hard place. This is not a recommended place to find oneself. However, it is often a perception of where one is, if not a reality.

The flip side of this is to be a living stone wherever you are. With this oxymoron we can begin again.

- Imagine supporting new life—a living stone can gather moss.

- Imagine computer generated images and what Pixar could do with a living stone.

- Imagine how this might be paralleled by a different phrase—a steadfast or compassionate lover.

- Imagine a living stone, dismissing the idolatry of destiny, saying, "So sorry, here let me help you up so you can try life again," when someone stumbled across a self-proclaimed fate.

- Imagine the witness, "Once I was just a stone; now I'm a living stone, a merciful stone."

- Imagine picking yourself up and skipping yourself across a pond setting off ripples of joy in the lives of others.

- This image originally referred to Jesus, and as disciples setting out to follow a way leading to a transformation of the world, we might use it as an image for ourselves.

- Let's form a band—Rolling Living Stones.

- Let's recognize ourselves as members of Living Stone Congregation.

Two important keys wrap around this passage. From the NRSV:

Verse 3: "If indeed you have tasted that the Lord is good" you will be able to escape the destiny mode.

Verse 10b: "...once you had not received mercy, but now you have received mercy" and if such change can be mine, it can be anyone's at anytime.

Remembering these bookends may help put what comes between them in a better light. Without these comforting arms we get pretty privileged and exude exceptionalism.

1 Peter 2:19–25
Assured [4]

Woe be to the preacher who doesn't start with verse 18. This important context of involuntary servitude is crucial to avoid issues of abuse that forget such a context.

In the context of not having a choice, the choice of suffering rather than death can make sense. Elseways the choice of suffering rather than not suffering is nonsense.

Suffering for what is right gives small comfort, but sometimes it is the only comfort available. Though necessary, it is simply difficult to spread a table for enemies or be generous with family (note the parallelism so enemies and family can be interchanged).

As The United Methodist Church approaches yet another General Conference, GLBTQI persons who have devoted themselves to the apostles' teaching and fellowship, to the breaking of bread and the prayers, still find themselves suffering within the family (which has turned enemy). There is no credible suggestion that this will change anytime soon.

This is sad for our GLBTQI family members and it is sad for a church that doesn't respond to those continuing to be hospitable toward those who hurt them. Discrimination does not go unnoticed. A result is that, day-by-day, more and more people are not being added to the number of those finding new hope and health through the witness of Jesus. (Take a look at the drop in percentage of "Christians" measured against the population and the rise of the Nones.)

We can no longer take Peter's advice about putting up with injustice, particularly for some false unity. He notes what Jesus didn't do but falls short on what Jesus did do—revealed in his body the injustice of the dominating system of state and religious institutions, was proactive in bonding community to itself as a non-blood-based family, and trusted a vision of being beloved when others did their best to humiliate him.

We are not called to be a single sheep led to the slaughter, but a union of blessed people doing what needs to be done even in the face of injustice.

1 Peter 3:13–22
Assured [6]

"Now who will harm you if you are eager to do what is good?"
–NRSV

Well, anyone with a my-interest larger than a your-interest.

And so the necessity of a statement that has enough experience to know how real it is that good intentions are no guarantee of security—"You are blessed whether or not you suffer as you do what is right".

Be ready to keep on doing what your gentle and reverent hope leads you to, even as demands are made to prematurely prove or reluctantly deny your hope.

To argue with Peter for a moment, baptism does not save. It sets one on a course of living out an assurance of belovedness.

As we have known from of old—Baptism is resurrection. A lack of resurrection is a sign of the lack of baptism (even if one has been duly watered). Remember your Baptism and be Reborn in light of tomorrow.

1 Peter 4:1–8
Absent Saturday

Anyway. Anywise. Anyhow.

Anyway, given the suffering of the past, now, above all, maintain constant love for one another, for love covers a multitude of sins.

Anywise, given the suffering of the past, now, above all, maintain constant love for one another, for love surpasses a multitude of sins.

Anyhow, given the suffering of the past, now, above all, maintain constant love for one another, for love forgives a multitude of sins.

Anywhere, given the suffering of the past, now, above all, maintain constant love for one another, for love transforms a multitude of sins.

Any way you come at this one, the process of life is toward fuller life. Whether it is "Holy" Saturday or any other day, we are either participating in this game[1] that constantly adds new value, that persistently includes in more folks, or we aren't.

---

[1] For more on the use of the word "game": read the Nobel Prize winning *Magister Ludi: The Glass Bead Game* by Herman Hesse.

1 Peter 4:12–14; 5:6–11
Assured [7]

Proofing text is daunting work. Proof texting is fun. We are always proof texting, so it's good that it's fun.

Peter suggests humility now, to later receive an exaltation. Who wouldn't want to be exalted? So, some humility now may well be worth trying. In fact, if we do it well enough, we may even hurry any exaltation.

Of course there is a tension between humility and constantly looking around to see if this is a time of exultation that we have been exalted. Now? Now? Now? Are we there yet? Am I there yet?

Indeed, it is past time for exaltation—"I have glorified G*D; it's time to get my reward in kind. Have I done enough humility and glorification yet, G*D? Surely so."

... I guess not. Let's sing another round.

---

sometimes we get the feeling
time is running out on us
it has been almost 40 days
[or is that years?]
almost twice what we need
to begin a new habit
or break an old one
almost midlife crisis

something ought to be happening
'round here somewhere
what do you think?
has it happened
and we missed it again?
about to happen?
eventually, right?

well, let's hang in a bit longer
we haven't hit bottom quite yet
let's try praying once more
perhaps another refrain
what's our discipline say
when lion-sized doubts arise?
protect one another

2 Peter 1:16–21
Mountain Top to Valley

We know what we know. Our eyewitness is a key to the whole of life's mystery. For us it is no *mythery*; we heard the conversation about belovedness as though we were in the same room.

Surely one of the great detectives would mutter, "Sounds like you were an earwitness."

Whatever. One of the great motives is love spurned. When G*D sang out, "And you are my Beloved", all those other suitors heard themselves being rejected. A passion to crucify comes from being a rejected lover.

Our eye/earwitness was not an interpretation. What we saw and heard was what there was to see and hear. Our experience led to our belief and our belief now leads our experience. Presuming a premise sure makes belief easier. In fact we no longer have any use for doubt—"What is spoken by God is understood by us; so listen up as we tell you what God says"—doubt not.

In your experience of today's church, how are we doing with the issue of interpretation? Does an interpretation by a majority make it more true than an interpretation by a small group? What is our "eyewitness" experience that affirms a multiplication of belovedness, not a scarcity of same? A part of our witness may be the injury caused by Peter's very assurance of his rightness and his preemptive use of God-Truth that denies an alternative experience. Peter's transfigurational experience is not the basis of my "morning star" experience.

Luther was ready to do without James. *The New Interpreter's Study Bible* intro says 2 Peter is "among the least read of the biblical canon." I'm prepared to follow Luther's lead and claim 2 Peter to be a house of rigidity we can do without.

1 John 3:1–3
Honoring Day

Whom does G*D not love? There are those who would tie this question to some given reality such as gender, race, sexual orientation or temporary state like enemy of the day or breakers of social norms such as corporations causing wide-spread harm and murderers. Some consider such as these as outside G*D's love and unworthy of our love.

Again, whom does G*D not love?

If this suggests that all are children of G*D, how do we proceed to single out saints? Would it be because they are more lovable or more loved?

Is what is to be revealed some additional quality of loving on-ward, some saintliness?

To be a child of G*D who doesn't claim to be the only child of G*D is a blessing to one and all. It seems to take a heap of living and walking with others to pull this off. It is worth it. We don't get to a compassionate image of G*D by tinkering with our image of G*D, but by beginning to practice compassion. This practice allows us, then, to see this quality in G*D. This may be part of a great circle dance with G*D practicing compassion to be able to see this quality in us and as we are seen into compassion we see G*D having more compassion....

Revelation 7:9–17
Honoring Day

Who are the ones who come out of great ordeal? Those who are loved? Those who have named the right god?

No matter where they have been, what they have done, the consequences they have borne—all are loved beyond themselves.

There is a happy response to understand past knowing that one is loved. It is here portrayed as a universal joy we all blend into. This may be very satisfying for whatever is receiving such a paean of praise.

Less satisfying is knowing that we are but part of an adoring crowd. There is only love of G*D left, no love of Neighb*r. While exciting, it is but a thin veneer of exaltation covering nothing else. All in all, for all its noise and show, a very static scene.

If this apocalyptic literature is to mobilize us into action in this world, it is important to return to a question of who now is later going to celebrate. May it be the ones we love. And so we expand our love base that all may rejoice.

---

tears will be wiped away
this is a grand vision

ordeal sufferers
suffering ordeal sufferers

to live toward it
we identify current tears

rivers of tears
falling from above

huge racking sobs
tender whimpers

springs of life
rising from below

from whence do they arise
man's inhumanity to man

meet in middle age
to cleanse our eyes

to wipe away such tears
a new humanity is revealed

who are we
who are they

wounded healers
healing wounded healers

loved lovers
lovers loved

Revelation 21:1–6a
New Year's Day

Again we reprise a resolution of a deity's duality. G*D will be with the good guys. Everything is set right. Where there was crying and laughing there will now be only laughing. (If we read a bit further we find the criers being separated out for a second or final death instead of a new or final birth.)

Is this your vision of G*D with us—only good from now on? All choices are resolved? A static smile of pleasure is always present? Is this the year you have before you? What does it mean for G*D to dwell or tabernacle with us, to move into the neighborhood? How would our love of G*D change if G*D were our Neighb*r and would G*D then so love a Neighb*r as to cast them adrift forever on a burning lake?

Appendix — Sunday Designations

Past Designation	New Look
Advent	Needed Change
Christmas	Blessed Body
Holy Name of Jesus	Naming Day
New Year's Day	New Year's Day
Epiphany	Guiding Gift
Baptism of the Lord	Beloved
Presentation of the Lord	Old Welcomes New
Transfiguration of the Lord	Mountain Top to Valley
Lent	Conviction
Annunciation of the Lord	Creation's Conception
Ash Wednesday	Self-Recognition Day
Liturgy of the Palms	False Dawn Sunday
Liturgy of the Passion	Premature Fear Sunday
Holy Week	Clarification Week
Maundy Thursday	Courage Thursday
Good Friday	Annihilation Friday
Holy Saturday	Absent Saturday
Easter Vigil	Hopeless Hope Vigil
Easter/ Resurrection of the Lord	Assured
Easter Evening	Opened Heart Evening
Ascension of the Lord	Our Turn to Witness

Pentecost	Energy to Witness
Trinity Sunday	Live Together
Season after Pentecost	Community Practice Propers 3–29
Visitation of Mary to Elizabeth	Elizabeth and Mary Meet
Holy Cross	Relic Day
Thanksgiving	Thanksgiving
All Saints Day	Honoring Day
Reign of Christ/ Christ the King	Evaluation Day

Abbreviations

The following are abbreviations of Bibles referred to and used:
CCB—Christian Community Bible: Catholic Pastoral Edition
CEB—Common English Bible
CEV—Contemporary English Version
IB—The Inclusive Bible: The First Egalitarian Translation
JANT—The Jewish Annotated New Testament
JB—The Jerusalem Bible
JSB—The Jewish Study Bible
KJB—The King James Bible
MSG—The Message
NIB—The New Interpreter's Bible
NJB—The New Jerusalem Bible
NISB—The New Interpreter's Study Bible
NRSV—New Revised Standard Version
REB—The Revised English Bible
SB—The Schocken Bible, Volume 1
SFB—The Spiritual Formation Bible
WSB—The Wesley Study Bible

WW—indicates paraphrase or translation by the author.

About the Author

Wesley White has been partnered/married with Brenda Smith White since 1972. He is father to two: Shai, daughter; Brandon, son; and grandfather to Nathan and Nicholas.

Wesley grew up outside a small town in southern Wisconsin, went to a one-room country school, and graduated from the University of Wisconsin—Whitewater with a degree in Sociology. He served for 2 years in the Peace Corps in the Philippines. After returning to the United States, Wesley graduated with an M.Div. from Garrett-Evangelical Theological Seminary in 1971 and served in ordained ministry for 38 years before retiring. He is also a trained and registered Transitional Intentional Interim Ministry Specialist and has served three congregations in that role.

Wesley has received recognition for work on inclusion from the Wisconsin Commission on the Role and Status of Women and other justice issues through the Perry Saito Award of the Wisconsin United Methodist Federation for Social Action.

His current work is with LovePrevailsUMC.com to remove a false testimony within the church about the incompatibility of LGBTQI persons and Christian teaching.

Production Details

Manuscript: formatted in Apple Pages
exported to Adobe Acrobat

Cover: *Abstract Pattern of Lines,* Volodymyr Lebid
Image Credit: www.123rf.com/phot_19491840_
abstract-pattern-of-lines.html
llebbid / 123RF Stock Photo
Design Consultant: Amy DeLong
Typography: Title is Trebuchet MS

Book Typography: Headings: Helvetica, 11 and 12 points
Text: Optima, 10.5 point

Book Graphics:
Pages 239 and 240: Cerezo Barredo provides copyright
and royalty free graphics from a Latin America Liberation perspective. I have used them over the years
and appreciate receiving explicit permission to use
two in this context, even though that wasn't needed.
To find a Year A graphic that suits you go directly to
www.servicios_koinonia.org/cerezo/indexAgraf.php
or www.TextWeek.com

Publisher Logo: designed by Susan Eaton Mendenhall of
www.JazzArt.biz for use as a logo for *in medias res.*
It represents being in middle of things as a way of
life—lifting the past to make way for the future.

Other illustrations and charts: Wesley White

Printer: CreateSpace, Charleston, SC

Copies Available: Amazon.com, CreateSpace.com, and other
retail outlets.

Made in the USA
Charleston, SC
17 December 2013